ECHAD:

an ANTHOLOGY of LATIN AMERICAN JEWISH WRITINGS

general editors —

ROBERT & ROBERTA KALECHOFSKY

255 Humphrey St., Marblehead, Massachusetts 01945, U.S.A.

First Printing, 1980
Second Printing, 1984

Library of Congress Catalogue Card Number: 79-88853
ISBN: 0-916288-06-4

Echad, an anthology of Latin American Jewish writings / general editors, Robert & Roberta Kalechofsky. — Marblehead, Mass. : Micah Publications, c1980.

282 p. ; 23 cm.

Includes bibliographical references.
ISBN 0-916288-06-4

1. Jews in Latin America—Addresses, essays, lectures. 2. Latin American literature—Jewish authors—Translations into English. 3. English literature—Translations from Spanish literature. 4. English literature—Translations from Portuguese literature. 5. Latin America—Ethnic relations—Addresses, essays, lectures. I. Kalechofsky, Robert. II. Kalechofsky, Roberta.

F1419.J4E25 980'.004'924—dc19 79-88853

Typeset by Ed Hogan & Ronna Johnson
Aspect Composition
13 Robinson St., Somerville, Mass. 02145

Printed by McNaughton & Gunn, Ann Arbor, Michigan 48106

Cover design by Robert and Roberta Kalechofsky.
Production and technical assistance: Robert Kalechofsky.

Acknowledgements:
"Growing Up Jewish in Guatemala," (c) 1974, *Present Tense,* The American Jewish Committee. Reprinted with permission of author and publication.
Clarice Lispector, "Love" and "The Chicken" first appeared under "Amor" and "Uma Galinha" in *Laços De Familia,* (c) 1960 Clarice Lispector. Reprinted with permission of Carmen Balcells/Agencia Literaria, Barcelona, Spain.
Alberto Gerchunoff, "The Anthem" and "The New Immigrants" reprinted from *The Jewish Gauchos of the Pampas* with permission of publisher. (c) 1955 Harper & Row, Publishers, Inc.
Jaime Alazraki, "Borges and the Kabbalah," (c) 1972 *TriQuarterly.* Excerpts reprinted with permission of author and publication.
Saúl Sosnowski, "Contemporary Jewish-Argentine Writers: Tradition and Politics," *Latin American Literary Review,* Vol. VI, No. 12, Spring-Summer, 1978. Reprinted with permission of author.

Benno Weiser Varon, "The Diplomat and Dr. Mengele," *The National Jewish Monthly,* May, 1979. Reprinted with permission of author.
Isaac Goldemberg, *The Fragmented Life of Don Jacobo Lerner,* Persea Books, Inc., New York. (c) 1976 Isaac Goldemberg. Excerpts reprinted with permission of author.
Gerardo Mario Goloboff, *Caballos por el fondo de Ojos,* Editorial Planeta, Barcelona, 1976. Excerpts reprinted with permission of author.
Alicia Steimberg, *Músicos Y Relojeros,* (c) 1971 Centro Editor De America Latina S.A., Buenos Aires. Excerpts reprinted with permission of publisher.
Diego Viga, "El Suicidio Del Tartamudo Y El Sueño Del Psiquiatra," from *Las Pecas De Mama,* Editorial "Minerva" Quito, Ecuador, 1970. Reprinted with permission of author. "Cibernética" and "Meditaciones Alrededor De Una Tía" from *El Diagnóstico,* Editorial Casa De La Cultural Ecuatoriana, Quito, 1969. Reprinted with permission of author.
Julio Ricci, "el Shoyhet" from *El Grongo,* Ediciones Géminis, Montevideo, 1976. Reprinted with permission of author.
Teresa Porzecanski, "Parracidio" from *El cuento uruguayo contemporáneo,* (c) 1978 Centro Editor de América Latina, Buenos Aires. Reprinted with permission of author. "Identificación" and "Primera Apologia" from *Esta Manzana Roja,* Editorial Letras, Montevideo. Reprinted with permission of author.
Samuel Rovinski, *Ceremonia De Casta,* Editorial Costa Rica, 1976. Excerpts reprinted with permission of author.
Yaacov Hasson, "Iquitos: The Jewish Soul in the Amazon, Notes of A Voyager," *Nuestro Mundo,* July, 1969. Reprinted with permission of author.
Esther Seligson, "Un Viento De Hojas Secas," *Luz de dos,* (c) 1978 Editorial Joaquín Mortiz, Mexico. Reprinted with permission of author. "Luz de dos," part IV, *Luz de dos,* reprinted with permission of author.
Ben Ami Fihman, "Mi Nombre Rufo Galo," "La Venganza," and "Contrafuerte," *Mi Nombre Rufo Galo,* (c) 1973 Monte Avila Editores, C.A., Caracas. Reprinted with permission of author.
Isaac Chocrón, *Rompase En Caso De Incendio,* (c) 1975 Monte Avila Editores, C.A., Caracas. Reprinted with permission of author.
Dr. Josef Goldstein, *Agarismo: Un metodo Bíblico contra la esterilidad,* Caracas, 1965. Excerpts reprinted with permission of author.
Alicia Segal, "Una Visita Sin Antesala," "Alguien Si Pone El Dedo En La Llaga," and "El Musiu," *Entrevistados En Carne Y Hueso,* Liberia Suma, Venediciones C.A., Caracas, 1977. "El hembrismo," *Cuarta dimensión,* Sintesis Dosmil, Caracas, 1975. Reprinted with permission of author.
Elisa Lerner, *En El Vasto Silencio De Manhattan: Drama Poética.* Excerpts reprinted with permission of author.
César Tiempo, poetry from *Sabatión Argentina,* (c) 1933 Sociedad Amigos de Libro Rioplatense.
David Unger, "Market Day" and "Public Bathhouse in Zunil" published with permission of author.
Jorge Plescoff, "Exercises in Comprehension," *Ariel: A Quarterly Review of Arts and Letters in Israel,* No. 48, 1979. Reprinted with permission of author. "Number Forty," "Number Seven" from *Exercises in Comprehension;* "The Agony of Being" from *The Mist of Dawn,* reprinted with permission of author.
Isaac Goldemberg, "El Rabino De Staraya Ushitza," "Epitafio," "Crónicas" published with permission of author.
José Kozer, poetry from *Este Judío De Números Y Letras,* Ediciones Nuestro Arte, Santa Cruz de Tenerife, 1975. Reprinted with permission of author.

Table of Contents

Introduction

The history of the Jewish presence in Latin America begins with Columbus. It is a history intricately enmeshed in the religious politics of fifteenth century Spain, a fascinating and labyrinthine history, but too tangential to the purpose of this anthology to elaborate upon here. Suffice it to say that of the ninety souls who sailed with Columbus on his first voyage, six were Jews, known as Marranos or Conversos. Their names are known. Two achieved distinction: Rodrigo de Triana (also known as Rodrigo Bermejo) was the first to sight the coastline of the New World from the masthead. The second, Luis de Torres, whom Columbus refers to in his diary as "one who had been Jewish and who knew Hebrew and some Arabic," was the first man to step ashore on the soil of the New World. Six Jews, not Conversos, but professing Jews, also accompanied Columbus on his second voyage. Their names are also known: Juan de Ocampo, Antonio de Castri, Efraín Benveniste de Calahorra, Alveno de Ledesma, Iñigo de Ribas, and Garcia de Guerrera.

Such names with such accents sound strange to the Ashkenazi Jew, to the Jew from Eastern Europe, from Scandinavia, from Germany. It is time to become acquainted. Judaism, religion, people, and history, is deep and broad and global, fragmented and unified, separated and whole. This century, this post-holocaust generation century, finds us, not weakened but, to our surprise, in the process of self-discovery, of where we have been and where we are everywhere: in China and India, in Africa and Scotland, in Europe and in México; and the process of self-discovery is the process of recovery, and of establishing a humane and humanly possible definition of "universal" and "particular."

The poet, Czeslaw Milosz, in *Bells in Winter,* wrote: ". . .the Universal is devouring the Particular." In our search for unity, harmony, brotherhood or sisterhood, much emphasis is often placed on the universality of mankind, or on Christianity or Islam as universal religions. But universality is a virtue mainly with respect to the common denominators of mankind: the aspirations to beauty and glory, the plain and enduring requisites of freedom, love, friendship, faith. It ceases to be a virtue when it usurps the particular, when it homogenizes human beings, when it seeks to ignore the differences which history, geography, time, space, and culture, weave in each person. Human beings, to be human, require a locale, a "time-space axis." Love, human love, not theoretical or philosophical love, but the everyday love of everyday human beings, is rooted in the familiar and the particular. Human love, as Orwell pointed out in his essay on Gandhi, is particular and particularizing. We love this person or that one, this place or that. Love distinguishes and by distinguishing, confers respectability. To be loved is to be singled out, to be called forth. It is the particular which teaches us to love, which lifts out the differentiating and determining detail of place or person from the anonymity of mass.

Differences are real. The particular is real. Jews must learn that about other Jews, both religious and secular Jews must learn that about each other, the Oriental Jew about the European Jew, the Israeli Jew about the American Jew. People everywhere must learn that about other people. The Christian must learn that about the Jew. Jewish history is not Christian history, and the Jewish religion is not the Christian religion. There may be correspondences, a common source, but the differences are real: they reflect the accumulation of history and an angle of vision. In Isaiah's great harmonic, the lion lies down with the lamb: neither are transformed, one into the other; the boundaries of their beings remain; the other way, their obliteration for the sake of harmony, would be a travesty on the order of the universe.

The particular and the universal are not antonyms. All human beings partake of both, some with greater consciousness than others, a few even with joy. The particular and the universal do not contradict each other, do not cancel each other out. They sustain each other, in the cosmos, and in the deepest reaches of the individual soul.

All this I discovered as a writer and put down in a notebook somewhere: that if a writer set out to be a universal writer, he would surely be second rate. Homer knew the world through the Greeks. Dante caught fire from the local conditions of his particular Christian world. He even put his personal enemies in hell—and you can't get more particular than that.

It is in the climate of the particular that our emotional and sensory life first takes root. No philosophical system or esthetic principle can ignore this.

From my own groping as a writer, as an American writer, as a Jewish writer, as an American-Jewish writer, not being able at first to figure out which end of the see-saw I belonged on, I discovered the concept of balance. I was both. How obvious! I could never be anything but. How could these eyes and ears, first bred on the sights and sounds of a Brooklyn street, be anything else? But in the infancy of that world, all Jews spoke with a Yiddish or Brooklyn accent, all Jews spoke like me; all Jews were white like me; all Jews came from Europe. My past was only a hundred years old.

In the normal process of things, I was disabused of this ignorance. At sixteen, a Jewish girl from Alabama came north to visit her grandmother, who was our neighbor. She spoke accordingly with her own accent, a deep southern accent. The effect upon me was not laudatory. I refused to believe she was Jewish. I, born to this city which claimed a fourth of the world's Jewish population, was the provincial who knew nothing about Jews anywhere else.

Since then it has been a voyage outward for me: the discovery of Chinese Jews, Yemenites, African Jews, Black Jews, Nordic blue-eyed Jews, Spanish dark-eyed Jews, Bedouin Jews, Iranian Jews, Uruguayan Jews. And I have discovered that in the perspective of history we are not any one thing that anyone ever told me we were. We are not city-dwellers or country-dwellers. We show up in many ways, depending upon the circumstances of time and class and country. Jews have been soldiers in the Roman army, colonizers with William the Conqueror, and sailors with Christopher Columbus.

In the nature of their multifarious existences over the globe, in the diversity of their customs as Jews and as citizens of any particular country, in the recognizable unity of their God and their history, in their everlasting and everlastingly tried loyalty to themselves as Jews, in the homelands in which they find themselves, and in the permanent homeland of their religion, the Jews are the paradigm, the metaphor for the interconnectedness between the particular and the universal.

Hence, this anthology: to affirm this fact.

This volume is not intended solely as a literary, esthetic presentation, but also as a human literary presentation: to capture, as well as possible, the spectrum of Jewish life in Latin American countries through newspaper articles and interviews as well as in poetry, fiction, and scholarly articles. Nor do all the writings reflect Jewish life per se. Indeed, some readers may wonder what is Jewish about some of the writings, while others may be surprised at the persistence and familiarity of themes.

Jewish emigration to South America, particularly to Argentina, received its greatest impetus at the same time that Jews from Eastern Europe came to the United States, around 1890. Many of these Jews who came at the end of the nineteenth century, whether to North or South America, had a common background in Eastern Europe. Some of those who came to Argentina, came on the wave of socialist-agrarian idealism, founded and supported by Baron de Hirsch, to establish Kibbutz-like settlements on the open pampas of that country. Emigration to the New World, whether to North or South America, whether by Jews or non-Jews, is closely related to conditions in Europe. Hence, for Jews, we find another "wave" of emigration to places like Venezuela, Mexico, Dutch Guiana, in the late 1930s and the years following. As the political climate in some countries in Latin America became less viable for Jewish life, other countries, for political or other reasons, maintained or achieved this viability. For the Jew, the Argentina of today is not the same country it was for him in 1890. We should keep this in mind when reading, for example, the excerpt from Alberto Gerchunoff's book, *Los gauchos judíos,* written as a paean to a land of freedom.

What connects the writings in this anthology is that they represent the spectrum of Jewish thought and sensibility in Latin America, a blend of Judaism, Eastern Europe, a particular country, and the influences of Spanish and Indian cultures. Isaac Goldemberg's poem, "Chronicles," blends the religious imagery of the Peruvian Indian and Judaism, while Alberto Gerchunoff's novel combines social references of Sephardic and Ashkenazi Jews. In the totality of these writings is the ferment of cultural mixture. Several works, like "The Shoyhet" by Julio Ricci and "Borges and the Kabbalah" by Jaime Alazraki were included for their expressions of how the Jew, his person or culture, is reflected in the eyes of the non-Jew. Borges' interest in Jewish culture is well known.

All the writers in this volume, except for Alberto Gerchunoff, are contemporary and all others, except Clarice Lispector, are living, ranging in age from their thirties to their seventies. Some, like César Tiempo, span the literary Jewish history of their country. Many are now living outside their native country, several in the United States.

I want to thank Saúl Sosnowski, editor and publisher of *Hispamérica*, for his help and suggestions, and equally Professor Estelle Irizarry of Georgetown University, for her help, and both for their patience with the necessity of correspondence; and my husband for all the intangible conditions of support. I want to express regret that writers like Bernardo Verbitsky of Argentina, who recently died, could not be included in this volume, and that writers like César Tiempo are inadequately represented.

Most titles and names of awards, prizes, institutions, and schools are kept in their original Spanish for the sake of dignity, particularly those that are readily understood in their context.

Finally, both my husband and I want to thank the National Endowment for the Arts, which helped make this anthology—conceived at first as an intuition—into reality.

Roberta Kalechofsky
Marblehead, Mass.
June, 1979

Hablar de Judaísmo en términos globales como si la "herencia judaica" sólo le perteneciera a los askenazis o a los sefaradíes, es un absurdo, puesto que *lo judío* no estriba ni en una pureza de sangre, ni en una uniformidad de origen, ni, mucho menos, en una rigidez de pensamiento y de actitud. Si por peso filosófico contara, sería la herencia sefaradí la más fuerte; si vamos a hablar de un cierto misticismo o de un resurgimiento con tintes literarios, lo askenazi estaría más cercano en el tiempo. Pero si de fidelidad a la Ley escrita y de preservación oral se tratara, ambas visiones, y, dentro de ellas, la multiplicidad de enfoques, conforman ese cerco que ha mantenido al Judaísmo vivo hasta hoy en día. Ni askenazis ni sefaradíes tienen el privilegio exclusivo de la pervivencia de la judeidad. Para fortuna del Judaísmo, la contradicción y la oposición son sus elementos germinativos.

¿Es posible seguir fomentando en nuestros hijos un antagonismo no sólo anacrónico sino—y a corto plazo—de efectos disgregantes para todos en cuanto a identidad y, para lo judaico en relación a su posibilidad de seguir constituyendo un manantial de aguas vivas?

Aquí Estamos is a bimonthly review of Jewish interest published in Oaxaca, Mexico. The following is an excerpt from its editorial of January-February, 1978. Esther Seligson, whose stories are included in this anthology, is one of the editors. The following is an excerpt from an editorial written by her.

To speak of Judaism in such global terms as the "Jewish tradition" as belonging solely to the Ashkenazic or the Sephardic is absurd. That which is Jewish does not rest on blood or race, nor does it rest on uniformity of origin, nor even less on rigidity of thought and action. If we speak of philosophy, then the Sephardic tradition is the weightier; if we speak of a certain mysticism or of the resurgence of literary themes, then the Ashkenazi tradition is closer to our own times. But where fidelity to Torah or the oral tradition is concerned, both visions, and within both these visions, the multiplicity of their views, form the continuous circle that has maintained living Judaism to this day. Neither Ashkenazim nor Sephardim have the exclusive privilege of having preserved Judaism. It is the good fortune of Judaism that opposition and contradiction are its germinative elements.

Ought we then to continue to foment in our children an antagonism which is not only anachronistic but—considering the narrow dwelling-ground—effectively disperses our communal identity for others as well as for Jews themselves, with respect to our continuing desire to be a source of living waters.

Trans. by Roberta Kalechofsky

Gerardo Mario Goloboff

from

Caballos por el fondo de los Ojos

Rifke's queasiness might not be due just to the sea. The rolling isn't so bad today, but last night it was different, some of the waves actually came as far as the people. Almost everything got soaked. Nobody has anything that isn't damp and full of salt. She says she can't even keep down a piece of *broit.* Garfinkel looks at me and laughs, "bread" he says. And when I tell her he starts laughing again, hugs me, saying "son," "a son," and I stare down at the ropes, the cables, the people sitting on the deck, the children crying, and the sea that is now calm and gray.

Mazeltov, Rifke, "rejoice." There will be peace and food. Papa set his heart, let them go with you, he told Garfinkel, who will they die for if they stay, over there will be good and rich lands. God does not love these wars.

He was sitting as always in the straw chair while Garfinkel, standing in front of him with his hat on, listened and said yes, that might be. Between the two stood a table and on it only the Book and a bowl of water. Garfinkel said he was sorry to bother him, but since he had been called, he could enter. There was great commotion in the house and throughout Kitay. Also the son of Num is going, also Isaac, also him. Papa is happy, whatever he does is what God loves. The *kohanim* Garfinkel is in charge of everything, but he needs the authorization and advice of him who is more than a *kohanim,* almost more than a *Rebbe,* a living wise man. Num never lifts his eyes from the Book, day and night seated in the straw chair, his mission is to read the written teachings and to guide the men of the village. He sleeps sitting in front of the table and the Book, a lighted candle between his hands so that at dawn the flame will wake him and he won't be abandoned to sleep. On the table, a bowl and a towel: in the night he might touch his hair or his beard, and that uncleanliness must be washed off as soon as he opens his eyes because the Book must not bear any stain, the hands of the Talmudist must be cleaner than the cleanest wind of Israel.

The ship gives a sudden lurch, two hundred people shout and pray, their bundles roll from one side to the other, they must go down, this might be as bad as the other storm. Rifke takes the steps slowly, certain now that she must be very careful of herself, it will still be days before they reach America.

• ◦ • •

> "Whoever has not felt the play
> of drama between the thing and
> the word, cannot understand me."
>
> —Vicente Huidobro

Arg-entine.

Arj-entine.

Argentina. First comes the country of speech: you have to make a language from the roots up. A language that to resound like *tug* and mean "day" must become *day* through and through, with its light, its air, its unknown birds. You have to work hard so that to pronounce becomes to feel. So that with all the intensity of the mother word you embrace everything you want to express. So that expression and sensation keep to their banks, and saying "day" is like saying *tug,* because *tug* is not night, not darkness, not cold, it is sun bright morning open sky.

To start babbling again, be a child again, and those muscles in your throat aching because they've never been used before, balking clumsily and then forcing out fragments of sounds, ragged consonants, broken syllables.

To build a home out of the language so that this land will not ignore you. Because if you don't, everything stays the same, alien in its uniformity. The mother words are no help now, it won't even help to call on the assistance of *Got: Got* too has changed to "God," and to ask His help in the village tongue with mud and pasture all around is to direct Him to a place where the divine hand cannot find you. You must call Him here, to this pile of sand, so that He can bring water and rest. Here He can begin His work over; almost everything is still to be created, except solitude. His word must bring forth fields and hearths. In Kitay He was called to watch over what already was, so His work would not be lost. Here He is summoned by a planet that has yet to be created.

There is no house, no table, no tablecloth, and no other clothes than what you see. Intimacy is the wide earth and a few strangers looking on. You sink your hands in the earth as always; you watch the men come back but without knowing them. Babel. We are together but we miss the thread, the bond that makes equal: that *broit* which is *bread* for all and which in everyone satisfies the same hunger, the same thirst, the same fatigue, the same sleep, the same pampa. Above it we will raise up adobe, thatch, logs, iron. Beneath it we will place future crops and sunflowers. But for now an insurmountable legacy divides us: to speak is to create distance because the same thing is different, or rather, it is changed to a noise that says something else, bodiless, weightless, colorless. "Land" is not *land,* not what you walk on, dig up, water. It isn't loose, brown, black, hard.

It can't be broken, nothing from it can be eaten. It isn't to be measured or smoothed. With "la-und" and with "la-and" and with "land" you come closer and closer, but the name still lacks a family. It's too busy with opening and closing the mouth, a new inflection, discovery. The people will come later.

You will begin by standing straight and tall, gaining strength, growing deeper. Once taken in, you will start to learn and grow in unity, a dominion understood by others: those men who watch and pick up their gourds and drink a beverage more bitter than tea. You must hear all these things in their own spoken country for sea, ship, stars, hidden passports, lost baggage, wars, pogrom, Kitay, to be remembered without fear.

You must build the courage of speech, root the sounds and the silences. Something becoming what you mean to say but not diluted on your lips. Which isn't land and only "land," but also *land,* something of worth, of weight. The word in its being, with all its music. Equal only to itself. The unique, the unexchangeable, the richest of all names. Inimitable in its breadth and depth. A language for coming together, for forgetting, for beginning to believe in the new. Filling empty spaces, being learned through resistance and difficulty so that men can know themselves and be known. And understand that breaking an almost eternal habit is harder than building a world.

Trans. by David Pritchard

Gerardo Mario Goloboff *was born in 1939 in a suburb of Buenos Aires. He has been active in literary circles in Argentina, and was an editor of* Nuevos Aires, *a review of fiction and critical thought. He has had a book of poetry published,* Entre la diáspora y octubre, *and his poetry has been translated into French, Greek, Italian, Macedonian, Norwegian, and Serbian. He is presently teaching Spanish American literature and civilization at the University of Toulouse-Le Mirail, France.*

Saúl Sosnowski

Contemporary Jewish-Argentine Writers: Tradition and Politics

In addition to the plight and pressures suffered by the general population under the current military regime, the large Jewish community (measuring about 350,000 persons) has to contend with a renewed wave of anti-Semitic outbursts. The alleged presence of individual Jews in the various guerrilla movements; the alleged participation of some Jews in high financial scandals, further serve to fuel those elements that in the past have not required any excuse to launch into virulent campaigns. Bookstalls along main avenues show the renewed prosperity of Nazi literature. Repeated threats against the Jewish population; slogans, paint bombs on synagogues and the occasional machine-gunning of Jewish owned stores, have caused justified alarm and protests of Jewish institutions. As of this writing there has been no change in the situation.

This paper does not pretend to address directly the question of whether an Argentine-born Jew is in fact—in the eyes of the general population—a "real Argentine." It intends, rather, to view the position of several Argentine-Jewish authors *vis-à-vis* this issue. The larger and more complex issues of acculturation and assimilation are ever present and, as such, an intrinsic part of each author's relationship to his respective environment.

The selection of the authors underlines the real distance that lies between the initial enthusiasm of the newcomer to a potential paradise and the more rigorous probing of basic values and official versions of local history in later works. The reduction of an ample sampling of Jewish-Argentine authors to these few should not ignore names like Samuel Eichelbaum, Bernardo Verbitsky, César Tiempo (né Israel Zeitlin), José Rabinovich, among many others; it is based on the knowledge that their views are basically represented by those who have been selected.

The journey from Eastern European villages to the new land; birth in an unknown environment; growing pains in a society seemingly without restrictions, are some of the sequential factors that have modified the respective authors' views and molded their degree of severity in questioning the component elements of their heritage and their country.

Like other Jewish immigrants who were bound for the new agricultural settlements, the Gerchunoffs sensed a wave of liberation from Russian anti-Semitism and the constant disquieting threat of pogroms. They were leaving behind—so they thought—intolerance and prejudice;

they were heading toward a republic that held that all men are equal, toward a land that would not force them to continue in practically prescribed trades but would re-establish the mythified biblical setting of the Jew as a farmer. Illusions and desires were forceful. The newcomers had to believe in the newly opened gates. The charter that Baron Hirsch established[1] and the need to survive in an unknown and at times hostile environment, required new skills, new habits, at the same time demanding a radical change in outlook towards a new open country; a lengthy process of acculturation that was to face them with new loyalties.

The lessons of acculturation were well learned by Alberto Gerchunoff (1889-1950), one of the best known Jewish-Argentine authors. The scant and fading memories of his native Russian village of Proskuroff enmeshed with tales of endless persecutions, were confronted with new realities in the new settlements of the provinces of Santa Fe and Entre Ríos. New and invigorating myths replaced those of previous generations. Jewish traditions started to fall into different categories: the desire to be an Argentine, a man with a history that is inscribed in the very soil that he learned to work, forged visions that were rooted in the initial ecstasy of the newcomers. For the writer's father, captivity, bondage, the perpetual wandering among nations, had ended in 1891 in the Moisés Ville colony. For Alberto Gerchunoff, the son, the centennial of 1910 was the Passover celebration of the new land: delivered from Czarist Russia, the Jews had found their homeland in a country that offered new hymns of praise: the *Haggadah* was joined to the Argentine national anthem. These are the relationships that can be drawn from *Los gauchos judíos*—translated into English as *The Jewish Gauchos of the Pampas*—[2] the composite of generally brief sketches of Jewish life in the new farming communities, that Gerchunoff published to join in the festivities.

Even the murder of his father by a drunken gaucho—as told in "The Death of Reb Abraham" in *The Jewish Gauchos*—did not dispel his youthful enthusiasm. He understood the individual responsibility of the murder and its impact on him, but it did not lead him to reject the newly found *milieu* and its potential opportunities. Shortly thereafter, the family moved to another colony and they became full-fledged farmers. His outward appearance—Gerchunoff recalls in his "Autobiography"[3]—was that of a gaucho. This was the first step into a world that he described in quasi-messianic terms. The impact of nature causes a radical change: origins are obliterated; nature itself makes him an Argentine. This expression should not be taken lightly: it is Gerchunoff's strong determination to become part of a *national* entity that undermines his analyses of the Argentine socio-political crises and enables him to continue an elegiac remembrance of earlier days. After having worked for several years as a journalist he still did not elaborate in a critical fashion the role that the national oligarchy and foreign interests played in the deterioration of his idealized country. Although he did espouse some liberal and even mildly socialist causes, Gerchunoff, significantly, worked as a literary critic for the conservative daily *La Nación.* For its publishers he must have been a model of what the new Argentine brought by the immigrant waves should be: he saw more the patriotic chauvinism of the Jews, not their plight. Although, in fairness, I should mention that he joined others in repudiating public attacks on Jews in Buenos Aires, his articles on the European events that culminated in World War II and later, and his extensive defenses of the legitimacy of Israel as a homeland for displaced Jews.[4] He stated, however, that there are no "religious questions" in Argentina, failing to see the ramifications of the anti-immigration, nationalist laws of residence or, even in a literary context, the products of the well-known cycle of *La bolsa* [The Stock-Exchange].[5] He saw the Jews, tempered by centuries of suffering, developing under changing conditions. He himself, after all, occupied several official positions and he knew of some Jews who held University chairs. What mattered to him is Argentine citizenship. In his "Autobiography" of 1914, he wrote, "Argentina is Palestine for the Jew, the promised land, in the strict sense of the Scriptures is the land of freedom." This line of thought led him to state: "I do not aspire to sing only Jewish life: I am above all an Argentine and my being an Argentine orients my existence as a man of letters."

Gerchunoff was and remained a member of an elite group of men which constantly expounded the benefits of the land of the free, as if the land could be abstracted from the class that ruled it. His apparent longing to join that class, a misdirected sense of gratitude and loyalty to his adopted country, prevented him from an accurate reading of the country's ills and from a rational defense that might support the contention that Argentina in fact was the "promised land." A posthumous collection of some of his essays was published with the quasi-messianic title of one of them: *Argentina, país de advenimiento* [Argentina, Country of the Future].[6]

Jewish history in Argentina did not conform to Gerchunoff's pastoral version. The contradictions of a system that embodied the roots and causes of its economic and political crises and eventual demise continued to exacerbate the literary production of those who questioned the liberal version of Argentine history sanctioned, as it were, by the Constitution of 1853.

I do not want to leave the impression that Gerchunoff's writings should be dismissed. On the contrary, his writings responded to a definite historical need. They reflect the initial impulse of the immigrant who seizes and consolidates his first opportunity to surround himself with geographical limits. In other words: he can perhaps be seen as the landless historical figure in search of a territory on which to ride out/write out his past and on which it is possible to establish a new system that will negate any chance of the past's continuation.

The arrival in a new land may signal the abandonment of previous traditions and the assumption of a history rooted within specific borders. This, in turn, may lead to a shift in emphases, to the total commitment to one of these alternatives to oblivion or, as we shall see, to the search for some sort of equilibrium that would balance multiple and conflicting interests within a self-defined role. This is not to say that we are facing a simple dialectical procedure that may cancel some elusive middle ground when faced with idealized ends. Gerchunoff's unabating desire to be Argentine serves to gloss over a critical view of his newly acquired country because the possession of a national identity in itself is the reward he needed to obliterate a label that did not give him "nationhood." Argentina lends him its citizenship; Gerchunoff displaces his original ties to an issue of secondary importance.

History has dealt with this concern. In recent years, the descendants of Jewish immigrants (many first-generation Argentines) have not proven to be as self-indulgent as some of their elders. Confronting history with facts, tradition with immediate needs, and Argentine and Jewish interests with the more encompassing issues of imperialistic struggles, they have encountered a complex and entangling web that does not lend itself to unidirectional or clear-cut solutions. It is to some of these authors that I shall now turn my attention.

* * *

To be Argentine and to be at the same time a Jew conscious, if only subliminally, of an inherent difference in relation to the rest of the population, demands an approach to history and traditions that questions the meaning of certain rites, that demands a lesson from the all-too-easily forgotten events of World War II, that, in the last analysis, requires finding the meaning of those problems *within* the concrete setting of current Argentine history and its socio-political context. This posits the following: there appear to be two worlds that dispute the attention and, eventually, the participation of the person involved. There are, in fact, two languages with their respective cultural code that signal different messages to those who have to opt for one or strive to integrate some elements of each into a more global concept of self-identification and of one's role in society. These are the forces at play in the case of Germán Rozenmacher (1936-1971).

Shortly before his tragic death and at a time when Peronism and its possible meanings were being re-evaluated, Rozenmacher saw himself confronting other members of his generation and stating: "I was neither a Peronist nor an anti-Peronist: I was a Zionist, a sort of lunar creature (I cannot say that it was terrible: it was just so), that placed me in the position almost of a tourist *vis-à-vis* what was taking place."[7] "Tourism" is not a word to be associated exclusively with misunderstood Zionism. The relationship of the tourist to Argentina takes on new dimensions when its contents are linked to Judaism and the role of Jewish traditions and rites in a *milieu* that presents itself as different, in a context that negates extraneous elements in its midst. For Rozenmacher, Judaism and "Argentinism" are mutually exclusive. To be one it is necessary to renounce the other or reach an uneasy truce of constantly diminishing returns. Rozenmacher did face facts. The problem lay in the instruments used to apprehend those facts.

In his play *Requiem for a Friday Evening,*[8] a young man refuses to accept the burden that his father needs to thrust upon him: to continue the tradition of the cantors of the village of Capule, to be another link in the tradition that ties the Abramsons to their people. The refusal by the son is coupled to the announcement that he intends to marry a non-Jew. The father cannot accept the situation and although, with a last-minute gesture, shows his love for the son, the break between them is unavoidable.

The scene takes place in bleak surroundings. When dealing with Jews, all of Rozenmacher's scenarios portray the misery of the immigrants who failed in their pursuit of "Amerika"; they also accentuate the pervasive grayish tone with which Rozenmacher sees the tradition into which he was born. It is housed in an infinitely sad space that suffocates its believers and chokes off any possibility of renewal. It emphasizes that its inhabitants are no longer enclosed in their *shtetl,*[9] that although their material situation is not what was evoked in long forgotten dreams, they are in a country that offers other unnamed alternatives. After all, David claims, he has written a thousand pages of a potential novel; he is not, therefore, just another clerk. He also has a girlfriend of the land. . .all of which are new, elusive and mistaken readings of the situation. Viewers and readers of *Requiem* can only support Sholem, the father, stubborn and firm in his beliefs and in the sense of historical continuity. Sholem does speak a foreign language, he is concerned with persecutions and anti-Semitism, he is preoccupied with money because his family's daily economic survival is at stake. It could not be otherwise. The social concern that transmutes these elements should have been a determining factor in David's decision. But the son only sees himself as a stranger who has to listen to tales of a past that isn't his, who is tired of speaking an uneasy mixture of Yiddish and Spanish. He feels the need to break out through, we are led to believe, his writing. Yet, as an aspiring writer (intellectual?) he does not analyze the situation of his peers for, to begin with, he has not recognized them as such. The required analysis would have thrust him once again into the surroundings that he rejects, it would have demanded a thorough reappraisal of the function of money in the capitalist system, a re-evaluation of that system and the participation of Jews in it. Part of that analysis would have led him to face another truth: Argentina sees him as a Jew and the noun-turned-epithet underlines once again "outsider," a status that cannot be changed by acquiring a marriage license with a daughter of other immigrants whose name is María.

In a thought-provoking essay, *Ser judío* (1967),[10] León Rozitchner indicates that when in Argentina he is pointed out as a Jew, the body into which he was born, with its surrounding geographical and cultural context, has been taken away from him. The label restricts his breathing space, his space is, in fact, reduced to the limits marked by his own body, a body that is dislodged from the land into an abstraction. To be called "Jew" clearly means "non-Argentine" and it is the others who have the power to cancel an historical attachment to the native land. This, as Rozitchner points out, leads to a shattering and easily achieved possibility: the Jew can have his roots denied by those who transform their epithets into unequivocal actions.

María is not to be construed as a solution to a Jewish presence in Argentina; it constitutes its self-denial. The fresh air and the new blood do not clear the cultural diaspora, it replaces it with different elements that seal the past into an historical category that can be shelved with other remnants. This approach does not deal solely with an abstract belief in codified religious laws; it faces the question of the concrete geographical settlement of a group of people. When dealing with Rozenmacher, it is useful to recall that Zionism does not consist of an occasional donation to the Israeli National Fund; it embodies the possibility of uniting lofty ideals with concrete purposes in a specifically defined territory. In other words, it is necessary to examine within these proposals whether the native land is in fact, as Rozitchner wills it, "tierra originaria," whether all land, or any land, is a reality that allows imagination to materialize and assume a corporeal definition. We deal, as in reference to Gerchunoff, with geography and its ramifications. The certainty of its possession allowed Gerchunoff to underline a newly found nationalist embodiment above all other concerns, which on occasion, served to open gates to a more universal acceptance of Jews by those who find emphasis on such elements distasteful. The apparent meaning of *Requiem*—pain at the break with the past, but nevertheless a necessary break in order to form a new and nominally less restrained or prejudicial society—perhaps allowed the production to be repeatedly presented on the official network of Argentine television. In spite of the author's stated goals, its ideological content is basically reformist. It postulates, moreover, a no-exit situation without engaging in an analysis that may have laid bare the underlying reasons for the conflict, rather than taking recourse to obvious and superficial levels that emphasize only the dramatic outline. The work engages a problem without facing it, glossing over basic impulses in lieu of dissecting structures that would confront social and political prejudices with a national project that in Argentina may have proved fruitless. Such a procedure may have led to Albert Memmi's disturbing insights. David's exit from his father's house and his eventual marriage to María can be seen as a liberating step, or can it? Is the new contract with María a deed of independence or a relationship that will hinge on the degree of uprooting that each will be able to tolerate? "Is it not possible that in the last instance this is a way of consuming the oppressor transformed now by the sign of love?"[11] Moreover, the incorporation of the oppressor—according to Memmi—transfers to it the stigma of the minority's label.

We may conclude this reading by underlining that the complex relationships between "Jew" and "Argentine" have not advanced in this case. Rozenmacher's play does serve, however, to mark the level of discourse on the topic when the issue is not subjected to the analysis it requires and when the labels serve solely as markers instead of signs that point to deeper causes in which alienation is rooted.

If this work had been part of a concrete and thorough project, the following step should have been an examination of Jewish immigration, its various components and purposes, the Jews' participation in the Argentine political process, and, perhaps more significantly, the dynamics that have ruled the relationship between Jewish communities and governmental institutions. Rozenmacher has dealt with Jewish motifs as well as with issues based on Argentine politics and guerrilla resistance to the seemingly never ending stream of reactionary dictatorships. But we should take into account that these two worlds never meet in his literary production. Rozenmacher himself did participate in "light" political activities and added his name to pro-Arab declarations during the Six Day War. In his work, he did not view all the components as integral parts of a pattern whose axis traverses the collapsing enterprise of the Argentine bourgeoisie and the wider conflicts of the world powers with their consequent effects on local communities on one hand, and with Israel and its ties to those communities on the other.

In Rozenmacher's works, the, for him, stifling presence of Jewish traditions is on one side and the local political explorations on the other. Judaism, restricted to what he has rescued of the traditions rooted among Eastern European Jewry, is only capable of producing success stories evidenced in material possessions or frustrated beings who cling to vain hopes while economic and emotional repression take their toll. In his literature, no solution is offered by the Jewish parents except a direct involvement with the community and the necessary steps to be named a success in that sector of society. The chasm that artificially separates these worlds is further evidenced by the partial success in depicting fragmentary reality. The attempt to understand the root causes that govern acculturation and integration into a national entity is marred by repeated frustrations.

Mario Szichman's (1945) novels—*La verdadera crónica falsa* (1972) and *Los judíos del Mar Dulce* (1971)[12]—seem, at first, to cover the space left by Rozenmacher's literary production. His characters are not so much concerned with the meaning of a Jewish heritage as with events that shatter daily the notion that the Argentine military are in control. Jewishness is transformed into folklore, behavioral patterns are formulated as puns that shift from a smile to an insolent sneer. The main drive is to recover the meaning of Argentine lives of Jewish ancestry involved and, perhaps later lost, in the struggle against right wing dictatorships. In *La verdadera crónica falsa,* the emphasis, at first, is not placed so much on modes of integration and lingering habits that distinguished the Pechofs from the other neighbors, but rather upon their direct participation in the daily pursuits of a family that has to survive, as others, in a political system that is being torn apart.

The Pechofs survive, unfold, and some develop politically, against the background of the then considered last phase of Peronism. The agony and death of Eva Perón in 1952 and the executions of Peronist sympathizers and innocent bystanders in the garbage dump of José León Suárez in 1956[13] serve Szichman to plot the significance of the family's presence in Argentina. Rather than engaging in soul searching and metaphysical questioning about the "Jewish condition," Berele-Bernardo reorganizes history. The family is put into a new framework; the elements that mold their lives can and should be seen against the background of Argentine history. For him, Yiddish does not necessarily estrange: it conjures up in few words a world with a behavioral code that is strange to the local sounds; it has its function and its useful purposes. Yiddish and Spanish are not, as in Rozenmacher, a source of alienation; they are signs of two coexisting ways of life; they are tools that contribute to the formation of beings who partake of both and who have no insurmountable conflicts in deciding that their concrete task is to engage the political forces that aim at the restoration of an apparently superseded period of history. His work is to restructure both Jewish and Argentine myths, and in so doing he attempts to unmask the contents and causes of their existence. Through an analytical process, his project aims to restore all to their original and rightful habitat.

Both Rozenmacher and Szichman deal with the urban population. In both cases, the Jewish families are set in generally oppressive surroundings under the increasing pressure of the city of Buenos Aires with its changing Jewish ghettoes, marked elitism and belabored material success as a defensive reply to outside hostility. The youthful narrator of Alicia Steimberg's (1933) *Músicos y relojeros* (1971)[14] is also placed in a predominantly Jewish neighborhood of Buenos Aires. Although narrated from a simplistic view and concentrating on conflicting elements in her family, the child poignantly seizes upon the dynamics of her petty bourgeois Jewish family, its negative behavior, the snappiness between her mother and sisters and the older generation, and the ruling economic factor that sets categories and defense mechanisms that attempt to deny wealth as success (we are—she says—poor but intellectual; they, at most, will be "chancho burgues," bourgeois types). It is the child with her fragmentary insights into the family's behavior and drives that emphasizes the dissolution of the large family unit into smaller units. These units are concerned with their own narrow projects and the drive towards material triumphs. Marriages and burials are performed by a Rabbi: rites whose sense has been lost by the family are continued because the community is bent upon preserving them—there is no inquiry into the role of rites as cohesive communal forces—as the non-Jewish surroundings keep building inroads. Alicia Steimberg herself cannot understand an abstract God and thus visits churches with outward beautiful signs of a God she does not see in the Synagogue. But the main thrusts—and in this we find a common bond with Szichman's insolence—are elaborated with disarming humor. It is the faint smile of the narrator's eyes that denounces the false pretensions of her family and their slow but sure disintegration. Its members wear masks that are wearing thin; they perform in roles for others while the stage is crumbling under the child. In her affirmation of, as it were, intellectual prowess there is, obviously, an immediate defense against money as a criterion for advancement. There is also an incipient elaboration of the use of the intellect as the other means of asserting one's presence and recovering a segment of concrete reality in a city that may obliterate its inhabitants.

I would not like to insist on a theme (urban vs. rural living) that can be found with variants throughout literature. The fact remains, however, that in dealing with Argentina we must remember that a great initial effort was made by Baron Hirsch to turn Jews away from urban living—and its resulting occupational and trade distribution—and settle them in the countryside. Primarily, the effort was designed to save Jews from persecution in Eastern Europe—Czarist Russia for the most part. It was also designed to retrain people in their original historical occupation. In this aspect, there is an obvious connection with one of the primary Zionist goals; the great difference lies in the geographical setting of the homeland. The results of the experiment can be seen—on a literary level—in, for example, *Los gauchos judíos.* A limited number of immigrant Jews fought natural and cultural obstacles and basically succeeded in the initial endeavor to settle down in the countryside and work as farmers. But centuries of urban living were not superseded by one generation of farmers. The children and grandchildren drifted towards the cities.[15] Once again, as city dwellers, they had to restructure their lives and work and submit to the pressures that other urban Jews were already facing.

In light of this fact we shall consider another author: Gerardo Mario Goloboff, born in 1939 in one of the Jewish colonies, Carlos Casares, lawyer, essayist, poet, who, like many other Argentines, had to leave in recent years for another life of exile. Goloboff is the author of *Caballos por el fondo de los ojos,*[16] a novel published just last year and, I believe, one of the most successful to date in blending what we may draw from literary theoretical advancements with an incisive examination of a Jew's condition in Argentina.

Herman, the main character, faces the white sheet that covers the bullet-riddled body of his son. The white sheet is also the blank sheet on which the blood of his son starts to trace the family's history. Ink and blood on the white cover of a death brought upon by governmental repression, rewrite a journey which began four generations earlier. The bright-eyed illusions of an as yet undefined "better future" end in a blank stare at the sudden demise of all possible continuity.

In the Russian village of Kitay, amidst degradations and persecutions, a group of families set out on a journey to a land depicted by images of peace and tranquility, of religious tolerance and respect. The life in the Argentine countryside was, as everywhere else, a mixture of joy and sorrow, but it also was the concrete arrival and possession of a land that was open to newcomers. The immigrants had to learn new ways and they did; they had to learn the new language, call the world by its new names, and their sons did. The new generation was abandoning its European past. In passages and brief references that vaguely remind us of Gerchunoff's *Los gauchos judíos* and *Entre Ríos, mi país* (1950), we read of an exultation at the new-found opportunity to recover the taste and sense of the earth, the quasi mythical reenactment of a collective and national rebirth. New national myths slowly replaced the old; more encompassing concerns transcended the immediate preoccupations of the farmers; wider horizons lured some of them and their children to explore urban living. Buenos Aires, a city of turmoil, of activism, of expansion for small socialist and anarchist cells, of strikes and conflicts is also a place for opportunity to develop and to prosper. "Success" rules the conduct of the immigrants. After all, an underlying cause of their journey was also "to make America" and America is synonymous with glory, wealth and all that is considered positive by the establishment. America, some thought, can also be Zion if joy and peace cover the land. Argentine and Jewish history—the adventuresome grandfather claims—are repetitions of the same archetype of repression and defense of individual and tribal or national rights. But ideals slowly succumb under daily pressures. Herman grows up knowing of his father's Socialist ideas and activism; of the pressures brought upon his family by false hopes and the opportunism of certain Peronist leaders and recent political converts to its ideological plans. Demagoguery replaces concrete social proposals. Betrayal of promises and opportunities mark Herman's generation. Herman himself will later engage in the manipulation of money: a fetish that reproduces itself from a fictitious paradigm. Herman does not fulfill a productive role, he is an insurance agent and businessman with increasing speculative powers. No trace is left from the past's production of raw material, from his own family's past as farmers. The distance between the past and earth, between agricultural production and the manipulation of capitalist opportunities creates a vacuum. His family will fall into the hold of that vacuum. Any chance he may have had to recuperate from ethical losses, any analytical concept that may guide him through the recurring questions of his duties as a Jew and as an Argentine will also vanish. Within a conceptual framework—not to be found in Rozenmacher's proposals—the narrator pursues Herman's actions and motivations to their limit. Neither he nor the analyst who will later guide him through his own past will offer an answer. The analyst points the way; Herman refuses to see it. Condemned by his own manipulative position and commitment to a system that gave him monetary and social success—although at the price of personal alienation—he can only strive to ease his son's path in his search for an alternative to the system that he himself upholds with his work and his standing.

Herman needs secure (insured!) walls, yet he knows they are non-existent. He has learned that assimilation is not the answer, that for him there is no promised land in faraway places, that Socialism is not an answer. All he has is a vague and unprogrammatic notion that there must be "something" as yet undefined and unstructured that must be better than what he has.

He does not accept, however, what has been the answer for others. Nora, who started as just another woman in a long line of extramarital relationships, who later succeeded in offering him an alternative which he has failed to accept, tried another option: she moved to Israel where she strived to build her life in a society she feels can also be hers. In Nora's case, assimilation will acquire a different meaning. It will not be the obliteration of one's past history into someone else's desire; it will be the continuation of a not forgotten link in a land on which history recovers its original purpose. Herman has lost his opportunity to fight for either cause in either land because excessive and suffocating introspection and inner searching have sealed his options. Knowing that his mother died while giving birth to him, the complex desire and attachment to his physical mother and the mother earth notion, separate him forever—so he believes—from any chance to possess the land and thus be one with it.

Two deaths mark his inability to actively perform a redeeming role. On the one hand, his mother's death and the potential ties to the family's political tradition mark his rejection of the formal opportunities of his father's career as a socialist politician. On the other: his son's death during a revolutionary act. Between them lies Herman, now confined to endless reexaminations and to be guardian of his son's body. Dead is his heritage; dead is his continuation.

Yet, what seems at first to be a wholly nihilistic interpretation of the middle class Jew, is again reexamined: it is the blood-stained sheet that covers Herman's son that leads to a thorough reexamination of his origins.

The novel does not unfold in a linear narration. It is a complex structure that recreates the multiple events that led to the final scene in the morgue: the evidence that the descendants of the Jewish farmers did learn the original language that opened up the country's reality to them. That the longevity once promised by God in a dream of Herman's great-grandfather lasted the announced four generations; and Roberto once again became vulnerable to oppression. Perhaps more than this: it shows that the settlers' hold on the country was perpetual, that death was the risk and the price paid for their nationality to be finally acknowledged by all the inhabitants; a negative recognition in death.

The final page of the novel evokes the original moment of departure from Europe: Num, the great-grandfather, has, as always, seen *The Book* and then tells his people to go. They shall some day encounter joy and peace; in a distant future, only he who will make a path of his own blood and walk on it will have the land. The first generations will be seeds and footprints on which the others to follow will recognize and pave the way.

More than recreating a Jewish setting by means of folkloric depictions of home life and communal ceremonies and thus shutting itself in an anti-solution, *Caballos por el fondo de los ojos* presents itself as an open structure, a thorough probing of Jewish life in the way that it should be analyzed and assimilated: in the reading of man's reaction to oppression, in its confrontation with negative forces that have to be replaced in order for the original searchers to find their peace on their earth.

* * *

As we have seen, the presence of the Jew in Argentina has been viewed by these authors from different perspectives. Their analysis—or lack of it—is clearly determined by class position and interests and by their respective abilities to view critically the options that this presence allows. Whether the solution is total assimilation, acculturation, the subservience of either the Jewish tradition or the Argentine social demands to the other, a total commitment to Argentine interests or to Israeli interests (when these interests clash), is a question that remains open after these authors have offered their response or have questioned the list of options. One element, however, remains clear: any discussion of the subject has to be undertaken from a position that recognizes the two basic components of the authors: their Jewish background and their Argentine citizenship. Against those who tend to eliminate the first, Rozitchner writes that the negation of one's origins actually incorporates the anti-Semitic view of Jews. Furthermore, he states, it eliminates the possibility of recovering the positive elements of Judaism. It is on the basis of these elements, on a clear knowledge of being Argentine Jews, that we—continues Rozitchner—should participate in the national process. The contributions to the nation should be made by people who know their origin, who accept their history without shame.[17] Only those who are fully conscious of their history's meaning, can freely elaborate the meaning of their participation in their native countries; they can understand that a process of true liberation is not limited to simplified disjunctions and to the quick adherence to some all-too-easily-called popular movements.

In closing, let me once again quote Albert Memmi: "For a Jewish writer, true courage, real exile, would surely be to begin to talk as a Jew to all men." "To be a Jewish writer means to necessarily express the Jewish condition, to offer it to the other, or to a certain degree, to have it accepted by others."[18] When this is understood, the common struggle for liberation from oppressive forces will not be seen as separate from this condition. It is in order to see—among other elements—this process that I have chosen these writers. Their collective reading does not conform to a dialectic process. It does show several different approaches to a problem that when recognized and properly elaborated ceases to be a problem and becomes a basis for future action. [June 1977]

FOOTNOTES

1. Baron Maurice de Hirsch (1831-1896) established the Jewish Colonization Association in London which, together with the Alliance Israelite Universelle, was instrumental in the establishment of agricultural settlements in the Argentine countryside and the safe passage of Jews to them primarily from Czarist Russia. The feeling of the Jewish settlers towards their benefactor can be appreciated in a speech pronounced by Alberto Gerchunoff on December 8, 1931, included in *El pino y la palmera,* [*The Pine and the Palm*], a collection of essays and speeches published in 1952, in Buenos Aires, by the Sociedad Hebraica Argentina, pp. 33-36.

2. Translated by Prudencio de Pereda, New York, Abelard-Schuman, 1955.

3. This "Autobiography" was written in 1914 and has been included in the posthumous collection, *Entre Ríos, mi país,* published in 1950.

4. Gerchunoff's *El problema judío* [*The Jewish Problem*] was first published in 1944 and reissued a year later as a separate book by Ediciones Macabi of Buenos Aires. It can also be found in *El pino y la palmera,* pp. 135-69.

5. A notorious anti-Semitic novel stressing the alleged control by Jews of the Argentine economy published by Julián Martel in 1891 that ran several editions and marked a literary cycle that is still being studied and debated by critics.

6. Buenos Aires, Losada, 1952.

7. "Testamento de Rozenmacher," *Primera plana* [Buenos Aires], No. 446, August 17, 1971, p. 46.

8. First staged in the IFT theater of Buenos Aires in 1964, later published by Talía.

9. In Mario Diament's *Conversaciones con un judío* [Buenos Aires, Timerman Editores, 1977], Máximo Yagupsky, a product of the Jewish agricultural settlements in Entre Ríos province, indicates that those who agreed to travel to Argentina, his grandfather among them, did so on the condition of being allowed to maintain their traditional modes of behavior. Although they became farmers, their lifestyle did not change from the one they pursued in their European villages (p. 155).

10. Buenos Aires, Ediciones de la flor, 1967, p. 36.

11. *La liberación del judío* [Translated from the French, *La libération du Juif*, by Leonor E. de Lieban], Buenos Aires, OSA-Diálogo, 1973, p. 169 ff.

12. *La verdadera crónica falsa,* Buenos Aires, CEDAL, 1972, is based on the original *Crónica falsa,* Buenos Aires, Jorge Alvarez, 1969. *Los judíos del Mar Dulce* was published by Galerna-Síntesis Dosmil, Buenos Aires-Caracas, 1971.

13. The novel is based on investigations carried out by journalist Rodolfo Walsh which were published in *Operación masacre.*

14. Buenos Aires, CEDAL, 1971.

15. Máximo Yagupsky attributes the drift towards the city to the cultural attractions of the urban centers more than to economic reasons. *Conversaciones con un judío,* pp. 164-65.

16. Barcelona, Planeta, 1976.

17. *Ser judío,* pp. 47, 64, 99.

18. *La liberación del judío,* pp. 156-57.

Saúl Sosnowski *was born in Buenos Aires in 1945. Educated in Argentina, Jerusalem and the United States, he received a Ph.D. from the University of Virginia, and is Chairman of the Department of Spanish and Portuguese at the University of Maryland. He has published two books,* Julio Cortázar, una búsqueda mítica *and* Borges y la Cábala: La búsqueda del Verbo, *and is the founder and editor of* Hispamérica.

Alberto Gerchunoff

The Anthem

from *Los gauchos judíos*

During their first years in the colonies of Entre Ríos, the Jews knew very little about the new homeland. Their conception of the Argentine people and customs was a confused one. They admired the Gaucho, and feared him, and they conceived of his life as a thrilling amalgam of heroism and barbarism. They had misinterpreted most of the gaucho tales of blood and bravery and, as a result, had formed a unique conception of their Argentine countryman. To the Jews of Poland and Bessarabia, the Gaucho seemed a romantic bandit, as fierce and gallant as any hero of a Schummer novel. The factory girls in Odessa had avidly read Schummer after their hard day's work. Now, the farm girls in Entre Ríos did the same thing.

In the synagogue—constituted by one or another ranch-house in Rajil—the old and young men discussed their ideas about Argentina. The enthusiasm they felt for the free life here—something they'd dreamed about during the dark days in Russia—had not softened a bit. All felt a fervent love for this country, however new and unknown it seemed. The hope they felt was as fresh as the new black earth their plows turned; the new hope and the new earth made their own selves feel new, their bodies young.

On Saturdays, until midday and after, the men would stand at the door of the synagogue—not far from the corral in this instance—and recall their sufferings and exodus, as if the immigration from Imperial Russia had been the historic Exodus of the Bible.

They talked; they argued. José Haler, who had done his military service in Russia, once maintained that Argentina had no army.

"What do you know about that?" Elder Isaac Herman almost shouted at him. Elder Herman was a bent old man, palsied and infirm, who taught the children of the colony their prayers. He opposed José energetically. "You don't know anything, you! You're a little soldier boy, that's all. What do you mean, Argentina has no army?"

"Anybody can understand that, Elder Isaac," José said. "Here in Argentina, the Czar is a President and he doesn't need soldiers to defend him."

"And what about those that we see at the railroad station at Dominguez? What about those, eh?"

The question confused José. It stopped him. He could not satisfactorily explain the presence in Dominguez of the sergeant whose saber in its rusted scabbard was so frightening to the children.

On another afternoon, a neighbor brought news of a coming festival in Villaguay. He told of the arches and flags and banners being erected in the streets of the municipality. This news was commented on everywhere and another colonist proposed that they find out the reason for the festival.

The colonists did not know a word of Spanish. The young men had quickly taken up the dress and some of the manners of the Gauchos, but they could manage only the most basic Spanish phrases in their talk with the natives. It was decided, nevertheless, that their Gaucho herdsman, Don Gabino, a comrade of the great Crispin Velazquez and a veteran of the Paraguayan War, should be consulted about the matter. Don Gabino thought that the preparations might be for some local fiesta, or might be for a coming election, perhaps. This idea seemed very logical at first, but it was later rejected. Finally, it was the Commissary for the colonies, Don Benito Palas, who cleared up the matter of the preparations for the Jews and explained to the Shochet, in eloquent yet simple form, the full significance of May 25th, Argentina's Independence Day.

The idea continued to interest the colonists of Rajil, and in the nightly conversations and rest periods of the day they talked about the date. Each one had his own idea about the significance of what had happened on May 25th, but all felt its genuine importance. Finally, it was suggested that the colony celebrate the great anniversary.

It was Israel Kelner who first offered the idea. Israel had once gone to Jerusalem to organize the immigration sponsored by Baron Rothschild. An eminent Hebraist who had been publicly praised by the Shochets of Rajil and Karmel, Kelner enjoyed great prestige in the colonies, and often delivered the principal address at ceremonies held in the colony. Now, he took a trip to Las Moscas, and learned from Don Estanislao Benitez all the necessary details about the 25th of May.

The commemoration of the day was decided upon, and the Mayor and Shochet were designated as organizers for the festival. Jacobo, the Shochet's helper, who was the most acclimated of all the young men, put on his best pair of gaucho pantaloons and rode from house to house on his smart little pony to announce the holding of an assembly that very night in the synagogue.

At the meeting, the details of the celebration were discussed and it was decided first not to work on the holiday, of course, to bedeck the doorways of the houses with flags, and to hold a big meeting in the clearing, at which Elder Kelner would deliver an appropriate speech. It was decided, furthermore, to invite the Commissary to the festival as well as the Administrator of the colonies, Herr Bergmann, a harsh and unsocial German who had little feeling about the occasion to be commemorated.

During the preparations, a further difficulty arose. It was discovered that no one knew the colors of the Argentine flag. It was too late to do anything about it now, and so the preparations had to go on.

Finally, the great day came.

The dawn found Rajil bedecked like a ship: the doorways were covered with flags and banners of all colors. The Argentine colors were there, too, though the colonists did not realize it. A mild sun shone bright but not too warm as it lit up the flat countryside and bathed the yellowed shrubs and the white walls of the huts with its new warmth. The Commissary sent his little band, and they swept into the music of the National Anthem as soon as they arrived at the colony. The hearts of the Jews filled with joy at the sound and, though they were still confused about what this date meant, the thought of this patriotic festival they were celebrating in their new homeland filled their spirits with a new happiness.

The service in the synagogue was attended by all the men and women. Their Jerusalem tunics shone white and resplendent in the sunlit room as they listened to the Rabbi bless the Republic in the solemn prayer of *Mischa-beraj,* a special prayer in praise of the Republic.

After the reading from the Sacred Book, the Mayor spoke. He was a less learned man than the Rabbi, but he knew how to keep people enthralled. He used many gestures of the synagogue preachers, and he would often tear at his chestnut-colored beard.

"I remember," he said, "that in the city of Kishinev, after that most terrible of pogroms, we closed our synagogues. We did not want to have to bless the Czar. Here, in our new country, nobody forces us to bless anyone. That's why we bless the Republic! That's why we bless the President!" Nobody knew who the President was, but that didn't seem to matter.

Immediately after the Mayor's speech, the people left the synagogue and gathered in the clearing. The wild flowers of this season shone brilliantly on an improvised arbor near which the band stood and played the Anthem, lustily and continually. The young men of the colony were showing off their horses, and the native boys from the breakwater district stood in a group, watching silently, but keeping themselves well supplied from the trays of sweets and pastries. The demijohn of wine waited on the arrival of the Commissary for its opening.

It was growing late when Don Benoit Palas appeared with his escort, carrying the Argentine flag. The ceremony began. The Commissary drank his cup of wine and Elder Israel Kelner stood on the dais to speak. In the simple Yiddish of the people, and in the name of this colony, he saluted this country "in which there are no murders of the Jews," and illustrated his feelings with the parable of the two birds—a story that his neighbors had heard on many occasions.

"There was once a bird imprisoned in a cage of iron. He believed that all birds lived as he did, until a certain day when he saw another bird flying freely through space and flitting from tree to rooftop and back again. The imprisoned bird grew very sad; he rarely sang. He thought so much about his imprisonment that he finally got the idea of breaking out and picked at the bars of his cage until he was free."

Jacobo explained the story to Don Benito, who, being a native, could make little of the involved discourse. In his answer to Elder Kelner, Don Benito recited the stanzas of the Anthem.

The Jews could not understand their meaning, but they recognized the word "liberty," *libertad,* and, remembering their history of slavery, the persecutions suffered by their brothers and themselves, they felt their hearts beat faster at the word. *Libertad!* It was here. It was theirs. Speaking from their souls, with their truest feelings, they answered the word with one voice. As they did in the synagogue, now they exclaimed together: "Amen!"

. . . .

The New Immigrants

The morning the new immigrants were expected, some two hundred people went to the station at Dominguez. The immigrants were expected on a ten o'clock train, and their colony was to be established outside San Gregorio and close to the forest where, according to local legend, cattle thieves and tigers abounded.

Spring was coming everywhere, and the green fields of the meadows were already well dotted with daisies.

The station was crowded and the people speculated about the new arrivals from Russia, especially about the Rabbi from Odessa, an old, learned Talmudic scholar of the Vilna Yeshiva who had been to Paris, it was said, and had been very courteously received by Baron Hirsch, the Father of the colonies.

The chief and the sergeant of the Villaguay constabulary had come to the station to assist in the arrival, and were talking quietly together. Other Gauchos were there, playing jackstones while a number of the Jewish colonists watched.

The Shochet of Rajil had drawn the Shochet of Rosch Pina into a discussion in the hope of confusing him before so many people. They were talking about the Rabbi among the expected immigrants, and the Shochet of Rosch Pina was telling some things about him. He had known him in Vilna where they studied the sacred texts together. The new Rabbi was a fine person and he knew the Talmud almost completely by memory. He was a member of the group that had gone to Palestine to purchase lands before Baron Hirsch had thought of launching this project in Argentina.

The man had never practised as a rabbi, the Shochet said. After he finished his studies, he had become a merchant in Odessa, but he often contributed to *Azphira,* a periodical, written entirely in ancient

Hebrew.

Later, the two Shochets debated a complicated point of domestic law, and the Shochet of Rajil quoted an idea of the divine Maimonides on the sacrifice of bulls.

Awaiting the new arrivals recalled deep and lasting memories for most of the crowd. Many remembered the morning on which they had fled the unhappy realm of the Czar. Then they recalled their arrival in this promised land, in this new Jerusalem they had heard proclaimed in the synagogues and had read about in the circulars carrying little verses in Russian, praising the soil of this country:

"To Palestine, to the Argentine,
We'll go—to sow;
To live as friends and brothers;
To be free!"

"Don Abraham," the sergeant said to the Shochet, "here comes the train."

A sudden rush of talk spread. Behind the hills, in the clear morning, the thread of the engine's smoke was seen.

When the train puffed in, the immigrants descended from two coaches. They looked drained and miserable, but their eyes shone with bright hope. The last to descend was the Rabbi. He was a tall, broad old man with a pleasant face and a thick white beard. The colonists gathered around him; he was overwhelmed with greetings and wishes of welcome. The Shochet of Rajil, Don Abraham, worked his way to the Rabbi's side and took charge. He led him away from the station. They were followed by the colonists and the long line of immigrants, with their bundles and their children. The immigrants seemed to be losing some of their misery as they moved in the soft morning air and stared at the beautiful countryside.

When the lines had moved a little away from the station, Don Abraham mounted the stump of a tree and made a speech of greeting—well interspiced with Hebraic quotations. The new Rabbi answered for the immigrants with the quotation of a short verse from Isaiah. He spoke about czarist Russia then, telling of the horrible sufferings of his people there.

"Here," he said, "we shall work our own land, care for our own animals, and eat bread made from our own wheat." The Rabbi was filled with a thrilling enthusiasm, and he made an imposing and prophet-like figure with his great beard waving in the wind. When he stepped down from the stump, the Rabbi embraced the sergeant and kissed him warmly on the mouth.

Then, in the full warmth of the morning sun, the caravan started for San Gregorio.

Alberto Gerchunoff (1884-1950) *was in his time one of the most famous journalists in South America. He wrote for* La

Nación, *the leading daily of Buenos Aires for forty years, and eventually became its editor-in-chief. His family was one of the agricultural colonists inspired by Baron Maurice de Hirsch's Jewish Colonization Association (ICA), and they came from Russia to a colony in Argentina, known as Entre Ríos. Here Gerchunoff was raised in the colony of Moisés Ville, reading Russian and Yiddish, speaking Spanish, loving the pampas and deeply admiring the life of the gauchos. His book,* Los gauchos judíos, *is dedicated "to the revered memory of Baron Moisés Hirsch, founder of the Jewish colonies in the Argentine Republic." Now out of print,* Los gauchos judíos *captures the idealism and optimism of the early Jewish immigrants to Argentina.*

Poetry by César Tiempo

Verses to a Dictionary And to the Neckerchiefs (Worn by the Gauchos)

With you, it is not impossible to define
creatures and things with the simplicity
of the fish whose scales streak the sea with blue and gold,
Or of the sea itself that swells with the gracefulness of the fishes.

Not even with that propriety,
constricted, harsh, tight, rigid
with which we quote you when the truth requires;
and what could be truer than truth itself?

We look for a precise definition
and we see that that silken tongue is a scarf
worn by the ostentatious gauchos of our land,
a fluttering caricature of the heart

And the blue smile of that breast strap
and the clinging summer of the blouse
and the bright mullion that illuminates
the face of whoever wears it;

Multicolored and varied like
Laban's flock, the ranks of
neckerchiefs display their colors to the world,
their polychromed and shimmering shield.

They come from a simple, elemental world
where forms have a common root.
They know the profound language of shade
and like their masters, their destiny is mortal.

They lack the inner brilliance of precious stones
but not of the epicarp (is not color also a fruit?)
and like sorrow, they gather at the throat,
for not in vain is man their creator.

Flabby lexicon! Etymology and flimsy
semantics: your definition fails to persuade:
we want it as clear as our romantic
and wild happiness at being heedless and alive!

trans. by Antonio J. Dajer

Romance of the Gambler's Girls (Romance de las Hijas del Chamarilero)

Reb Menashe Dorogofsky
what beautiful girls you have!
the brunette enchants me,
also, the red-head.

The trampled plants of our century
spring again from their feet
the curve of the Hebrew sky
which claimed my faith.
—the feast of Tabernacles of my life
new tablets of the law—
Adonai stretched out this bridge
with the figure of a woman
between my harsh dreams
and the dreams of Israel.

Sparkle of their laughs
and honey rose of their skin
are mirrored by the anxious water
of the world when it sees them
as golden as God commands
here and in Jerusalem.
The girls of this gambler
seem like the daughters of a king.

Reb Menashe Dorogofsky
what beautiful girls you have!
which will I choose
for a nuptial feast
if the brunette is made of roses
and the red-head of honey?

I would take them both
and the dowries which you give with them,
and with my tricks
I will know how to keep them;
for in hunting my fortune,
my verses are my decoy:
we will live with the happiness of the refrain:
"There are not two without three."
Restocking the branches
of the blonde trunk of Sem.

Thread of gold, thread of silver,
Reb Menashe, now you see it:
thread of gold: your daughters,
and of silver as well—what do you say!

trans. by Shepherd Bliss
and Roberta Kalechofsky

A Series of Verses to the Venerable Ancient Whose Portrait Hangs In the Window of a Lottery Agency

The Avenida de Mayo
glows with a virginal light beneath the Sabbath sky.

That light strikes
the window pane that displays your portrait:
Laban amidst a flock of gaily colored lottery
tickets, green, blue, and purple.

The skullcap, the flowing beard and the patriarchal
eyebrows give you a holy countenance
that beckons the unsuspecting sheep that wander
among the musical squabbles of the
asthmatic klaxons.

Why, with that haloed prophet's head,
to reveal the mystery of the coveted number
must be easier for you than it was for Jehovah
to create you from a bit of reverie and
another bit of clay.

Your sons and your servants
sell miracle bread:
tickets for a quick spin among the clouds
with its share of loops and crash landings.

They compete with their Creator
even during the sacred serenity of the Sabbath,
and you preside with that fathomless smile
and those Talmudic whiskers over their worldly needs.

With the mortal wisdom of the returning voyager,
your gaze that wandered through the starless night
now regards who knows from what lofty perch
the snake dance of the final sin.

Now in the Gehenna where golden and bloody faggots of flame
crackle and burn
your soul will be scourged by sombre angels,
deaf to your cries.

No passerby will know, seeing your kindly eyes,
the agony which mercilessly consumes you from within
while the impetuous waves of traffic surge on
beneath a sky that is bursting open, crystalline, restless.

Israelite! You who lead
another reprobate life
beyond the shallow glare of your windowpane,
I alone understand you!

Ah, if you would only show me the secret number
I would abandon myself with you over the mouth of hell
to pass a consecrated Sabbath of idleness
that would gladden the sleepless sea of your dead Sabbaths.

trans. by Antonio J. Dajer

Dirge for a Bar that Has Closed Down

The slow and green river that winds through
the blanched street of the Jewish Quarter
kept watch over your agony.
From my old table
I used to see him
approach your windows with
restless eyes. And as he wandered away beaten,
his responsory was a lamentation
on the winding streets of Callao and Corrientes.

Your unexpected departure
changed the course of the routine
lives of those bourgeois with their hesitant
and improbable fancies;
of those bourgeois who at the same hour
and with the same unction every day
abdicate the counters of their clothes stores
and, passing the sceptre to their wives,
enter with uncovered heads
at midafternoon—flashing
a smile—through the same familiar doorway
and with the same bland gestures
join the gesticulating circle
which, seated in a corner, struggles
—with its Russian tea and its philately—
to preserve the Wailing Wall
(While the implacable daughters
attached to the complicit nuptial telephone
and shaking the wires with guttural r's
begin to arrange charming rendezvous
in the lobby of the "Etual"
—adventures with insipid endings,
with episodes in your Family
Room, whose gravest folly
is to break each other's heart,
passionately, more or less,
or parsimoniously,
but with no harm intended. . .)

They too were forced to emigrate,
those youths addicted to drink
who hailed Castelar as a co-religionist
along with Maimonides and Gabirol;

some: steadfast Zionists
who between "cubano" and "san martín"
before the dulled mirrors
declaim in precise terms
and cast their eyes like nets for the woman playing
  the violin;
and the others: experts on the Hebraica
with the pomposity of asses,
who know nothing of Mosaic Law
and break all the Commandments
Upon whom the University
bestows a title and the leisure
to give us performances
of their unfolding vanity.

And the friends whose scattering
you caused. Even now
their passionate dreams and wholesome happiness
gleam in your lounge.

And my stunted novel
a bit vulgar—a bit wistful
with the most beautiful girl in it
whom no one ever knew.

Bar that shattered my final scheme,
now that I see you from the viewpoint of
my loneliness, lost in this swarming city,
I think that if you had not closed down,
I might have prevailed.

The slow and green river that winds through
that blanched street of the Jewish Quarter
kept watch over your agony.

From my old table
I used to see him
approach your windows with
restless eyes. And as he wandered away, beaten,
his responsory was a lamentation
On the winding streets of Callao and Corrientes.

trans. by Antonio J. Dajer

Freckled Childhood
(Niñez Pecosa)

I certainly had an obscure childhood
but intensely my own,
a childhood which wanted to be dashing
but had the features of a caricature.

Yes, a caricature. For example:
that absurd love for Sophie,
the rabbi's wife whom I saw
every night, profaning the temple.

(To think that Tolstoi was the sentimental
bridge that almost united us
that Passover afternoon
I read "Resurrection," languishing.)

And this precocious, burning fever for Mariadela
—her father my namesake and matchmaker—
Where can I find four mad phrases
and an ending worthy of a novel?

trans. by Shepherd Bliss
and Roberta Kalechofsky

César Tiempo *was born Israel Zeitlin in the Ukraine in 1906. Along with Alberto Gerchunoff, his family's emigration to Argentina belongs to the phase of early Jewish settlement in that country. His poetry and work has been known for some time in the United States to such admirers as Donald D. Walsh who, with H.R. Hays and Dudley Fitts, translated some of Tiempo's poetry for the* Anthology of Contemporary Latin American Poetry, *published in 1942 by New Directions. As Walsh pointed out in his article on Tiempo for* Revista Iberoamericana *(November, 1945), more than any other Jewish writer of Argentina, Tiempo was the interpreter, the defender and the conscience of the Jews of Buenos Aires. As director of the periodical,* Critica Y El Sol *and of the review,* La Columna, *Tiempo played an important part in the literary development of Argentinian Jews. His first volume of poetry,* Versos de Una *was published in 1923, and his talent was acclaimed. The volume was republished in Buenos Aires in 1977. Now ailing with the discomforts of age and glaucoma, César Tiempo may justifiably be regarded as "dean" of Argentinian Jewish poetry.* Libro para la pausa del sábado *(1930) received the literary prize, el Primer Premio Municipal de Poesía in the same year. This volume was followed by two more books of poetry whose titles reflect a similar theme:* Sabatión argentino *(1933) and* Sábadomingo *(1938).*

Alicia Steimberg

from
Musicians and Watchmakers

My grandmother knew the secret of eternal life. It consisted of a set of rules that were so simple, it was hard to believe that she should be the only one who knew and applied them. From time to time we shared in the ritual and in this way we too were guaranteed at least a good portion of immortality, if not the whole lot.

One of the ceremonies of her practice consisted in bringing Swiss chard to a boil and eating it right away, pouring off the cooking water and sprinkling the vegetables with the juice of two large lemons. In the more elaborate form of this procedure, the vegetables were cooked beneath a lemon tree. As soon as they were ready, an incision was made into two lemons hanging in the tree above the pot, so that the juice which dripped onto the chard would retain its full ration of vitamins. That's how we avoided "eating corpses."

My grandmother used to say that ninety percent of all human ailments came from constipation. Everybody at home suffered from it and there was a continuous exchange of recipes to rid oneself of this trouble. In spite of all her knowledge regarding the subject, my grandmother was the one who suffered the most. Whenever she managed to move her bowels, she'd go about with a big smile on her face, tell everyone the good news and was even able to make a joke or reminisce about spring in Kiev.

"That was what you'd call spring! And it would arrive after a winter which also had been a real winter! When it already seemed as if the cold and the snow would last forever, a morning would come when she would pull the curtains open and see torrents of rain coming down. As soon as the water had run off, the sun would suddenly come out and everything would burst into blossom and the orchards would be chock full of cherries. Sweet cherries, not like the ones we have here. And it would be the same thing the next day, and the day after, and so on—not like here, where nobody knows what spring is really like."

That's how my grandmother would speak of her native country, when the well-being of her intestines put her into a good mood.

I don't know whether Otilia ever had the illusion of being pretty. Perhaps—on some summer afternoon, when she would take the trolley down Ninth of July Avenue, riding with her fiancé, a handsome fellow who looked like Clark Gable and who was younger than she. You'll want to know how she landed him. It was at a dance, where she and her next younger sister each found a fiancé.

The young men were friends. They had come to Buenos Aires not very long ago and were making a living in any way they could. They also went out and had fun, as bachelors do. For forty cents, they would enjoy a day in the sun: ten cents for the trolley that went to the Municipal swimming pool, ten cents for the return trip, ten cents for an orange drink and ten cents for a salami sandwich. They basked in the sun, in their woollen swimming trunks, their little moustaches and their innocence, and talked about the future.

"Listen—you going to get married?" Clark Gable asked.

"Well. . . .no. . ." was the answer. "I'm going to travel. . . ."

Nevertheless, they did get married, within one month of each other, and soon after that conversation by the swimming pool. Otilia and Clark Gable married first (the luck of the plain one!). I participated in all the preparations. Grandmother installed herself with a bag of rolls in the yard of the house in Donato Alvarez. She cut each roll in half and put them together with some stuff in between. Platters laden with those rolls, together with soft drinks and beer, were placed on trestle tables which were put up at night in the yard. I don't know whether there was anything else, because I rarely managed to get close, and when I did manage, I'd be smothered with wet kisses by all the aunts, asked to tell them my name and how old I was, and whether I loved my little brother.

Neither did I manage to see much when the glorious moment arrived and the brides—first one, then the other—left the house of their parents and acquired the privilege of being supported by a husband. At that moment, all the guests crowded around the bridal canopy which was lit by an electric light bulb. Clark Gable and his friend were tall; their heads were tilted beneath the canopy, with the little lamp resting upon their hair which was pressed down with brilliantine. Apart from this one small inconvenience, everything went well. I stood there on tiptoe, craning my neck in vain, and heard the solemn voice of the Rabbi who initiated the ceremony by invoking God's blessing. I was a little girl, but I already knew that one was expected to be very moved. I also knew that the smell of jasmine came from the neighbor's garden, because in my grandparents' garden there were only geraniums. I also noticed that more than one of the guests would turn around in the middle of the ceremony, showing a considerable lack of reverence, in order to cast a glance upon the trestle table. I learned something during the first of these weddings: Not to stay until the end of the ceremony and get caught between the canopy and table. That's what happened the first time and I was almost squashed.

Several years before, another wedding had taken place in this house, as a consequence of which I was born and, three years later, my brother (of whom I had to say whether I loved him). Once Otilia and Amanda were married, there was still Mele left, a fourth sister who was to remain single for many years to come. Finally she too got married, which was a good thing, because if she hadn't—what a heartache for her mother!

Shortly after Otilia and Amanda were married, Grandfather became sick and I no longer visited the house in Donato Alvarez. I heard nothing more about my grandfather until one day I was taken to the Chacarita (because my grandfather who was an atheist, a socialist, and a vegeterian, was cremated according to his wishes, and therefore is not buried among our relatives in the Jewish cemetery). Before I was taken to his funeral services, nobody told me that he had died. They did not want to upset me. We stood for a while and looked at the box. It was impossible to imagine that Grandfather could be in there. Otilia and Amanda were not there, because of their "condition." My cousins were also born within a month of each other: first the son of Otilia and Clark Gable, and then the one of Amanda and Clark Gable's friend. Amanda and her husband later moved to General Pico and we lost contact with them.

An era had come to an end, one which had been long and difficult for my family, but pleasant and much fun for me. I used to smell the cookies Grandmother baked, listen to Mele, Otilia and Amanda as they rehearsed some didactic play for the Drama Group of the Socialist Party, and watch a windmill being created on a canvas that Mele was painting. The picture did not interest me as much as her palette did, for it was covered with all kinds of blobs and peaks of colors.

Otilia and Clark Gable installed themselves in one room of the house, into which they managed to stuff a wide bed with night tables, a dining table with chairs, a wardrobe, a dresser and a side table. In a jar which Otilia called her "centerpiece," there was a bunch of artificial flowers that she herself had made. When Chubby was born (that's how he was called, because that's what he was), they also had to fit in a cradle.

Motherhood did nothing for Otilia's looks. She did not get any prettier—only fatter. It was impossible to imagine her the way she had looked when she had been engaged; slender, with her blue linen sailor dress, white high heeled shoes and bangs on her forehead. Clark Gable, on the other hand, was now thinner than he used to be, but still good looking, cheerful: always telling jokes. From time to time the mother and the sister of Clark Gable came to Entre Ríos for a visit. They were "ladies" and had leisure and were in a position to travel. They also had shrill voices and they used a contraceptive method which consisted in jumping again and again from a table to the floor after they "had relations" with their husbands. They were famous for the number of abortions they had given themselves; there was not one in the family who had had less than 30 or 40.

Otilia and Amanda willy nilly had also turned into "ladies." Otilia chose the names for her children among those which appeared in the society notes of the local newspaper. The same names as those of the children of Mrs. Peralta Ramos or Mrs. Martinez de Hoz. She avoided the obviously Catholic names, such as combinations with Maria.

Amanda, who was less pretentious and more sentimental and who loved to sing tangos, gave her children names of celebrities. They were called Evaristo, Azucena and Greta. This last concession—or deviation—was due to her passion for foreign actresses.

With this matter of names a long family tradition was broken. All the female cousins of Otilia and Amanda had been called Dora and all the male cousins had been called Leon. In order to distinguish one from the other, they were classified as Dora, Dorita, Dorucha, Dora the tall, Dora the short, Uncle Joe's Dora; Leon, Leoncito, Leoncho, Leon of the watchmaker's, and Leon the lawyer. When everyone was together, there was no confusion at all. Each one knew very well who he was and who the others were.

Now that three of her daughters were married, Grandmother was pleased. At the weddings of other relatives which were not held in her arbor but in halls that were rented for the occasion, she allowed herself to be photographed with her daughters, her sons-in-law and her grandchildren, all dressed fancy and with new shoes. I learned to distrust the smiles which they also wore on these occasions: when Grandmother returned from a party and put on her housedress, she showed her true face; the mirror of an existence full of suffering at the side of a silent husband and daughters who were constantly fighting with each other, always at odds, and nursing resentments for no reasons. According to what I heard them call each other during these arguments, the four of them were bitches, snakes, malicious egotists, idiots and misers. I tried to discover these qualities in their faces, but apart from the fact that they were overweight and not pretty, I could see nothing more.

After each fight they would swear to be enemies forever. But then they would meet again at a wedding or a funeral, their faces covered with rouge and smiles, showing off their small children, and soon they were on good terms again and, for a time, peace reigned.

Once we did have a picnic, and everything went wrong: ants, mosquitoes, overflowing garbage cans spoiled everything. "When a poor person wants to have fun. . . ." said Mele, the one who married so late and who, like the rest of her sisters, was a great "nasher." Grandmother tried to cheer us up, telling funny stories which had happened to other people she knew: one fellow had had bad luck in business and had been left out in the street; another one had to interrupt his studies because of money problems; another had to cancel a trip; again another had just had his sixth daughter... She would laugh till she cried and never noticed whether or not the others shared her amusement.

The same things were not so funny when they happend to Grandmother. Then she would fall into despondency, the grey rings under her eyes would show clearly, and she would consider the unhappy event to be one more proof of her unlucky star.

In spite of her bad experience with marriage, she was a great advocate of marriage. She advised the girls to go to parties with pretty, low-cut dresses, to wear lots of jewelry—(never mind, whether it was real or fake—as long as it was shiny)—and to keep their eyes sharp for the boys.

"No use being shy," she would say. The way to act was like that relative who took her daughter to dances and whenever she would meet a boy, she would approach him and say: "Young man, may I introduce you to my daughter." The baffled victim would not stop to think that not only did he not know the lady to whom he was being introduced—which was only natural—but neither did he know the lady who was making the introduction—which was not so natural.

This strategy never failed. The victim would blush, would shake hands with the girl and ask her to dance. The mother would sit down with the other mothers who looked at her askance out of envy, since their daughters were still standing on the other side of the hall, pretending that they were delighted to be talking with each other, while others were already preparing their trousseaus or pushing baby carriages in the park.

There were afternoons of visits to the house in Donato Alvarez. The family from Constitución would arrive, plant wet kisses on my face and ask whether I loved my little brother. Once they brought their grandchild to play with me, but he coughed a lot; so they would not allow me to come close. I looked at him from a distance, sitting on the first step of the stairs leading to the terrace. When everybody was busy talking, I went up the stairs, but on the top step I slipped and tumbled down, and landed on top of Otilia who was waiting for me with her arms open. The heel of my shoe went into her nose. Later, while she dipped a piece of cloth into brine to stem the blood, she gave me her furious glances. She didn't say anything to me because, after all, I was a little girl, but I'm sure that from that moment on I too was in her eyes like all the others: a bitch, a snake, malicious, egotistic, an idiot and a miser.

My grandfather, who was the only man in the house, never participated in these chats. He remembered the time when he was the one who had given orders to these daughters. He knew they were happy when they laughed a lot, but if they chattered too much, he would give them a laxative. He was convinced that all strange behavior was due to irregularity. "Do you remember your father?" Grandmother would say when she had one of her attacks of nostalgia. "How he would give you Josselin tea?"—and she would shake with laughter at the memory.

Grandmother was eleven years old when she emigrated from Kiev to Buenos Aires. She was sent to school and learned Spanish very well. She could sing tangos like a sick bird. . . Scaa-a-a-a-ars-

trill, trill, trill,—indelible sca-a-a-aars, of a wou-ou-ound—trill, trill, trill.

She never spoke about how she came to marry Grandfather. She gave birth to her daughters, one after the other, without any difficulties. Each one appeared before the midwife did, eager to be born and to start fighting with the other. Times were bad. There was unemployment. And eviction. At a benefit dance, money was collected to find a new home for them and for other poor people. The newspaper published an article about this party. Several people made very good use of the opportunity, and several young girls were presented to society. Various engagements followed. In successive issues of the newspaper, photographs appeared of formal engagements, of weddings, and of births of first children. The young mothers chose names for their historical children. The same names that Otilia's children have.

Before they got married Otilia and Amanda were salesgirls in La Piedad where they sang to the customers the praises of the odds and ends they had for sale. Mele, the one who had a hard time finding a husband, never worked outside the house. Sometimes she sewed and helped with the domestic chores, and when she finished she would paint. She painted flowers, sailboats at sunset, Dutch girls with tulips, haystacks and farmhouses. She copied the pictures from postcards she had.

On Sundays everybody had dinner at the house in Donato Alvarez. The fiancés of Otilia and Amanda would come too. They made the house more cheerful. They were great talkers. They brought bottles of wine and put us on their knees, and we had to read for them, and show them what we knew. I would recite, I would sip Father's port and say that I loved my little brother, and the women did not fight.

Their engagements were announced as late as possible in order not to give other unmarried girls a chance to flirt with their fiancés. It was also necessary to establish relations with the families of these future husbands. And in this Amanda was an expert. The moment Clark Gable's friend showed signs of weakening and realized that, travel or no travel, he was headed for matrimony, Amanda began to visit her future in-laws.

I went with her for that first visit, because she felt that the presence of a child makes the situation more relaxed. While one gives the child candy, asks her to recite some poetry, asks her stupid questions, and compares her with other children of one's own family, the time passes.

Clark Gable's friend had two unmarried sisters: Lia, who was very thin and colorless, and Marta, much younger, with curly hair and a protruding lower lip, who blushed for no reason. Lia had a special way of pronouncing the "r." It was not just a guttural "r," but it sounded almost like a "kh." It was she who opened the door and led us across a dark courtyard to a room, at the entrance to which there was a rusty box with a star of David, for contributions to Eretz Israel. As soon as I sat down in my chair, Lia looked at me and said: "Oh, how pkhetty," and gave me an oily cookie. It was Amanda who interested her. She devoured her with her eyes, from her curly hair with the brilliantine, to her nails with the purple red nail polish, and the aquamarine ring. "Come, Makhta," she called to her sister, "Amanda and her niece have akhived."

"Poor girls," Amanda said later. "They were crazy about our visit—you should see how they live in that house. . . ."

• • ◦ •

"Children—what for?" Grandmother said. "Why bring unfortunate creatures into this world!" Mele, who had finally married, was not thinking about having children, the way other married people do.

This gave rise to two questions: one, whether Mele, if she had wanted children, could have had them, considering her age; the other: what did Grandmother mean by "bringing unfortunate creatures into the world"? Did she think that children of Mele's would be unfortunate? Because they would have old parents? Because Mele used to go around with her mouth open and had swallowed live flies two or three times in her life? Or did Grandmother think that any child that came into this world, whether or not it was Mele's, would be unfortunate? Unfortunate, because some catastrophe was about to happen? Another war, or the end of the world? Unfortunate, because all Jews are unfortunate—or all the members of our family?

I couldn't ask any of these questions aloud, because supposedly I had not listened to the conversation. I was supposed to be in my room, learning the equation that says that A is equal to A, which can be proven by some absurdity.

Grandmother and the sister of Leon the watchmaker, the one who had a crazy daughter in the madhouse, had pulled chairs out into the yard and were sitting there, talking and moving their heads in their way which indicated sadness.

One thing was certain: Mele looked very pleased when she left the house with her husband, Uncle Thomas (Tevie to his friends), a timid man with grey hair and mustaches who had certain difficulties explaining what he did for a living. Through these conversations that I was not supposed to hear, I discovered that he worked at a window at the Hippodrome. I don't know what was wrong with this kind of work, but he probably knew, since he avoided talking about it. Or perhaps he felt inferior in our particular family which, though it was now going through rather hard times, had been a distinguished family in which everybody had been either a musician or a watchmaker, which could be traced all the way back to King David. (By "musician" is meant a cantor in the Temple, and by "watchmaker" someone who repairs watches.) There has never been a butcher or a tailor in the family, which would have tarnished our name. During her engagement, Mele received Thomas every Sunday in the dining room. He always brought some sweet meringues for tea. After the wedding they lived at our home for several months. They had the room in the front toward the street, 30 meters from the bathroom. When Mele and Mama had a fight, Mama would lock the door of the dining room, which was the only covered passage to the bathroom. It was a great inconvenience when it was cold or when it rained. Thomas would run through the yard, sheltered under a huge umbrella. He had a funny way of running, Thomas. He ran with short little steps, his back bent, and he would progress so little that I could not understand why he was running: walking would have gotten him there just as quickly. One afternoon, when we exchanged confidences, Mele told me the story of Thomas, and then I understood.

When Thomas was a small boy in Poland his father taught him to do farm work. When Thomas made a mistake or became tired, his father would hit him with the same whip he used for the horses. When Thomas tried to run away, it was of no use: a man runs faster than a boy, and there went Thomas, running with his short little steps, with his back bent under the whip of his father. After I had heard this story, I always looked away when I saw Thomas running through the yard of the house.

As soon as they were able to, Mele and Thomas rented a small apartment and left the house. They stuffed it full of furniture so that it was almost impossible to walk through and Thomas, even had he wanted to, was not able to do any running there. This late marriage was without a doubt the happiest in our family.

"You are lousy with money—you take care of Mother!"

That's how the conversation ended and Mother hung up the receiver with a bang. Grandmother left the house a week later, preceded by Clark Gable who carried her suitcase. After that, Mama and Otilia broke off relations for a long time. Otilia made various unsuccessful attempts to send Grandmother back home.

I went from time to time to see Grandmother. I would find her depressed, absent minded, or suffering from the symptoms of that strange illness which had attacked her ever since anybody can remember, and which no doctor had been able to diagnose. They all said that she was healthy, remarkably so for her age, and they would at most prescribe some vitamins. "The doctors don't know anything," she would insist, and would take her own precautions. A medical student from the neighborhood who gave people injections and took their blood pressure, would come promptly whenever she called him. He would sit down next to her and proceed with great circumspection to pull the gadget for taking blood pressure out of its case, wrap it around Grandmother's arm, which she, experienced in these matters, would let hang limply by the side of her bed. In the meantime they would talk about all kinds of things: whether the weather was hot or cold, or about some plants in the yard. Then the young man would show Grandmother the readings on the gadget, which in turn would determine the mood of the house for the next few days. Even when her blood pressure was normal, Grandmother was a time bomb. Some annoyance, some row—and the pressure could go up and kill her. "You'll be the death of me," she would say, whenever anybody did or said anything she didn't like.

Once a year, on a certain date, there is a big party in the Home for Elderly Jews. The old people dress in their best clothes and invite the community to spend a Sunday in the home. It's a big social occasion. Picnic tables are set up, and all kinds of booths for the sale of food and drink, clothing and accessories, and "ladders" for raising money: whoever contributes the most, climbs to the highest rung. Otilia and Clark Gable never missed this day since their situation had improved—in contrast with our own family, which had remained chronically in straitened circumstances. But that did not matter to us, because we were intellectuals, and they, at most—and that is stretching it quite a bit—could only reach the level of bourgeois pigs.

After taking charge of her mother, Otilia then saw the home with other eyes. She looked less at the jewelry others wore, or at the amount the Circle of Jewish Ladies contributed to the Home, and more keenly at the faces of residents. She wanted to find out how they lived. "Never," she thought at first, after her inspection. But each time Grandmother was "impossible," Otilia had another fight with her sisters, because she wanted them to take care of Grandmother. The only things she achieved during all the years Grandmother was in her house, living with her, was that she got her to live with Amanda in General Pico for three months. At the end of the three months, Amanda sent her mother back, claiming that she herself was not feeling well.

Grandmother did not die of high blood pressure. When she was in her eighties (though she never admitted to more than seventy-eight), she had to undergo an operation. At that time I was already far away, away from them all. I learned through a phone call that she was ill, that she was going to have an operation. It was also through a phone call that I learned of her death.

The coffin was placed in a rented hall, closed according to Jewish custom, and covered with a black cloth embroidered with the star of David. I don't believe this was done because of any instructions on her part. It is not possible that she should have made any provisions for her death, since she did not believe she would die. Contrary to Grandfather, who had believed in absolute death and in ideals and had wished to burn into Nothingness to prove his point.

The decision to bury Grandmother according to Jewish tradition must have been Otilia's who could not afford to jeopardize her standing in the community.

It was raining when they carried the coffin from the funeral chapel to the cemetery of Tablada. It was raining when we waited for the corpse to be washed and the coffin to be carried to the temple.

The ceremony was short. Standing around the coffin, we listened to the Hebrew lamentations of the Rabbi. I did not understand what he said, but this ceremony was the most beautiful event in which I had seen my grandmother participate. Then they buried her—it was still raining—in a place far away from the entrance. The best sites, those by the main avenue, had long since been reserved. They had been reserved for those distinguished dead who are still alive, but who know how to take their rightful place.

Trans. by Miriam Varon

Alicia Steimberg *was born in Buenos Aires in 1933.* Musicians and Watchmakers *was her first published work. It was a finalist in a competition organized by publishers from Barcelona and Caracas.*

Jaime Alazraki

Borges and the Kabbalah

When asked a few years ago about his interest in the Kabbalah, Borges replied, "I read a book called *Major Trends in Jewish Mysticism* by Scholem and another book by Trachtenberg on Jewish superstitions.[1] Then I have read all the books on the Kabbalah I have found and all the articles in the encyclopedias and so on. But I have no Hebrew whatever."[2] These remarks, considering the number of interviews Borges has given, come rather late. Except for this single statement, nothing else has been added on the subject since Rabi's essay, "Fascination de la Kabbale,"[3] and Rabi's contribution lies in his merely having called attention to Borges' familiarity with Kabbalistic texts. I shall attempt to show how far Borges' acquaintance with the Kabbalah goes beyond the few accidental tracks left in his writings as a result of his readings. Ultimately, as André Maurois puts it, "Borges has read everything" that exists ("and all the books that don't exist," adds John Barth), and it would be unusual not to find in his prose some imprints of the material which, as is the case with the Kabbalah, exerted on his mind such an enthralling fascination.[4]

The impact of the Kabbalah on Borges' work far exceeds the random quotations or allusions the casual reader may find and which, after all, only confirm the interest Borges conceded above. Behind his transparent texts there lies a stylistic intricacy, a certain Kabbalistic texture, a spellbinding characteristic to which Borges finds himself attracted.

To the question, "Have you tried to make your own stories Kabbalistic?" he replied, "Yes, sometimes I have."[5] For the Kabbalists, as one of the classic texts shows, "every word of the Torah has six hundred thousand faces—that is, layers of meaning or entrances," and the ostensible aim of the Kabbalah seems to be to reach these profound layers. Borges' writings offer the reader a similar challenge. Most of his narratives do not exhaust themselves at the level of literal meaning—they present an immediate and manifest layer and a more oblique and allusive one. It is the latter which generates in his stories a Kabbalistic aura whose source goes far beyond a fortuitous familiarity with the Kabbalah.

1. A Scrutiny of Borges' Kabbalah Library

In "Death and the Compass," Borges examines some books on the Kabbalah from his own library. Echoing Cervantes' device,[6] Borges includes among the volumes of the murdered rabbi's complete works his own essay, "A Vindication of the Kabbalah," collected in the volume *Discusión.* Contrary to what happens in *Don Quixote,* where Cervantes' pastoral novel *La Galatea* receives from the curate a favorable although not excessively generous comment, the reference to Borges' essay in the story goes without any remark at all. However, the mere inclusion of an essay written by the same author who now writes the story produces an effect similar to the one achieved by Cervantes in the famous passage. Essentially it is the effect produced by the theater within the theater, by literature becoming the subject of literature. In this operation, Borges attains a literary magic he himself has poignantly described:

> Why does it make us uneasy to know that the map is within the map and the thousand and one nights are within the book of *A Thousand and One Nights*? Why does it disquiet us to know that *Don Quixote* is a reader of the *Quixote,* and Hamlet is a spectator of *Hamlet*? I believe I have found the answer: those inversions suggest that if the characters in a story can be the readers or spectators, then we, their readers or spectators, can be fictitious. (*OI,* 46) [7]

Among the books that Borges attributes to Rabbi Marcelo Yarmolinsky there figures "a literal translation of the *Sefer Yetsirah.*" The Book of Creation is a brief treatise on cosmologic and cosmogonic matters. It was written between the third and sixth century and represents, with the Book *Bahir* (twelfth century), the embryo out of which the bulk of the Kabbalah grew and developed. Its chief subjects are the elements of the world, which are sought in the ten elementary and primordial numbers—Sefiroth—and in the twenty-two letters of the Hebrew alphabet. Together these represent the mysterious forces whose convergence has produced the various combinations observable throughout the whole of creation; they are the *thirty-two secret paths of wisdom,* through which God has created all that exists. In his essay, "On the Cult of Books," Borges again refers to the *Sefer Yetsirah.* This time the reference is a long paragraph in which he furnishes some basic information on the book, describes its purpose and method, and brings in a quotation which may or may not be taken directly from the text, since this is the most widely cited passage of the Book of Creation and Borges might well have found it in the books and articles he read on the subject: "Twenty-two fundamental letters: God drew them, engraved them, combined them, weighted them, permuted them, and with them produced everything that is and everything that will be." At any rate, the long reference is an indication that the inclusion of this title in Yarmolinsky's bibliography is as important with regard to the murdered Talmudist as it is with respect to Borges' own interest in the Kabbalah. It shows also, however, that the aura of fantasy created by those enigmatic and often esoteric books springs, rather than from Borges' intention, from the reader's unfamiliarity with these works and authors, although Borges—undoubtedly—is aware of their puzzling impact on the reader.[8] The same holds true for the other books mentioned in the list. Thus the

History of the Hasidic Sect and the *Biography of the Baal Shem,* attributed to Yarmolinsky, are slightly modified versions of two works by Martin Buber: *The Origin and Meaning of Hasidism*[9] and *The Legend of Baal Shem.*[10] Borges' acquaintance with Buber becomes apparent in the story "The Sect of the Phoenix," where he quotes him, and in the essay "On Chesterton," where he directs the reader to Buber's classic *Tales of the Hasidim.*[11]

The last book mentioned in the list, *A Study of the Philosophy of Robert Fludd,* although not directly concerned with the Kabbalah, is not foreign to its doctrine. Several of Fludd's (1574-1637) postulates are amazingly close to those of the Kabbalah. The English Rosicrucian maintained that the universe proceeds from, and will return to, God; that the act of creation is the separation of the active principle (light) from the passive (darkness) in the bosom of the divine unity (God); and that the universe consists of three worlds: the archetypal (God), the macrocosm (the world), and the microcosm (man). He was a follower of Paracelsus, whose prescriptions for the making of the homunculus bear astonishing similarities to the golem-making formulae of the Kabbalists.[12]

Lönnrot, the "pure logician" of "Death and the Compass," carries these books off to his apartment, "suddenly turning bibliophile and Hebraic scholar" (*A,* 67). Borges could as well have said "Kabbalist," since Lönnrot attempts to solve the mysteries of the seemingly ritualistic murders in the same manner that a Kabbalist deciphers the occult mysteries of the Scripture. The arithmetic value of the dates of the murders and their geometric location on the map become important and revealing. Before Lönrott can establish these symmetries in time and space, he devotes himself to perusing Yarmolinsky's books. Borges does not miss the chance to unfold his erudition on the subject. Thus, one book revealed to the investigator "the doctrine that God has a secret name in which. . .His ninth attribute, Eternity, may be found—that is to say, the immediate knowledge of everything under the sun that will be, that is, and that was" (*A,* 68). The ninth attribute mentioned in the story takes us to the very core of the Kabbalah's cosmogony—the theory of the *Sefiroth.*

2. The Doctrine of the *Sefiroth*

Borges' first explorations into the subject of the Kabbalah are found in his second collection of essays, *El tamaño de mi esperanza* (The Extent of My Hope), published in 1926. There, in an article entitled "A History of Angels," Borges leaves a testimony to his first readings on the Kabbalah. He mentions two books, Erich Bischoff's *Die Elemente der Kabbalah* (1914) and *Rabbinical Literature* by Stehelin; even more important is the fact that the passage contains the germ of his more mature essay, "A Vindication of the Kabbalah," of 1931. Yet it is in the earlier article, "A History of Angels," where he writes literally about the theory of the *Sefiroth.* Relying on Bischoff and Stehelin, Borges explains that "to each one of the ten *Sefiroth,* or eternal emanations of the godhead, corresponds a region of heaven, one of the names of God, one commandment of the decalogue, a part of the human body, and a class of angels." He adds that Stehelin "links the first ten letters of the Hebrew alphabet to these ten heavenly worlds. Thus the letter Aleph looks toward the brain, the first commandment, the heaven of fire, the second name 'I Am That I Am,' and the seraphim called Holy Beasts."[13]

Perhaps the most direct bearing the doctrine of the *Sefiroth* has on Borges' work emerges in the story "The Aleph." The theory of the *Sefiroth* postulates that there are two worlds and that both represent God. "First a primary world, the most deeply hidden of all, which remains insensible and unintelligible to all but God, the world of *En-Sof* (Infinite); and secondly, one joined unto the first, which makes it possible to know God, the world of attributes."[14] The ninth *Sefirah,* as pointed out by Borges, is the source from which the divine life overflows in the act of mystical procreation. The world of *Sefiroth* is described as a mystical organism, and the most important images used in this connection are those of the tree and of a man. This tree is the unknown and unknowable God, but it is also the skeleton of the universe—it grows throughout the whole of creation and spreads its branches through all its ramifications. All mundane and created things exist only because something of the power of the *Sefiroth* lives and acts in them."[15] This notion of God's externalization is summarized in a passage of the *Zohar* (Book of Splendor): "The process of creation has taken place on two planes, one above and one below, and for this reason the Torah begins with the letter Beth, the numerical value of which is two. The lower occurrence corresponds to the higher; one produced the upper world (of the *Sefiroth*), the other the nether world (of the visible creation)."[16] The pantheistic character of this outlook comes openly to the surface in the Spanish Kabbalist Joseph Gikatila's formula, "He fills everything and He is everything." The theogony of the *Sefiroth* and the cosmogony of creation represent two aspects of the same act. "Creation," says Scholem, "mirrors the inner movement of the divine life. . . .It is nothing but an external development of those forces which are active and alive in God Himself. . . .The life of the Creator pulsates in that of his creatures."[17] The last assertion does not differ, even in its formulation, from Borges' own pantheistic formula, "Every man is an organ put forth by the divinity in order to perceive the world" ("The Theologians," *L,* 124).[18]

The Kabbalistic notion that conceives the Torah as a vast *corpus symbolicum,* representative of that hidden life within God which the theory of the *Sefiroth* attempts to describe, is paraphrased in Léon Bloy's *L'Ame de Napoléon* (as quoted by Borges in his essay "The Mirror of the Enigmas"): "History is an immense liturgical text, where the *i's* and the periods are not worth less than whole verses or chapters, but the importance of both is undeterminable and is profoundly hidden. . . .Everything is a symbol." Borges' own comments underline the affinity between Bloy and the Kabbalah:

> Bloy. . .did nothing but apply to the whole Creation the method that the Jewish cabalists applied to the Scripture. They thought that a work dictated by the Holy Spirit was an absolute text: a text where the collaboration of chance is calculable at zero.[19] The portentous premise of a book that is impervious to contingency, a book that is a mechanism of infinite purposes, moved them to permute the scriptural words, to sum up the numerical value of the letters, to consider their form, to observe the small letters and the capital letters, to search for acrostics and anagrams. . . . (*OI,* 128)

For the Kabbalists, the letters of the Torah are the mystical body of God, and from this it follows that the Creation is just a reflection or emanation of the Holy text; hence the Midrash "God looked into the Torah and created the world," and the story told in the Mishnah about a scribe (of the Scripture) who, when asked about his occupation, received from his teacher the following advice: "My son, be careful in your work, for it is the work of God; if you omit a single letter, or write a letter too many, you will destroy the whole world . . . ."[20] The whole idea is put in a nutshell in the Kabbalistic axiom: "What is below is above and what is inside is outside,"[21] from which the *Sefer Yetsirah* infers that "on the basis of the lower world we understand the secret law according to which the upper world is governed." The Kabbalist Menahem Recanati adds his own exegesis to the axiom: "All created being, earthly man and all other creatures in this world, exist according to the archetype (*dugma*) of the ten *sefiroth.*"[22] The text that best shows the spell of the *Sefiroth* on Borges is a passage from his story "The Theologians," in which he gives in a condensed formula the pantheistic essentials of the theory. "In the hermetic books," he says, "it is written that what is down below is equal to what is on high, and what is on high is equal to what is down below; in the *Zohar,* that the higher world is a reflection of the lower" (*L,* 123). From this Borges derives one of his favorite motifs—"every man is two men"—which has ingenious and fertile effects on his narratives.[23]

3. The Legend of the Golem

Borges' debt to Gershom Scholem is acknowledged in a couplet from his poem "The Golem": "But all these matters are discussed by Scholem / in a most learned passage of his book" (*SP,* 113). The book is Scholem's *Major Trends in Jewish Mysticism,* undoubtedly the most authoritative work on the subject and a model of scholarship. Borges could not have chosen better. Paradoxically, however—and this is one of the voluntarily involuntary mistakes in which Borges delights—the information for the poem does not arise from the "learned book," *Major Trends. . .*, which hardly devotes a few lines to the question of the golem, but from other sources.[24] Later Borges resourcefully explained in his "Autobiographical Essay" that he twice used Scholem's name in the poem "as the only possible rhyming word" for golem.

The poem represents one of the most felicitous expressions of a main theme in Borges' work—the world as a dream of God. More than in a *topos* of seventeenth-century literature, Borges finds in the religions of India a new foundation for his idealist outlook on reality.[25] Nevertheless, this theme of the world as God's dream is not motivated by only one doctrine, or "perplexity," as Borges calls it. "The Circular Ruins," for example, embodies the Buddhist belief in the world as the dream of Someone, or perhaps no one, but at the same time it casts in the mold of fiction the idealist notion which postulates the hallucinatory character of all reality. Borges' avid erudition, however, does not stop at these two sources. He searches for new formulations of the same basic idea, for new versions of a same metaphor, until he arrives at a brilliantly concise assertion—"Perhaps universal history is the history of the diverse intonation of a few metaphors" ("Pascal's Sphere," *OI,* 6). Therefore, it would be mistaken to point to one source as the motivation of the poem or the story, or to single out one exclusive intonation of a metaphor as the only "perplexity" Borges intends to reinterpret in his fiction. One of the enchanting features of Borges' art is precisely the combination of very diverse constituents, the blending of various intonations into one unified tone. In this process, the metaphors of history were converted into what they essentially are—into metaphors of literature.

Thus the story "The Circular Ruins," which seems to be inspired by Eastern beliefs,[26] is no less imbued with the doctrines of the Kabbalah than the poem "The Golem." Tale and poem are variations of the same theme: a man (a magician in the story, a rabbi in the poem) dreams another man into existence, only later to find that he too, the dreamer, is but a dream. In both instances, the creative powers of man seem to be competing with the creative powers of God. In reconstructing the legend of the golem in the poem, Borges makes use of a long Kabbalistic tradition from which the legend originates. This tradition has its beginnings in an old belief according to which the cosmos was built chiefly from the twenty letters of the Hebrew alphabet as presented in the *Sefer Yetsirah* (Book of Creation). If man can learn how God went about His creation, he too will be able to create human beings. This power is already attributed, at the end of the *Sefer Yetsirah*, to Abraham, who "contemplated, meditated, and beheld, investigated and understood and outlined and dug and combined and formed [i.e. created] and he succeeded."[27] A Midrash from the twelfth century goes even further by stating that "when God created His world, He first created the *Sefer Yetsirah* and looked into it and from it created His world. When He had completed His work, He put it [the *Sefer Yetsirah*] into the Torah [Pentateuch] and showed it to Abraham. . . ."[28] The secret is therefore in the Torah, which is not only made up of the names of God, but is, as a whole, the one great Name of God, and yet no one knows its right order, for the sections of the Torah are not given in the right arrangement. If they were, everyone who reads it might create a world, raise the dead, and perform miracles. Therefore the order of the Torah was hidden and is known to God alone.[29] The Kabbalists strove to find that hidden order, and the tradition of the Golem goes back as far as the prophet Jeremiah, who busied himself with the *Sefer Yetsirah* until a man was created. For the Hasidim the creation of a golem confirmed man in his likeness to God. Through Jakob Grimm's version of 1808, the legend achieved wide popularity and exerted a special fascination on authors like Gustav Meyrink, Achim von Arnim, and E.T.A. Hoffmann. This is not to say that "The Circular Ruins" is strictly an avatar of the legend, although the poem certainly is, but rather that Borges' familiarity with the legend of the Golem has impregnated his story.

The creation of a golem by man is parallel to the creation of Adam by God. As the golem is made from clay or mud, so Adam was made from the matter of the earth, literally from clay. The etymological connection between Adam and earth (Hebrew, ADAM*ah*) is very much stressed in the rabbinical and Talmudic commentaries on Genesis. Furthermore, in the Aggadah (the narrative branch of the Jewish oral law), Adam is designated as *golem,* which means the unformed, amorphous. Adam was said to be golem before the breath of God had touched him; and in a Midrash from the second and third centuries, Adam is described not only as a golem, but as a golem of cosmic size and strength to whom, while he was still in this speechless and inanimate state, God showed all future generations to the end of time. It was only after the Fall that Adam's enormous size, which filled the universe, was reduced to human proportions.[30] "His size [explains Scholem] would seem to signify, in spatial terms, that the power of the whole universe is concentrated in him. He receives his soul only at the end of Creation."[31]

In describing the efforts the magician makes to dream his creature in "The Circular Ruins," Borges interpolates this digression: "In the cosmogonies of the Gnostics, the demiurges mold a red Adam who is unable to stand on his feet; as clumsy and crude and elementary as that Adam of dust was the Adam of dreams wrought by the nights of the magician" (*A*, 59). Here Borges refers to certain Gnostic ideas, originally of Jewish extraction, according to which "the angels of Elohim took some of the best earth and from it formed man."[32] As in the traditional Midrash, this Gnostic Adam did not receive his soul until God and earth joined to make it. The idea that such an act of creation might be repeated by magic or other arts represents the backbone of the Kabbalistic tradition of the golem. It is this idea which one can perceive in Borges' story.

At first glance, the kinship of story and legend is hardly noticeable; "The Circular Ruins" is the story of a magician who sets himself the task of dreaming a man to later project him into reality, but the core of its theme is revealed only in the last paragraph: the dreamer too is but a dream; the creator too is but the imperfect creation of another creator; reality as a whole is but a dream of someone or no one. Thus focused, Borges' story begins to move toward the legend of the golem. Although the magician does not shape his intended son with mud or clay, as in the legend, but dreams him, the goal is still the same—the creation of a man. Yet the magician's dreams are not treated as such—that is, as intangible material—but rather as very concrete clay, as moldable substance: "He realized that, though he may penetrate all the riddles of the higher and lower orders, the task of shaping the senseless and dizzying stuff of dreams is the hardest that a man can attempt. . . ." (Recall that "golem" means "unformed matter.") And further on: "He then swore he would forget the populous vision which in the beginning had led him astray, and he sought another method." Before taking up his task again, "he cleansed himself in the waters of the river, worshiped the gods of the planets, uttered the prescribed syllables of an all-powerful name, and slept" (*A*, 58). When Borges writes "the prescribed syllables of an all-powerful name," we may surmise that he is thinking of the *Shem Hamephorash* or Tetragrammaton, which the Kabbalists sought by combining the letters of the Hebrew alphabet. Borges himself has paraphrased the Kabbalistic belief that when the miraculous *Shem Hamephorash* is pronounced over the golem made of clay or mud he must come to life: he "pronounced the Name which is the Key," Borges wrote in the poem "The Golem" (*SP*, 111). In his essay "The Golem" he had also pointed out that golem "was the name given to the man created by combinations of letters."[33] In "The Circular Ruins," the magician succeeds in dreaming a beating heart only after he has uttered "the prescribed syllables of an all-powerful name."

The description of the magician's dream is also reminiscent of the process of transformations (*temuroth*) of the letters as described in *Sefer Yetsirah.* Borges writes: "On the fourteenth night he touched the pulmonary artery with a finger and then the whole heart. . . .Before a year was over he came to the skeleton, the eyelids. The countless strands of hair were perhaps the hardest task of all" (*A*, 58-59). Similarly, in the *Sefer Yetsirah,* the letters of the Hebrew alphabet correspond to different parts of the human organism. Thus the double letters (beth, gimmel, daleth, caf, pei, reish, and taf) produced the seven planets, the seven days, and the seven apertures in man (two eyes, two ears, two nostrils, and one mouth). The twelve simple letters, on the other hand, created the twelve signs of the zodiac and thence the twelve months in time and the twelve "leaders" in man; the latter are those organs which perform functions in the body independent of the outside world—the hands, feet, kidneys, gall, intestines, stomach, liver, pancreas, and spleen (*Sefer Yetsirah,* IV-V). "One prescribed order of the alphabet produces a male being, another a female; a reversal of these orders turns the golem back to dust."[34]

Finally, Borges' magician dreams a complete man, but the dreamed being "could not stand up or speak, nor could he open his eyes." He resorts to the effigy in the destroyed temple, and the multiple god reveals to him that "its earthly name was Fire. . .and that through its magic the phantom of the man's dreams would be wakened to life in such a way that—except for Fire itself and the dreamer—every being in the world would accept him as a man of flesh and blood" (*A,* 59). In the Kabbalistic tradition, too, the act of animation comes with finding the right combination of letters as prescribed in the Book of Creation, an undertaking which normally demands three years of studying the *Sefer Yetsirah,* just as it takes a thousand and one nights for Borges' musician to produce his dreamed son. In both cases, animation comes only after exercising the divine power generated by the "all-powerful name."

Borges suggests in his tale that the dreamed man himself eventually becomes a dreamer and repeats the magic operation, and so will his son, and the son of his son, and so on *ad infinitum.* The golem of the Kabbalists does not reproduce, but it may grow endlessly in size. The only way of controlling this demiurgic growth is by erasing from his forehead the first letter of the word *Emeth* (truth), which makes the word read *meth* (he is dead). Once this is done, he collapses and turns to clay again. As fire can reveal that the magician's created son is a simulacrum, so the dropping of one letter can return the golem to his previous state as dust. Borges goes further by granting the dreamed man all the qualities of human life, thus bringing the golem-maker to a status no different from that of God. In the Kabbalah, on the other hand, the golem remains at a speechless level, a kind of docile Frankenstein,[35] with the exception of one Kabbalistic source—the *Pseudo Saadya,* where the golem is granted soul and speech.

Before sending his created son to another temple, "the magician imbued with total oblivion his disciple's long years of apprenticeship" (*A,* 60)—an idea of deep Kabbalistic roots. The "Midrash on the Creation of the Child" relates that "after its guardian angel has given it a fillip upon the nose, the newborn child forgets all the infinite knowledge acquired before its birth in the celestial houses of learning."[36] In a parenthesis Borges explains that the oblivion is needed "so that the boy would never know he was a phantom, so that he would think himself a man like all men" (*A,* 60), thus integrating a seemingly bizarre and unconnected idea into the sequential "rationale" of the narrative.

The exegesis of the Midrash comes from Eleazar of Worms (1232?), one of the pillars of German Hasidism: "Why, Eleazar asks, does the child forget? Because, if it did not forget, the course of this world would drive it to madness if it thought about it in the light of what it knew."[37] So no matter how different the two explanations may seem and how unlike their purpose, both share a common ground—the acceptance of a golem-making stage in which the dream and the child knew the mysteries of Creation. To be able to bear this world, the oblivion of that celestial or magical stage becomes inevitable. Scholem has observed that "in the root of the Midrash lies a remarkable variant of the Platonic conception of cognition as recollection, as anamnesis."[38] There is a moment in Borges' tale when the magician is about to recover the effaced awareness of that early stage, as if suddenly the recollection were to yield to a total illumination in which his origins became unveiled: "From time to time," writes Borges, the magician "was troubled by the feeling that all this had already happened. . . ." The revelation does not occur, but the hint provides one more clue to what Borges discloses only in the last line: the magician's own condition as phantom.

There is, however, one difference that separates the world-view of the Kabbalah from the outlook presented in "The Circular Ruins." In his story, Borges suggests that every man's reality is a dream and the god who is dreaming us is himself a dream. In the Kabbalah, God makes His creatures according to secret formulas that He alone knows; the first golem He created—*Adam Kadmon* (the primeval Adam)—was a creature of cosmic size and strength, and, furthermore, that first man was God Himself. It is in this light that one may understand the Midrash; "While Adam still lay as a golem before Him who spoke and the world came into being, He showed him all the generations and their wise men, all the generations and their judges and their leaders."[39] The Kabbalists managed to demonstrate this identity between God and Adam by means of *gematria* (isopsephism): they found that the numerical value of YHWH is 45 and so is ADAM's. As the Torah is but the name of God, Adam is God Himself. Before Adam, God dwelled in the depths of nothingness, and it is this abyss within God that was overcome in the Creation. Borges takes up where the devotion to monotheistic belief reined in the imagination of the Kabbalists. The Kabbalah goes as far as identifying Adam—God's golem—with God Himself. Beyond this point we are confronted with an infinite abyss of nothingness which is but the primeval and chaotic state of God before the Creation. Borges, on the other hand, echoing old Gnostic beliefs, implies that behind his dreamer there are perhaps innumerable dreamers: his golem-maker is a mere link in a long golem-making chain. He has said it masterfully in the last lines of a memorable sonnet, "Chess":

> The player too is captive of caprice
> (The words are Omar's) on another ground
> Where black nights alternate with whiter days.
>
> God moves the player, he in turn the piece.

But what god beyond God begins the round
Of dust and time and sleep and agonies?

(*SP,* 121-23)

° ° ° •

7. Unveiling the Seventy Faces of a Text

In the *Zohar,* as in Borges' fiction, one also finds the use of an old myth or motif and its subsequent reshaping into a new mode of thought. Moses de León takes the materials from the Aggadah and with them weaves his own fabric. He uses them freely for his own purposes and gives free rein to his imagination in making vital changes, emendations, and reinterpretations of the original. One example of this occurs in *Zohar* II, 124a. There, Moses de León converts a brief Talmudic tale which appears sporadically in the treatise of *Pesahim* 3b into a lively story on the same subject. When the Aggadah already contains mystical elements, these are duly emphasized and occasionally changed into an entirely new myth. A case in point is the mythology of the "great dragon" in the *Zohar* II, 35a, which has evolved from the Aggadah on the *Or ha-Ganuz* in the Talmudic treatise of *Hagigah* 12a. Borges' treatment does not differ essentially from Moses de León's. In the recreation of the myth of the Minotaur in the story "The House of Asterion," Borges' purpose is not mere virtuosity. Borges himself has suggested that the idea "of a monster wanting to be killed, needing to be killed"[56] is the fictional reverse or paraphrase of another idea stated in his article "A Comment on August 23, 1944, written during the war. There he said that Hitler would be defeated because he wanted to be defeated: "Hitler is collaborating blindly with the inevitable armies that will annihilate him, as the metal vultures and the dragon (which must not have been unaware that they are monsters) collaborated, mysteriously, with Hercules" (*OI,* 136). Yet Borges' own interpretation of his story far from exhausts its far-reaching implications. I believe it is in this story more than in any other that Borges' labyrinthine outlook has been most fully and richly developed.[57] The old and weary myth has become here an effective medium for bringing forth his own world-view. Like the Kabbalist, Borges creates a new myth out of the old one. He has read into the legend of the Minotaur a new meaning which not only redeems the old myth, but also justifies it. Borges, indeed, fulfills here a task similar to Pierre Menard's in undertaking to write a contemporary *Quixote.* In "Pierre Menard, Author of the *Quixote,*" Borges tells us that "Cervantes' text and Menard's are verbally identical, but the second is almost infinitely richer." This is just an exacerbation of the same attitude, of the same concept of literature according to which "one literature differs from another, either before or after it, not so much because of the text as for the manner in which it is read." "If I were able to read any contemporary page," explains Borges to prove his point, "...as it would be read in the year 2000, I would know what literature would be like in the year 2000" (*OI,* 164). In a strict sense, Borges' own narratives could be defined—applying this criterion—as different ways of reading the systems of philosophy and the doctrines of theology. "I am," Borges has said about himself, "a man of letters who turns his own perplexities and that respected system of perplexities we call philosophy into the forms of literature."[58] His stories are postures for reading those theories (which have made man what he is), but in the process the claimed "absolute truths" have become myths and marvels, humble intuitions of man's fantasy. Perhaps in this wise and skillfull turn of the kaleidoscope lies the revelation of Borges' art. If the essence of this revelation resides in the act of reading the new in an old text, we have simply come to the very point where the Kabbalah begins. These beginnings are described by Borges himself in his essay "The Mirror of the Enigmas":

> The notion that the Sacred Scripture possesses (in addition to its literal meaning) a symbolic one is not irrational and is ancient: it is found in Philo of Alexandria, in the cabalists, in Swedenborg.... The portentous premise of a book that is impervious to contingency, a book that is a mechanism of infinite purposes, moved them [the Kabbalists] to permute the scriptural words, to sum up the numerical value of the letters, to consider their form, to observe the small letters and the capital letters, to search for acrostics and anagrams....
> (*OI,* 125-28)

Now, one should ask what the Kabbalists achieved by means of this mystical hermeneutics. The *Zohar* is undoubtedly the most representative work of many centuries of Kabbalistic exegesis, but it is far from being the only one—there are literally hundreds of such books, many of them still in manuscript form. The *Zohar* shares some basic characteristics with most of those books: thus, for instance, a deliberately unsystematic construction, a tendency—rooted in Jewish thought—to avoid logical systematization. Scholem has illustrated the method (or rather the method's lack of method) of the *Zohar* with a very eloquent comparison: "Most of the fundamental ideas found in the *Zohar,*" he says, "were expressed only a little later in a systematically constructed treatise, *Maarekhbeth Ha-Elohuth* (The Order of God), but how dry and lifeless are these bare skeletons of thought compared with the flesh and blood of the *Zohar*!" And he goes on: "In the *Zohar* the most unpretentious verses of Scripture acquire an entirely unexpected meaning....Again and again a hidden and sometimes awful depth opens before your eyes, and we find ourselves confronted with real and profound insight."[59] The foundation of this imaginative wealth and fertility of thought lies in the belief that "the Torah is an inexhaustible well, which no pitcher can ever empty."[60]

Borges proposes a similar premise. When he says that "perhaps universal history is the history of the diverse intonation of a few metaphors," he appears to be postulating the opposite case, since he seemingly underlines the exhaustible character of *human* imagination.[61] But it is only the oblique formulation that creates this impression; actually, Borges is saying exactly the opposite. In the essay "The Metaphor," written in 1952, he offers the reader the prolegomenon of his idea, explaining that

> The first monument of Western literature, the *Iliad,* was composed some three thousand years ago; it seems safe to surmise that during this vast lapse of time every familiar and necessary affinity (dream-life, sleep-death, the flow of rivers and time, and so forth) has been noted and recorded by someone. This does not mean, of course, that the number of metaphors has been exhausted; the ways of stating or hinting at these hidden sympathies are, in fact, limitless.[62]

Consequently, "perhaps it is a mistake to suppose that metaphors can be invented. The real ones, those that formulate intimate connections between one image and another, have always existed; those we can still invent are the false ones, which are not worth inventing" (*OI,* 47). Taking this one step further, Borges implies that the task of the writer is not to invent new and original works but rather to reinterpret old ones, or—in John Barth's words—"to write original works of literature whose implicit theme is the difficulty, perhaps the unnecessity, of writing original works of literature."[63]

Borges' concept of metaphor (which for him is only a metaphor for literature) does not differ essentially from the *Zohar's* outlook on the Scripture: as the whole world is for the Kabbalists a *corpus symbolicum* (an idea that Borges has repeatedly quoted),[64] so the Torah is conceived, and to interpret it is, consequently, to unveil its "seventy faces" (i.e., infinite levels). Borges has referred to himself as "the man who weaves these symbols" (*A,* 95), and in a different context he has said that "art operates necessarily with symbols";[65] in addition, he has insisted on the idea that universal history is "a Sacred Scripture: one that we decipher and write uncertainly, and in which we also are written" (*OI,* 120), and he has likewise endorsed the belief that "we are the versicles or words or letters of a magic book, and that incessant book is the only thing in the world; or rather, it is the world" (*OI,* 120). For the Kabbalists, similarly, God looked at the Torah and created the world. The *Zohar,* like the literature of the Kabbalah at large, is an attempt to penetrate the hidden layers of that holy text; the results are those coined symbols and sometimes elaborated allegories by means of which a new, lucid, and original interpretation of the Scripture has been produced. Borges' narratives and symbols represent a similar attempt, with the difference that the text Borges reads encompasses "the almost infinite world of literature."

It has been asked whether the true interpretation of certain passages of the Scripture may not be found in the *Zohar* and nowhere else; I would like to ask if Borges' symbols—which claim not to be a reflection of the world but rather something added to it—do not imply a new understanding of man's confrontation with the world. Some of these symbols suggest that since man can never find the solution to the gods' labyrinth, he has constructed his own labyrinth; or, in other words, that since the reality of the gods is impenetrable, man has created his own reality. He lives, thus, in a world which is the product of his own fallible architecture. He knows there is another world, "irreversible and iron-bound," which constantly besieges him and forces him to feel the enormity of its presence, and between these two worlds, between these two stories—one imagined by God and the other fancied by man—flows the agonizing history of mankind.

FOOTNOTES

1. Borges is referring to Joshua Trachtenberg's *Jewish Magic and Superstition: A Study in Folk Religion* (New York, 1939).

2. See Ronald Christ, "Jorge Luis Borges, an Interview," *The Paris Review*, 40 (Winter-Spring 1967), 162.

3. See Rabi, "Fascination de la Kabbale," *L'Herne, J.L. Borges* (Paris, 1964), pp. 265-71.

4. See J.L. Borges, "Una vindicación de la cábala," *Discusión* (Buenos Aires, 1957), pp. 55-60.

5. Christ, *ibid.*, p. 161.

6. As every reader of the *Quixote* knows, in Chapter VI the curate and the barber perform a thorough scrutiny of the library "of our ingenious gentleman." The scrutiny represents a critical examination of romances of chivalry and pastoral novels to whose tradition Cervantes himself contributed *La Galatea.* This book, too, falls into the hands of the scrutinizers who decide to keep it because, the curate says, "that fellow Cervantes and I have been friends these many years, but, to my knowledge, he is better versed in misfortune than he is in verses. His book has a fairly good plot; it starts out well and ends up nowhere." Borges himself has referred to the effects of this "play of mirrors" in his essay "Partial Enchantments of the *Quixote.*"

7. I have further discussed the effects of this device in *La prosa narrativa de Jorge Luis Borges* (Madrid, 1968), pp. 87-88.

8. The last sentence was written before the appearance of *The Aleph and Other Stories* (New York, 1970). There Borges provides, for the first time, some enlightening "commentaries" on the background of the short stories collected in that volume. On "Death and the Compass," he says: "No apology is needed for repeated mention of the Kabbalah, for it provides the reader and the all-too-subtle detective with a false track, and the story is, as most of the names imply, a Jewish one. The Kabbalah also provides an additional sense of mystery" (*A*, 269).

9. Although this book was published in English in 1960, it collects essays published (1927) in Buber's *Die chassidischen Bücher* and his *Der grosse Maggid und seine Nachfolge* (1921).

10. The German edition dates from 1907.

11. There may be other references to Buber that I have overlooked.

12. For further information on this subject, see Scholem's *On the Kabbalah and Its Symbolism* (New York, 1969), pp. 197-98.

13. J.L. Borges, *El tamaño de mi esperanza* (Buenos Aires, 1926), p. 67.

14. Scholem, *Major Trends in Jewish Mysticism* (New York, 1961), p. 208.

15. For comprehensive information on the *Zohar,* see Chapters V-VI in

Scholem's *Major Trends.*

16. Scholem, *ibid.*, p. 222.

17. *Ibid.*, pp. 223-24.

18. This is not the place to elaborate on Borges' fertile use of pantheism in his fiction. I have treated this aspect of his work in my book *La prosa narrativa de J. L. Borges,* pp. 60-73. Here it will suffice to observe that the pantheistic notion that frames several of his stories stems from Plotinus, Spinoza, Sufism, Hinduism, Buddhism, and other sources, as well as from the doctrines of the Kabbalah. In some instances, Borges' contacts with the Kabbalah are indirectly established through authors who in one way or another echo Kabbalistic theories. Thus the world of *Sefiroth,* as described above, is found in Francis Bacon's *Advancement of Learning,* but now the theosophic symbols "tree" and "man" are replaced by the image of a book: "God offered us two books," writes Borges quoting Bacon, "so that we would not fall into error. The first, the volume of the Scriptures, reveals His will; the second, the volume of the creatures, reveals his power" (*OI,* 119).

19. The seed of this idea is already found in "A History of Angels," and is literally reproduced in "Una vindicación de la cábala."

20. Quoted by Scholem in *On the Kabbalah...*, p. 38.

21. *Ibid.*, p. 122.

22. *Ibid.*, p. 124.

23. In addition to "The Theologians," the motif can be traced in the following stories: "The Shape of the Sword," "Theme of the Traitor and the Hero," "Three Versions of Judas," "Story of the Warrior and the Captive," "The End," "The Life of Tadeo Isidoro Cruz," "The South," and "The Other Death."

24. One of them was undoubtedly Gustav Meyrink's novel *Der Golem,* which young Borges read while still a student in Geneva.

25. A concise exposition of this outlook as conceived by Eastern thought may be found in Borges' essay "Forms of a Legend."

26. I have discussed this in some detail in *La prosa de J.L. Borges,* pp. 53-59.

27. *Le Sepher Yetsirah,* Texte hébreu intégral, lu et commenté d'après le code originel de la Cabale par Carlo Suarèz (Geneva, 1968), p. 122. I use the English translation as it appears in Gershom Scholem's *On the Kabbalah and Its Symbolism,* p. 169.

28. The Midrash is "Neue Pesikta." Quoted by Scholem, *On the Kabbalah...*, pp. 177-78.

29. Scholem, *ibid.*, p. 167.

30. On the subject of the golem, see the chapter "The Idea of the Golem" in Scholem's *On the Kabbalah...*, pp. 158-204.

31. *Ibid.*, p. 162.

32. *Ibid.*, p. 164.

33. J.L. Borges, *The Book of Imaginary Beings* (New York, 1969), pp. 112-14.

34. Scholem, *On the Kabbalah...*, p. 186.

35. Notice that Mary W. Shelley's creature is also a close descendant of the golem.

36. Scholem, *Major Trends...*, p. 92.

37. *Loc. cit.*

38. *Loc. cit.*

39. Quoted by Scholem in *On the Kabbalah...*, p. 162.

. . . .

56. See Richard Burgin, *Conversations with Jorge Luis Borges* (New York, 1969), p. 41.

57. See my essay "Tlön y Asterión: anverso y reverso de una epistemología," *Nueva narrativa hispanoamericana,* I, 2 (September 1971), 21-33.

58. J.L. Borges, "Foreword" to Ronald Christ, *The Narrow Act: Borges' Art of Allusion* (New York, 1969), p. 9.

59. Scholem, *Major Trends...*, p. 158.

60. Scholem, *On the Kabbalah...*, p. 60.

61. For a penetrating article on this question, see John Barth's "The Literature of Exhaustion," *Atlantic* (August 1967), pp. 29-34.

62. Jorge Luis Borges, "The Metaphor," in "Up from Ultraism," *New York Review of Books* (August 13, 1970), p. 4.

63. Barth, *ibid.*, p. 31.

64. In a book review in his collection of essays, *Discusión*, p. 164, he says: "...for the mystics the concrete world is but a system of symbols."

65. *Discusión*, p. 141.

Jaime Alazraki *was born in 1934 in La Rioja, in the northwestern part of Argentina, near Chile, where he received his early schooling. He became involved in Zionist activities and went to Israel in 1956, where he lived on a kibbutz for two years and then studied at the Hebrew University of Jerusalem, where he received a B.A. in 1962 in Hebrew Literature and the Bible. He then came to New York, where he received his M.A. and Ph.D. degrees in Spanish Literature from Columbia University. He has been a professor in the Department of Romance Languages at Harvard University since 1978. He is the author of eight critical studies on Spanish American literature, four of which are on Borges, one on Pablo Neruda, and one on Julio Cortázar, which he co-edited.*

Jorge Luis Borges' *involvement and interest in Jewish traditions and literature is well known. He recently was awarded the Jerusalem Prize given by the city of Jerusalem to those outstanding authors who have shown an interest in Jewish matters.*

Victor Perera

Growing Up Jewish in Guatemala

Father

My parents were born in Jerusalem, a few blocks from one another, and were in their mid-twenties when they came to the New World—Father to make his fortune, Mother several years later as his intended bride. They were tradition-bound Spanish Jews, Sephardim, both descended from respected rabbis.

The marriage was a covenant between my father's Palestinian brothers and my mother's older sister. The courtship was entirely by mail—surface mail at that—so that pledges and passions had a month to cool on each crossing. By the time Mother arrived in Guatemala City, at age twenty-four, the bloom of their romance had faded, and they married "for convenience," as the third cousins they were.

I was surprised to learn when we went abroad that Mother carried those letters from Father in her luggage everywhere she went.

Father was the middle one of three brothers who shipped to America in the 1920s to pick the gold from the paving stones. In Jerusalem he had been a mathematics instructor at a girls' seminary. In Guatemala he began life as an itinerant peddler. (Why Guatemala? Father never explained this to my satisfaction.) Only recently have I come to appreciate the courage this required of him—an educated man of twenty-five, scion of respected rabbis and with only a few phrases of Quijotesque Ladino Spanish, reduced to peddling bolts of colored gingham to Indian laborers in a country so ignorant of his lineage it labeled him "Turk" and levied on his head double and triple the going rate in bribes, kickbacks, police taxes, and the other routine forms of graft.

And yet he grew to love his work. He took pride in his hard-earned position as one of Guatemala's leading merchants, and in his standing in the Jewish community as a loyal Zionist, a scholar and humanist.

Some years ago I came across a yellowed photograph of Father standing at the door of his textile shop the day it opened. The proud aura of ownership lights up his face. Father was to marry that store and consecrate his heart and mind to it with Talmudic ardor. Ourselves, his family, he fed, roofed, clothed, bedded down at night from an inherited reflex of duty. He had no real love for us.

Father was thirty-six when I was born, and nearly forty before I recognized him as my sire. By then the cares of business and advancing age had scored his brow and pinched his cheeks. I hero-worshiped Father from the start, as if from a premonition that his sway on my life would be brief. Any casual praise or word of advice from him stuck to my mind like a fly to flypaper.

A phrase that made a deep impression he spoke not to me but to a friend of his, as we strolled in the park: "The war will be good for business," Father said.

On another stroll with this same friend they discussed what private school I should go to. (Only the poor went to public school.) Father wanted a place where English was taught as a second language. "English is the most important language in the world today," I recall him saying.

When I was four Father's appendix burst and he had an emergency operation in his bedroom. His cries of pain ("Ay! Ay! Ay Mama! Ay Mama!") filled the house and rang in my ears for weeks afterward. More terrible than his titanic agony was the realization that titans, too, cried after their mothers.

With a boy-child's instinct I hoarded these proofs of Father's manliness:

His impressive phallus. It was deep-veined and thick, not overlong, a bull's neck crowned with all the totemic attributes of godhead. From this parent trunk his testicles hung like swollen fruit.

His gargantuan appetite. At the breakfast table I looked on in awed wonder as he drew and quartered a whole papaya and gobbled it down, block by block. Years later I learned Doctor Quevedo had prescribed this daily papaya for his poor digestion.

His enormous size. At five-and-a-half feet Father towered four inches above Mother and six inches above most of his female employees. This illusion vanished forever the day Uncle Mair arrived from Mexico with his new bride. Both were taller than Father by almost a head, and Uncle Mair was markedly bigger around the chest and shoulders.

His superhuman strength. This was evidenced by the ease with which he unscrewed jam and cookie jars, unstuck windows, raised and lowered the steel shutters outside the store twice a day. A special niche was carved on my pantheon the day I sat in his boat as he outrowed five of his male employees across Lake Amatitlán. (Was that race thrown, I ask myself after all these years, to flatter a vain boss?)

The manly way he rocked on the balls of his feet during the Shabbat services. His mere presence in the synagogue was imbued with patriarchal virility and mystery, so that in this setting his lightest pat on my head acquired profound significance.

His position of authority at home and in business. Father's rule in the home was unchallenged, at least in front of the children. He gave orders to Mother, who in turn gave orders to the cook, to my *china* (nanny) and to the two cleaning maids, Micaela of the "interior," who made the beds, and Eulalia of the "exterior," who swept the hallway. What took place in the bedroom, behind closed doors, was on a different plane of reality and I discounted it, although from my room I overheard quarrels in which Father did not always get in the last word.

The store was Father's true domain. He had twenty-five employees at his beck and call, all but six female; about a dozen of these looked upon him with an adoration far beyond the requisites of personnel loyalty. Ema, a pretty sixteen-year-old salesgirl of Mayan descent, was my own personal favorite. Father sent her to my bedside whenever I took sick, and she would tell me ghost stories. Once, when I was racked with coughs, pretty Ema placed her hand on my groin, which had a marvelously soothing effect.

I well remember the beatings he gave me. A restrained capacity for violence ranked high among my standards of manliness long before I got hooked on war films and comic books. Father beat me only three times in my life, in each case after sufficient provocation, and the logic of the punishment—if not the severity—was perfectly clear to me. What makes them distinct in my mind is the gap in each instance between my expectation (or lack of it) and the physical weight and texture of each beating.

The first time, he struck me because I'd left my school bag on a bus. This was not sufficient cause in itself, and I'm sure he would have forgotten the whole thing if I had let him. He hit me because I whined when confronted with the loss, and tried to weasel out of my guilt in a cowardly way. The slap was tremendous, a cosmic detonation that flung me across the floor. It was the sound of that slap more than the burning in my cheek that astonished and froze my tears for several seconds.

The second came when I traced muddy handprints on the walls after making mud pies in the patio for my baby sister. Then my astonishment sprang from the discrepancy between the misdeed and the punishment. I had often got off scot-free with far worse offenses. But the evidence was fresh on the walls when Father got home and, I suspect, there had been some contretemps at the store. The blow came lightning-quick, and once more I was knocked to the floor. When I pushed against the wall to get up, I made fresh mudprints but he did not strike me again, which I later thought illogical.

The third time, when I was eight years old, he beat me because I called Mother a whore. After that session I was confined to bed for nearly a week. In a sense Mother herself was responsible for my committing that offense. It was during Holy Week, when processions passed outside our house every afternoon. I was watching one of them from my bedroom window, although Mother had specifically forbidden me to, when I felt her behind me. At that moment an image of the Virgin Mary was trooping by, wrapped in clouds of incense.

"The Virgin," Mother said, pressing my shoulder, "is a whore." She used the Ladino word "putana."

The next time she provoked me, I flung the terrible word in her face.

I remember Mother's slow smile after I shouted the blasphemy. Yet it was not she who reported me to Father but my sister, Becky, who was barely five at the time. She remarked at the dinner table that I had called Mother a "bad name." Father, perking up, asked me to repeat it. I flushed, lowered my eyes, my tongue stuck to my palate. He then asked Mother, and she said she didn't remember.

"What did he call you!" Father shouted, his color rising.

"Putana," Mother said in a low voice.

Father lifted me up by the neck with one hand and dragged me into the hallway, removing his belt. This time I steeled myself. I thought I knew what to expect. But once more reality overwhelmed my worst apprehensions.

Father took out on me a lifelong rage that evening. I still bear the scars from that strapping. But if he had not administered it I would have thought that much less of him as a father, and that much less of him as a man. That beating grew, with the years, to be one of the enduring bonds between us.

Mother

One of the unforgiven remarks Mother made to me as a child was that she would have married differently—she never said "better" —if her father had lived long enough to afford her a dowry.

Mother bragged often about her father, Rosh Harabbim Yaakov Nissim of Jerusalem and Samarkand. Rabbi Nissim, as Mother told it, was the most learned man in Jerusalem. He was fluent in seven languages, quoted Talmud by the yard, and was not only widely respected but loved by everyone, above all for his brimming spirits and puckish sense of humor. Mother claimed both traits, with some justice, for herself.

Grandfather, the story went, longed to be Chief Rabbi of Jerusalem's Sephardic community but another rabbi, Moshé Ohanna—connected to *Father's* branch of the priestly tree—stood in his way. (At this point in the chronicle, Mother's face invariably darkened.) When a summons came from Samarkand for a head rabbi, Grandfather picked up his belongings and embarked alone, promising to send for his wife and children after he was settled. But then the First World War and Lenin intervened, and no word was heard from Grandfather for many months. At last he wrote to say he had remarried in Samarkand at the behest of his congregation, and was raising a second family. But he vowed to return to Jerusalem after the war.

Grandfather was as good as his vow. He was enroute back to Jerusalem with his new family when he caught typhoid in Bombay, and soon after died. His Russian wife and two children found their way back to Samarkand alone, without having set foot in the Holy Land. (Mother threw all this up to my Hindu bride the week we were married. "Forty-five years ago my father died of the typhoid, which he caught in Bombay," Mother remarked, out of the blue, to which my wife could find nothing appropriate to reply. She now thinks that an apology was expected of her. She having failed to extend it, Mother never forgave her.)

Her father's death when Mother was in her teens inflicted a wound that she will not permit to heal, a forever renewable sense of bright expectations forever dashed. From this unreduced grievance Mother carved out the formula that is the bedrock of her philosophy: "The world has thwarted forever all my bright expectations; therefore, the world is forever in my debt."

Most of Mother's worst faults sprang from this faulty reasoning, including her chronic laziness and neurasthenia, as well as her childlike dependence on Father to make all decisions and on four servants to do everything else.

There were compensating factors to balance the ledger:

Mother had been an authentic beauty in her youth. Among my treasures is a studio photograph of her at age seventeen, taken in Jerusalem. She is sprawled on painted grass, surrounded by painted sheep, in a Yemenite shepherdess' blouse and skirt. Her dull cotton stockings cannot disguise the shapeliness of her legs. Her face is a perfect luminous oval framed by waist-length braids, one of those prototype cameos of maidenly sweetness that were highly prized in the '20s. I am not surprised that she was coddled and spoiled by her mother and older sisters, and pampered in his turn by Father, at least in the early years of their marriage. She would also, I imagine, have been cosseted by her Russian stepmother, had that unlucky woman reached haven in Jerusalem.

The reverse side of Mother's sloth and irresponsibility was an infectious gaiety to which she gave free rein when the mood was on her, and which offset Father's abstracted solemnity for my sister Becky and me. Her spirits crested on motor trips to the coast. With a kerchief around her hair to keep out the dust, Mother would toss back her head and spill out a polyglot potpourri of songs all the way to the seashore. My favorites were "La Paloma," "Sur le Pont d'Avignon," "If You Were the Only Girl in the World," "Au Claire de la Lune," and, best of all, "Mama Inez":

Ay Mama Inez
Ay Mama Inez
Todos los negros
Tomamos cafe

(Oh Mother Inez, all of us blacks drink coffee.)

Mother sang in a pleasant, undistinguished soprano. You could see in her face how much sweeter her voice sounded to her own ears. It was on these trips, when the gypsy in Mother came out, that I loved her best.

But she was a gypsy in other ways, not all of them so attractive.

For one thing, she was childishly superstitious. Twice a month she went to Madame Fatima, on the arcade inside the Turkish quarter, to have her fortune read in the cards. She carried on a lifelong flirtation with astrology. A Saggitarius, she once stayed in bed a whole week because a hostile planet was menacing her star, and she dreaded committing a fatal misstep by getting up. Despite her fluency in seven languages and top-notch schooling at a French lycée in Jerusalem, Mother was not very bright. Or perhaps it was just that she had been dependent for so long, passed in trust from one doting hand to another—grandmother to mother to aunt to older sister to Father, like a family heirloom—that she never acquired the incentive to think for herself. I once gave her Ibsen's "A Doll's House" to read. She never got past Act I.

Mother's asthma was a cross we all had to bear. I suspect it was her way of punishing us for not being the golden family she might have purchased with a dowry. She went to bed every night with a man's handkerchief across her face, like a blindfold, because an Indian *curandera* (healer) assured her it would relieve the asthma. When her attacks remitted, she wore the handkerchief anyway, to ward off what she called "night vapors." For extended periods Mother used the asthma as an excuse for doing nothing in the kitchen, even when guests were expected. And she wore a tight girdle as an excuse for never bending below the waist.

When Father suffered his first coronary attack several years later, in New York, she pried into his mouth two large spoonfuls of her asthma medicine to stop his wheezing and coughing. Only my frantic call to the hospital and their prompt dispatch of an ambulance with oxygen tanks saved Father, whose lungs had to be pumped clear of water and Mother's medicine.

Mother deluded us all into believing her frail, when in reality she was strong as an ox and Father was the frail one. Since his death in Haifa thirteen years ago Mother has not suffered, to my knowledge, an hour's breathlessness from asthma.

Mother kept me in shoulder-length curls well past my third birthday, and would not buy me long trousers until I started fourth grade. At her Hadassah Club luncheons she was fond of showing me off as the unrivaled soft shoe prodigy she fancied herself to have engendered. When Becky was big enough, she featured us at Hanukkah receptions inside the synagogue as the flashiest child conga team north of Rio. She persisted in dressing my skinny frame in outlandish costumes. From firsthand report I know that she will even today whip out of her bag for a passing acquaintance in Tel Aviv a photograph of me in a black spangled *mariachi* outfit, age six-and-a-half, wearing a martyred grimace.

I have tended to speculate, given Mother's excessive physical interest in me, on what sort of bedmate she could have been to Father. For a long while I supposed she had to be as desultory and apathetic a lover as she was a wife and housekeeper. But one cannot presume to judge in these matters. Father was past thirty when they married, and I heard her accuse him more than once of of not giving her more children. The one time I surprised them *in flagrante* I was too confounded by the spectacle of jointed animality, and by the ensuing uproar in the room, to store away any clues.

Mar Abramowitz

Soon after my tenth birthday Rabbi Mishaan warned Father that he had neglected my religious education, and said I was in danger of growing up a godless heathen. Alarmed, Father looked up from his ledgers and registers and saw that Rabbi Mishaan was right. His first-born and only son, three short years from Bar Mitzvah, could not read a word of Scripture. This was hardly my fault. Our lingual tender at home was a secular hash of native slang and Ladino Spanish: "Manga tu okra, ishto, 'scapa, ya tus desmodres." (Eat your okra, animal; enough of your foolishness.") Hebrew was for off-color jokes and adult secrets.

Father's alarm grew when he learned that his only male heir was a renegade who stole visits inside the cathedral, whose best friend was a mestizo goy of scant scholastic attainments—a male heir, furthermore, who gaped imbecilically when you quoted Talmud at him or asked him to recite the Commandments.

Father's first step was to teach me a Hebrew prayer which I had to repeat every night before retiring. The second was more drastic. After years of getting by as three-holiday Jews we began observing the Sabbath. At dusk on Friday evenings Father took me to the synagogue, where he tried to teach me my Aleph-Bet. But his patience was short and his mind would drift continually to business matters. If I did not pronounce the syllables perfectly on my second or third attempt he would snap his prayer shawl in my face or slam the book shut, which instantly slammed my mind shut and turned my tongue to lead. After a half-dozen lessons I succeeded in memorizing the blessing to the Torah, which ends "Baruch attah Adonai, noten hatorah"—"Blessed art Thou, oh Lord, Who giveth the Torah." On the following Sabbath, Rabbi Mishaan called me to the Bimah and I recited the blessing before and after pretending to read a passage from the scroll, moving my lips to Rabbi Mishaan's words like a ventriloquist's dummy.

Father's lessons lasted only through Yom Kippur, after which the Christmas rush set in and he had to be in the store late on Friday evenings and all day on Saturdays. He gave up trying to teach me himself and engaged for my religious instruction a Polish war refugee, Mar Israel Abramowitz.

Mar Abramowitz did not attend services in our temple. With a dozen or so other Ashkenazi refugees from Eastern Europe he worshipped in a tiny downtown loft which was said, by those who had never been inside it, to smell of rancid butter and pickled herring.

Only on the High Holidays were the Poles and Litvaks allowed to defile our synagogue, and they had to sit toward the rear, next to the women.

Although I did not learn Hebrew for another two years, I was very early inculcated with the gospel of Sephardic caste. If all other Jews were Chosen, we were the Elect. We were sole heirs to a remote but glorious Golden Age whose legacy we could batten on, without any effort on our part, until the Day of Judgement. At the end of the Golden Age we had nobly suffered the Inquisition, which resulted in our Expulsion from Spain and resettlement in a place called the Diaspora. One day we would all reunite in the Promised Land, Eretz Israel, and begin an even more glorious second Golden Age, with God's blessing.

My earliest remembered "proof" of our legacy came at Yom Kippur. Toward the middle of the liturgy, before the blowing of the ram's horn that signaled God's presence among us, two men were summoned before the Ark: chinless, rail-thin Eliezer Cohen, a failure at business, and fat, famously henpecked Shlomo Kahan. Cohen and Kahan, whose names identified them as members of the priestly elite, first prayed in unison before the Ark. At a signal from Rabbi Mishaan they draped their shawls over their homburgs and turned to the congregation, faceless. They were instantly transformed into hieratic mummers, impersonators of God's mystery, as they swayed from side to side with both arms raised, chanting His words in antiphonal responses.

Of course, it never occured to me that Ashkenazim might have their own Cohens and Kahans to communicate God's blessing.

Mar Israel Abramowitz had been a successful lawyer in Warsaw before the Nazis came. Father said he had spent years in a concentration camp, but Mar Abramowitz did not talk of this and I never thought to ask him. I was not at all certain what a concentration camp was and had no special curiousity about it. I only knew that it was a place where Jews suffered.

Suffering appeared to be Mar Abramowitz's chief occupation. He was a thickset man in his middle fifties, with tufts of gray hair at either side of a squarish bald head. His bifocal glasses magnified a hollow look of grief in his eyes. His breath stank most of the time; nearly all his remaining teeth were black stumps. He had an ingrown right thumbnail which he continually stroked. It was several sessions before I understood that the sighs and moans punctuating our lessons had no connection with me.

Mar Abramowitz managed to teach me enough alphabet so I could read a little Hebrew, but his suffering got the better of him before we could start on comprehension. I soon learned to take advantage of his infirmity. If his breath smelled especially rank and he stroked his nail more than usual, I knew I could get out of doing the drills and coax him into telling Bible stories instead. I liked these exotic tales, which Mar Abramowitz delivered with a heavy Slavic accent and his usual grieved expression. As he got into them, however, his eyes would soften and he would grow almost eloquent, despite his poor Spanish. The Old Testament stories seemed to ease his suffering as much as they enhanced my tonic sense of truancy from serious study.

In my youthful wisdom, of course, I knew they were mostly fables. I lent no more real credence to a talking snake, the burning bush, the parting of the Red Sea, than I gave the prince who turned into a frog, or to Billy Batson's instant apotheosis into Captain Marvel with the magical word "Shazam." The fighting and killing, on the other hand, I understood perfectly: David and Goliath, Holofernes and Judith, the Canaanites and the Babylonians, these made eminent sense. The battle between the forces of good and the forces of evil, as I realized, as Tarzan and Kit Carson and Buck Rogers and President Roosevelt realized, was unending—part of man's natural estate.

There was a custom in our temple of auctioning off ritual honors on the High Holidays. Rabbi Mishaan would pace up and down the aisles, chanting the bids aloud in Hebrew (while keeping the score on the fringes of his shawl) so they sounded to my ears indistinguishable from the liturgy: "I have thirty-five to open the Ark from Isaac Sultan in praise of the Lord... Forty... Forty-five from Lázaro Sabbaj in praise of the Lord. Shmuel Benchoam bids fifty *Quetzalim* to open the Ark in praise of the Lord, Blessed be His Name...." On Simchat Torah, in reward for the scant Hebrew phrases Mar Abramowitz had dinned into my head, Father bought me the bearing of the Scroll from the Ark to the Bimah. I crept along the aisle with the red velvet Torah—junior size—hugged to my chest as worshipers crowded around to kiss it. The Scroll was weighted down with a chased shield, chains, silver horns and other ornaments, each separately bid for by the congregation. My fear of dropping the Torah and profaning Holy Scripture made my feet throb inside the corrective boots I wore for fallen arches. My performance of this ceremonial honor evidently assuaged Father's conscience, for he never bought me another.

One week Mar Abramowitz did not show up for our lesson because, Mother said, he wasn't feeling well. (She used the Ladino "hazino" to dignify his unwellness.) But I guessed he was only suffering. I pictured him crouched in a corner of his room, breathing his foul breath, stroking his ingrown thumbnail, the grief-stricken eyes sunk deeper than ever in their sockets. He failed to come the following week and the week after that. When he finally appeared, I hardly recognized him. He had shrunk from a corpulent middle-aged man to a wizened gnome. The sag of his shoulders inside the loose-fitting jacket gave him the derelict look of a tramp. Only his sunken black eyes had life. The bifocals exaggerated what I recognized even then as the haunted, pinpoint gleam of madness.

Mar Abramowitz had come to tell us he could no longer keep up my lessons because of his illness. His apology was rambling and disconnected and went on long after Mother assured him that she quite understood, and he was forgiven. Then, to my intense shame, Mar Abramowitz began to moan and cry aloud, right in our hallway, so that the sounds reverberated throughout the house. Mother fetched her handbag and placed in Mar Abramowitz' bony hand a folded bill. Brushing his eyes, he executed a courtly bow, pocketed the bill and kissed Mother's hand before he shuffled out the door.

Three years later, on returning from a trip to the States, we learned that Mar Abramowitz had hanged himself.

Victor Perera *was born in Guatemala in 1934 of Sephardic parents who themselves had been born in Jerusalem. He graduated from Brooklyn College in 1956 and received an M.A. from the University of Michigan in 1958. He has taught creative writing at Vassar College and is presently teaching at the University of California, in Santa Cruz. He was an interpreter-apprentice for the United Nations, and an editor-reporter for* The New Yorker. *His many articles, stories and essays have appeared in* The New Yorker, Harper's, The Atlantic, Commentary, Partisan Review, Antioch Review, Vogue, *and elsewhere, as well as in Spanish language publications, such as* Crisis *and* Excelsior. *He is also at present a Contributing Editor to* Present Tense.

Poetry by David Unger

Market Day

How the Indians live!
pigeon-toed, hunchbacks
dreaming of sunpowered escalators
after having schlepped
cords of wood
halfway from the stars,
their persistence
that of Tecun Uman challenging
Pedro de Alvarado's army
with a handful of poisonous arrows.
Sitting here
on this hillside slope
the clouds like a bib
around the mountain tops
I watch them secretly emerge
from a crevice or anthole
lean as picked bones
a shrewd smile spanning their faces
as if they were greeting Daffy Duck
masquerading as
Itzamna, God of Creation.
They snicker as I take
their photograph for ten cents,
the camera
a finely tooled machine
for what the mind should remember.

Public Bathhouse in Zunil

In the wake of sulfurous water
pushing through stone,
the Indian women peel themselves
on their bathhouse ledges:
one by one they fall in
like barrels of laughter while a gossipy smoke
hugs their brown bodies.
Their children, pilot fish dipping
and darting, trail after—
when they swallow water, they clutch
their mothers' breasts
as if they were the last surviving buoys.
This is High Mass,
life lived time and again
without Jacuzzis or Life Insurance,
sunrise, sunset
till a bubble breaks on the surface.

David Unger *is included in this volume both as a translator and a poet. He was born in Guatemala City, Guatemala, in 1950. He graduated from the University of Massachusetts in Amherst in 1973, and received an M.F.A. from the Columbia University School of the Arts in 1975. His poetry has been published in* Weid, Persea, Columbia Review *and elsewhere. In 1977 he was cited as "Outstanding Writer" for that year by* Pushcart Prize. *His credits as a translator are listed in the back of this volume.*

Diego Viga

Cybernetics

An engineer whom we shall call Atanasio, either because the author does not wish to reveal his true name or because none better has occurred to him, one particular night began to study the subject of himself, to search into his memories, to hold encounter meetings with himself.

It was an unhealthy preoccupation, contrary to his education, to his era, and harmful to his spiritual health. Atanasio was a modern man, a man of our happy and progressive times, as I have indicated by his professional title. But he was a very serious person and suddenly he began to have doubts about his sobriety.

These doubts were probably caused by the fact that he had not been sleeping well. He became a preoccupied man, and he decided to take a vacation in a luxurious hotel near the seashore.

But from the very first, he could not rest here either, and soon he could not sleep at all. On the contrary, what probably happened was that he could not sleep and therefore he could not rest.

Music from another room disturbed him, a horrible, extremely noisy music. This music would not have disturbed him had it not been for the noise that it made. Moreover, and even worse, it was dance music. Atanasio preferred to stay in his room and go to bed because he did not wish to dance—or, to tell the truth, he didn't know how to dance.

Because of this excessively noisy music, which originated in certain loud instruments and was motivated by the disgraceful desire of some people to dance, a desire he did not share, a desire he abhorred, he could not go to sleep. Because he could not go to sleep, he remembered himself again, and began to study himself again.

Self-knowledge had been recommended by certain gods in Delphi, though it was now out of style and out of use, as were these gods. It had also been preached and recommended by a certain old philosopher, who had been unemployed and who importuned those citizens of Athens who considered themselves obliged to do nothing to demonstrate their self-knowledge by debating without end, thereby losing the fight for existence. Finally, they gave him a small cup of poison to drink, which is a much more benign and humanitarian method of protection for society than some used in other parts of the world, and in other times.

Atanasio had never been interested in self-analysis before. He had occupied himself with machines, not with psychology, much less with psychoanalysis or with self-analysis.

The machines that interested him were those which were the greatest of all mechanical apparatuses, so marvelous, that they were just short of being pure machine: those computers, calculating machines, that were more certain, more serious, less equivocal than the human brain.

But some of these machines had recently demonstrated certain failures. They were in a nervous condition, irritable and willful. His employer maintained that this was caused by fatigue, the same as in human beings.

And taking advantage of this opportunity of exhaustion that sometimes upset the function of the machines, his employer recommended that he take a vacation.

But in such a way that doubts arose in him, whether it was him or the machines that were exhausted. Who has failed? Atanasio or the machines? Since the machines are superior to man, the electric cells in them superior to those formed by the substance of the nervous system, for everyone knows that one cannot trust the human nervous cells—Atanasio came to the conclusion that it was he himself who was exhausted, he himself who was not functioning properly, so that the seemingly thoughtful recommendation of his employer was really a reprimand.

Furthermore, and naturally, not being able to sleep, when one is in bed, one begins to remember the past in little bites.

That damn dance music!—noisy music from hell, produced by very primitive and despicable machines—and diabolical—for these machines had no other objective but to make unpleasant and useless noise. Such dancing, twirling without feeling, making inappropriate movements, put a serious man like himself in a ridiculous and undignified situation, who had already been degraded by such movements in other human beings which, without the certainties of an electronic brain, would have incalculable and unforeseen consequences.

Perhaps he, Atanasio, was frightened by the unforeseen and the unforeseeable.

This music with its rhythm—a rhythm that was noisy and cruel to one of his disposition, he considered to be an uncontrollable force. Atanasio's disposition said: sleep. But, to wish intensely, to wish ardently to sleep, is the surest way not to fall asleep. Thoughts circled in his head, circled unmanageably, uncontrollably, damned and damnable, and therefore in a vicious circle.

He did not wish to continue thinking. But he continued thinking just the same, continued thinking in circles. In a false circuit.

Other men—the other men who seduced women, they conquered—this seemed ridiculous to him, undignified, an insipid game. Atanasio was not an old man, though perhaps on the outside he was a "loner," a lover of solitude because he was afraid that others were better than him.

One is not able to calculate life exactly, rigidly, with precise intelligence. He was an intelligent man who served the intellect, was dominated by it. For him, intelligence was control, which is to say that intelligence was precisely that which was capable of being calculated, evaluated, anticipated by the machines.

The machines—!

God created man in His semblance at an immemorial time. Evil tongues twisted this doctrine around to maintain that it is man who created God in his image.

Then man created and invented the machines, now the machines know everything better than man does. Without the computers man would not have been able to create the atomic bomb.

Problems. Lacking sleep because he lacked sleep, Atanasio suffered from nostalgia, nostalgia for what had been. Worse, another problem arose. How to resolve the problem of man, or the problem of Atanasio. Who is man? Who is Atanasio?

Atanasio, well clearly—I am Atanasio. But who am I? How do I calculate myself? How and according to what rule: I would have to calculate the I—Beginning to calculate—and calculating to the rhythm of the dance music—a rhythm that was automatic—rather automatic—his interior rhythm, the rhythm of his interior machine, his own rhythm—but—.

Atanasio calculated and calculated—it was not difficult—his brain functioned surprisingly well to the rhythm of the dance music, in a night of insomnia.

Very well! His brain functioned very well, as well as a cybernetic machine—an automatically, regulated machine—that reacted, registered, and worked properly, without equivocation, while he never rested.

Excellent machine—!

Register—!

Mechanical brain—!

Now—a dream of satisfaction, satisfied—content—.

And now, again, he was not able to sleep, out of an obligation to the satisfactory result, to the internal pressure, the sanguine internal pressure he had built up.

This preoccupation with the sanguine pressure kept him from sleeping, and lack of sleep built more pressure in him: automatically, regulated machine, cybernetic machine.

Atanasio was pleased with himself that he had brought about this good machine, an exact, cybernetic machine, very reliable, trustworthy.

But why didn't he dance? Because he did not wish to dance, because he did not know how to dance because he was a machine. It was not requisite for a perfect machine to know how to dance. The machine is the product of the human brain—and the brain—better say the brain of Atanasio, was the product of the machines, produced to perfection by cybernetic machines, engendered by the machine, by cybernetic machines without frivolous dances—product of the machine, producing machines—product—producing—machine always mechanical, driven by its own power. But what if this is what precisely was immortality! Atanasio would have found the formula for immortality —machine creating machine. Once, a machine called the human brain, and now, at a later time—this other machine—the eternal and immortal machine. But why?

And who am I?

He woke—and looked at his watch—and began to get up after a few minutes.

Because his thoughts had to accommodate themselves to those people who had lived for centuries and millenia of history without cybernetic machines. How is it that they then produced—as if the immortal thought had surged up—the soul?—The immortal soul of man, then, is naturally the machine.

What were these past people like, what had they been like before the machine—?

How explain all this with his new formula for immortality. If, for example—if, for example, he himself, after several minutes or after several hours of insomnia was immortal, immortal due to the evolution of the machines, due to the interaction of machine and brain—he would not now want to lose his immortal soul. But his soul would then have existed before. If—if it had been able to record—, naturally, its transmigration—but he had not believed before in the existence of the soul or in immortality. He had discovered immortality and now he was beginning—he was beginning to agree—oh! if it were possible for a computer to help his memory—! But slowly, slowly, the memories were surging—a meadow—something about a meadow and food—yes, yes, he had eaten food—and someone had ennobled it with work—the machine— now he was beginning to be a machine in spite of his not being interested in dancing and in spite of his hating music.

But no, one day mankind discovered the automatic machines, with superior reactions, more rapid and more precise than his own. He had dedicated himself to these machines. He had evolved from them and perhaps Atanasio was the first of the new immortals, of the new man-machines.

But he had existed before. Eternity—vexatious eternity—one day, long before the cybernetic machine, man had discovered that he could use another's strength, brute strength, the strength of the animal. Then he put the horse to work.

Fields and food and salt—and after labor—mounted on a horse, carried by its muscles—and then harnessed, like a war horse—Atanasio, clearly, was beginning to accommodate himself to his former life.

In this way transmigration existed, and so did eternity.

In his former existence, he had been a horse.

He had been a horse, and from it man had resulted, and now he was being transformed into a machine. How pretty evolution was! How hopeful, how beautiful—! And he would not be a cybernetic machine forever—.

He accommodated himself to the past: pretty meadows and afterwards in the service of man, good oats with work and blows—still oats and an enclosed stable.

The music broke through his dreams of remembering. The idiotic dancing, the noisy embraces with the female of the species—Machines are not male and female, machines have no sex. Perhaps for this reason they are superior—and unlike man, they do not participate in stupidities—and now trying to accommodate himself to his former horselife—he thought, what of the mares?—no little mare neighed in his dreams—only oats and carrots, men mounted him for war, they gave him enough to eat, to satisfy him—no reminder of the feminine upset Atanasio's spirituality.

Another doubt arose, which tormented him—perhaps they had castrated the horse.

It was not important; eternity existed; horse—man—man, horse—man—machine.

And Atanasio was happy and slept profoundly well to the rhythm of the hated dance music.

Trans. by Roberta Kalechofsky

Diego Viga

Meditations on an Aunt

Reverend Father condemns doubt. He has to pray to ask for pardon.

But it does not pay for Hernan to pray. Furthermore, he knows that in the coming year they will send him to a secular school and that Uncle Dionysus says that that is much better for him. Uncle Dionysus is Mama's brother. Naturally, these adults have power, they have the right to send him to any school. At least, they assure themselves they have that right. There is always the possibility of rebelling, of turning oneself into an ignorant street boy. He ought to make up his mind if he wants to be such a street urchin, who is able to do dishonest things when he feels like it if he thinks he has something to gain from it, one who can play with anyone he wishes to without his father calling his attention to it.

These thoughts were unworthy thoughts, and Hernan knew this very well. It is much better to be a good boy, to eat in an elegant hotel where one can look forward to the good things on the menu. If you behave properly, no one grumbles at you. On the other hand, bad children are often exposed to dangers; but at times he envied these bad children and he even envied the poor children who were not enclosed in the cage of good conduct. Hernan told himself that he was now past the age of such doubts, he was already of school age.

However, at times doubts arose in him of their own free will. But it was worth the trouble to behave well—to behave himself according to the rules gave him the advantage of being able to observe people, even adult people without offending them.

For example, he would be able to observe the low cut of female clothes, in which place, he had heard it said, was a mysterious part of the woman—They also wore bikinis on the beach—allowing him to examine more or less—to contemplate their navels—though, with respect to the navels, the difference between men and women was nonexistent; but still he would stare with fascination at the feminine navel —but what of that which was above—Uncle Dionysus at times spoke in a dirty way and he was moreover a doctor—perhaps he spoke so freely because he was a doctor. Uncle Dionysus once said that this mysterious part of the woman corresponded to a cow's udders, and Mama had smiled and had called him a "devilish child."

Mama was his sister—it was very odd to think that Mama was Uncle Dionysus's sister, in the same way that Inesita was his sister. Now Mama—most certainly Mama had never worn a bikini, but always a very decent bathing suit—Moreover, Mama did not know how to swim well, which made Hernan feel superior, like an animal over a chicken. In Mama's bathing suit one could not see any division at all —moreover, he had been suckled, he had been nursed—still, he knew nothing exactly, or clearly. He was one who always had to guess, one whom adults always left in semi-obscurity.

He indeed knew about Aunt Nora, who wore a bikini—and at times Mama whispered about her to Papa, privately, that Aunt Nora —. He couldn't hear very well what Mama said, but it was clear that Mama did not like Aunt Nora very much, that she believed that Uncle Dionysus had married "a woman" like Aunt Nora. At times, he heard words on Mama's lips, such as "flirt," "too much, you know," "it's always being said," and "but those men—!"

Papa always answered on these occasions with a grunt. Hernan never knew whether it was an affirmative grunt or a negative grunt, or just a grunt of mellow opposition. Papa did not seem eager to have the exact sentiments of his grunt understood. If anything had an exact and definite direction, it was Papa's eyes. His glances directed themselves and fixed themselves, with black rays, towards the place where the upper piece of the bikini hid Aunt Nora's nursing apparatus. How odd that cows carried their udders between their hind legs, while women—.

Hernan, a bit ashamed of himself, told himself that this apparatus interested him because it suggested something about evolution—which was precisely what had awakened his profound and disquieting doubts.

Uncle Dionysus had said that there was a species relationship among the animals, that some had descended from others. Uncle Dionysus was very congenial, very congenial and interesting, so that Hernan resolved to study medicine when he was grown up. To follow in Uncle Dionysus's footsteps—but, being grown up seemed very like a distant future, as distant as the enormous boats that appeared as small as toys when they passed on the double blue horizon—the blue of the sky above the cerulean blue of the sea; the steamers that moved across the dividing line.

If the animals were our relatives and particularly the monkeys— he had watched some of these monkeys in a small zoo—they had higher bosoms—like those of women.

Evolution was obviously necessary, but it was illicit. Perhaps it was contrary to religious teaching. It was not possible that the world was created in six days and if Adam was descended from certain creatures, it was not possible that God had personally breathed life into him.

Hernan had an agreeably rebellious sensation which at the same time was frightening.

It was contrary to his religious teaching. But he was certain he would escape from these religious doctrines shortly in a way that his rebellion would not be so dangerous—but, still, what if they put him in hell. Papa had also liberated himself from these beliefs, but Mama— not reputable ladies like her—where, in fact, would Aunt Nora land if hell exists—something about her promised Paradise, so—it might not be necessary to send her to hell—only to purgatory—and purgatory—

purgatory had something attractive about it—.

Women are so disturbing! Even Aida, the mulatto who took care of Inesita, his small sister who is nothing better than a small nuisance.

Everyone played on the beach, browning himself in the sun.

Hernan returned to his oblique contemplation of the different nursing apparatus of the ladies, more or less hidden.

Aida's for example, was not very exciting, although sufficiently developed, brown, and covered with an ugly bathing suit—and Mama—well—that which at one time had nourished him lay outside his competence—and it would have been indecent. There remained Aunt's—magnificent Aunt's—Uncle Dionysus should be a supremely happy man, he had everything in the world. He was a doctor, he knew everything, he was a superior man, and he was married to Aunt Nora. He was able to caress her at any time—and at any place of her body—even without her bikini—clearly one had to be Uncle Dionysus in order to bring a Nora into the family and to this beach. Everything that was good was due him, and he had it all.

If only some day Hernan could transform himself into Uncle Dionysus, there would be a second Dionysus.

He asked himself a question about evolution, for he wanted to know more. The monkeys—how had they developed? He looked at Uncle Dionysus' strong hands, hands with refined but strong fingers—and his father's hands—shaggy like a monkey's—not appropriate for delicate work like those of his uncle's.

Mama's hands, white, small, chubby hands, with little expression in them—at one time, it had enchanted him for those hands to caress him, now they caressed Inesita—what they gave to Inesita in caresses had surely been taken from him—Aunt Nora's hands were fine and thin, with long, beautifully painted fingers. They were the most delicate hands, the prettiest, the most human, the summit of evolution.

And the feet!

The feet had been transformed into organs of support, in order to walk proudly, a bit swaggeringly, on two feet instead of on four—so Uncle Dionysus taught. This is elegant, but at bottom not practical. A dog or a strong horse can run a longer course for a longer time than man can.

In the meantime, Hernan continued to contemplate the feet. Papa's big toes were very gross and had short fuzz on the top. Mama's feet seemed to be domestic and honorable, small and chubby like her hands, with some ugly corns owing to the shoes she wore that were too narrow. Aida's big toes grew out, appeared separated from the other four, as if they had a fancy to grow in an opposite direction, like the thumbs on the hands, like the toes of a monkey's foot.

And Aunt Nora's feet, long and thin—and the toes also long, they seemed like the fingers of a hand, like intelligent fingers—.

But Uncle continued to teach that the foot-hand had developed from the foot-foot. It was the monkeys who had feet and narrow hands with long, delicate fingers, which appear so aristocratic to us. They are also dolicocephalic, which seems to some individuals to be a distinction and the sign of superior people.

What will become of the dolicocephalic? These were Uncle Dionysus's words.

Still more and more doubts arose in Hernan with respect to the evolution of the human race—The long and refined fingers, so pretty, induced in him a desire to be caressed by them—although they were like the toes—toes were not so human, but were Simian residue—still nothing took away from the beauty of Aunt Nora's hands and feet.

There arose then in Hernan's mind the suspicion that women belonged to another species, that they were not human, but simply and entirely female. That thought was very disturbing to him. Perhaps women had descended from another species—Papa with the fuzz of the monkey—while those with the beautiful feet with toes which reminded one of fingers—intelligent fingers, like Aunt Nora's—Hernan was very confused.

A small boat, formed by three logs fastened together, with a simple sail, approached the beach.

Uncle Dionysus proposed that they take a turn in this boat—"Who wants to come with me?"

—"It's too dangerous. I won't permit it," Mama screamed.

It would be delightful to show himself off as a good and obedient boy—but it would also be shameful to Uncle Dionysus, whom he wished to be like.

—"I am going with you, Uncle."

—"Arthur, say something to Hernan."

Papa's indefinite grunts indicated the prohibition—while the eyes of the head of the family remained fixed on the beautiful feet of Nora —straightening up slowly.

It was all very confusing—he had to escape—he had to flee—towards the ocean— to be like Uncle Dionysus—daring, unconventional—and at the same time, so knowing—.

"Are you dreaming, or obeying?" Uncle Dionysus asked, and Hernan noticed a certain scorn in his voice.

To escape his doubts—to show Mama that he was manly—already manly—.

"Don't look for adventures. Especially with a child," Aunt Nora advised. This decided him, that she had called him "chico"—he would show her, he would prove how manly he was, fearless, one who belonged to a superior species, to the strong sex, he would prove it particularly to her.

They got on to the boat.

Hernan conquered his fears, and his uneasiness was compensated by the frightened shouts of the ladies—he took them for admiration.

He was sharing something with Uncle Dionysus. He would be

like him, after all.

The waves carried them away, the salty water chafed his body and his face, whispering to him—the murmur of the ocean.

He realized that they were soon on the high sea. Now mountains rose above the high waves, like a horseman on a stallion. The air whistled through the sail.

And the world was full of happiness.

Trans. by Roberta Kalechofsky

Diego Viga

The Stutterer's Suicide and the Psychiatrist's Dream

There's an old German proverb which says that "if a person is planning to take a trip, he should be able to talk about it." Frankly, I'd watch out for that. I don't think that anybody should mention his travels to anyone. . . .

After putting it off for several years, I went to Europe via New York City, under the pretext of attending an International Science Congress. I planned to stop in New York for about 40 hours on my way back in order to visit some old friends and relatives. I wanted to see how much each of us had aged since the last time.

Just two hours before leaving home for the airport to fly to Europe, the Mendozas called me. Although they weren't exactly friends, they had always been pleasant. Besides, of course I remembered their son, Humberto. Everyone tends to feel a twinge of guilt if an acquaintance willfully takes his own life. This was the case with Humberto Mendoza. I was profoundly disturbed to find his name in the society page obituaries along with a series of announcements from friends, businesses and ministries offering their condolences to his parents. How had he died? And why in New York City? Had he gone there to seek medical advice?

Sometime after reading the news about Humberto Mendoza, I ran into a friend who confided to me that the entire city already knew the open secret that young Mendoza had committed suicide.

The guilt which I felt began as something completely unfounded. Humberto had been a student of mine, but he was one of those failures who abandons his studies and disappears. I had never considered his case as a tragedy, since his parents were more than comfortable; in fact they were influential people with magnificent connections.

As it is extremely painful for me to express condolences, I forgot to... Frankly, I wasn't even sure that I was obliged to do so, since I barely knew the family. Perhaps it would only reopen wounds which were just beginning to heal—especially the scar of his suicide.

It hadn't been my fault. Mendoza was no good at his studies because he lacked concentration, objectivity and self-confidence. What's more, he had an intense desire to race new cars down main streets. I once pointed out to him that this veiled timidity, his profound and hidden insecurity, is not a desirable quality in a doctor.

Besides, the boy stuttered. Surely that would be a deterrent to his professional pursuits, I thought.

At the end of the year Mendoza told me that he wouldn't return, most likely because he had failed several courses which meant he would fail for the whole year. I thought it was the best thing for him to do, and I inquired about his future plans.

"For the time being I'll work in Dad's company. . .later on we'll see. Maybe I'll study business administration, at an American university, of course."

"Perhaps our system is considered adequate to educate doctors merely as guardians of the health of future generations," I commented, not without a certain bitterness, "but for the sacred care of property, Business Administration, we are not sufficiently intelligent."

So much the better if this young man does go to the United States. Now I'm becoming nationalistic, I thought at the time. I'm actually concerned about this country.

After that I forgot Mendoza.

One day in the newspaper, naturally on the social page, I read an elegant article (with a photograph, you understand) about Humberto Mendoza, who had just been granted a scholarship by some American organization to continue his studies at a famous university. . .in New York City, no less!

I remembered thinking that the rich are always the ones to receive scholarships, and although Mendoza was neat and fairly well educated (with the exception of racing those high-powered cars), he wasn't exactly among the most intelligent.

Everything depends on pull, I thought, and of course those who have it don't need it. I pondered the endless theme of the world's injustices.

But I had enough to worry about and since Mendoza had left my tutelage, I forgot him. I don't know how much time elapsed without having thoughts of Mendoza cross my mind, until that phone call which I received just as I was departing for Europe. Of course I said that I'd be delighted to have the deceased's father pay me a visit.

Mr. Mendoza conducted himself in a commendable manner which hid his emotions and preserved his composure. I learned from him that Humberto had stayed in New York where he had studied business administration with reasonable success. The only thing which had held him back was his stuttering. So he had sought the services of a psychiatrist.

"Who, I believe," indicated the father, "is of the same background as you are."

He gave me the address of a Dr. A. E. Lewison (who being of European descent was probably called Lewisohn at one time.) What did the initials A & E stand for? Had his parents made the mistake of calling him Adolf? I know now that his name is Abraham Efrain. Humberto's father gave me the psychiatrist's address in Manhattan and begged me to locate him to find out what this doctor knew about his son. I couldn't refuse him, although I knew beforehand that my time in New York would be rushed.

On my way back from London, as soon as I arrived in New York and placed my suitcase in my cousin's apartment, I telephoned Dr. Lewison. Fortunately he was in. From his voice and pronunciation I knew that he had once spoken German. Since I was a colleague, he allowed me a bit of his precious time in his clinic on the following morning.

The reception room was impersonally decorated in bright colors like most North American clinics. The secretary, a reasonably attractive young woman who worked for several physicians, let Dr. Lewison know I was there and he received me promptly.

He was several years older than I was, with dark, sad, intelligent eyes that, perhaps due to his profession, reminded me of Freud's. That was the only resemblance, however. The eyes were framed by a heavy face, bald head, and white hair.

"Please have a seat," he offered. "You're from Ecuador, are you not? You weren't born there, I suppose?"

"Of course not. I was born in Vienna."

"And did you study there as well?"

"Naturally," I replied, "if one is born in a city that possesses such a famous Medical school. . ."

"I also studied and graduated in Vienna," he said, now speaking with a German accent which revealed that he hadn't been born in Austria. "I fled from the Russians to Vienna in World War I and like so many refugees, stayed in Austria."

We began to recall memories of unforgettable professors, clinicians, anatomists. . .

"I had the good fortune of being admitted to Wagner-Jauregg's lecture hall."

This reaffirmed my conclusion that Lewison was older than me because that famous Nobel prize winner had retired from teaching before I was able to attend his classes, though I saw him frequently.

"Did you ever attend Freud's classes?" I enquired somewhat naively. Because of his advanced age and debilitating cancer of the jawbone, Freud was no longer giving lectures during my time. I had the infantile need to boast that once I had had a discussion with the renowned gentleman. As a student, I had written a critique of one of his works and the elderly professor had responded to my respectfully insolent letter with a long and friendly explanation.

I remembered that Wagner-Jauregg, the head of Psychiatry, had been a confirmed enemy of psychoanalysis. (Freud had the title "professor," but he never actually headed a department at the university.) However, he was the only person unrelated to Freud who addressed him in the familiar.

"Many refugee physicians suddenly became improvised psychotherapists," Dr. Lewison continued, "because they had less difficulty pursuing that profession. Of course I too began as a psychotherapist, but I'm a doctor and once dreamed of devoting myself to neuropsychiatry. All of us study our patients' souls and I believe that we must realize . . .well, I don't wish to chat about matters which don't interest you."

"But they do. . .exceedingly," I assured him truthfully, "however. . ."

"I know your time is limited, just like mine and all the inhabitants of this high-strung island of Manhattan. To tell the truth, I often have more faith in Pavlov's behaviorism than in Freud, and I invariably apply the teachings, exercises and conditioned responses of the old country. Don't you think that speech patterns are primarily based upon conditioned reflexes."

I had, in fact, often said similar things to my students. Lewison and I were in agreement. By referring to speech patterns, he had raised the issue of my former student. Inevitably, I told him about my experience with that pretentious, scatterbrained, insecure young man.

"Good, once again we have something in common."

Great, I thought, unfortunately, what we have in common is that your treatment and my teaching both failed. Humberto Mendoza is dead.

"Stuttering always has psychological causes. The stutterer is a timid, insecure individual who had suffered certain psychological traumas. Perhaps in his early childhood, someone laughed at his baby talk. Or he had difficulty pronouncing his "r" or "s." Maybe it was caused by a premature sexual experience. But there are many other origins and I discovered with a little research that his defect was merely one involving the use of his respiratory apparatus. Therefore, I thought it unnecessary to bring up psychological motives. Usually in these patients a series of habits or conditioned reflexes have been established. . . The task of correcting them is extremely difficult, but they say that man is a rational being, so I sent the boy to a voice specialist. His affliction was aggravated by bad habits and a series of poorly directed conditioned reflexes, such as the excessive use of sharp tones and talking without using his diaphragm. He also had an inferiority complex about the feminine sound of his voice for which he compensated by sleeping with too many women in order to soothe his masculine pride. He was one of those patients for whom my treatment had very satisfactory results. Humberto Mendoza was convinced of the natural, that is to say physical-nervous causes of his defect and tried to remedy them with exercises suggested by a colleague of mine. Evidently, he was quite relieved to discover that his problem was not caused by some hormonal deficiency or a profound psychic trauma. So many young men mutter about psychic traumas without having any idea of what they are talking about. When I declared him cured, we were both quite pleased with the results."

Operation successful, patient dead, I commented silently, labeling myself a Sancho Panza for musing over worn out, humorless proverbs.

"In line with my responsibility, I followed up on Humberto Mendoza's condition, but I noticed something peculiar. Although completely cured of stuttering, he showed signs of distress, insecurity and depression. He never wanted to answer my inquiries. 'I'm a doctor,' I reminded him, 'How can I treat you if you don't tell me anything? You know very well that I depend on your communication to me.'

" 'I've nothing to communicate,' he said. 'You've done a magnificent job of curing me, and I'll be eternally grateful.'

"Dear colleague, you have reopened a wound," he said to me.

"By wound do you mean trauma?"

"Yes, yes. I don't want to use the word trauma. No one can be a good doctor, much less a trustworthy psychiatrist, in one's own case. I had forgotten the Latin American youth and now you come..."

"To annoy you?"

"It's no bother, believe me, it's no bother. On the contrary, for a long time I've tormented myself day and night trying to understand the cause of his suicide; a well prepared, premeditated act. An overdose of barbiturates followed by a hearty farewell drinking bout. It's common knowledge that alcohol and barbiturates interact with disastrous results. Besides, it might give the appearance that he accidentally overdosed because of his intoxicated state.

"But at least he was discreet. He acted quietly in his own bed at night with serious lethal intent. I tell myself over and over that I did everything possible to help him, that I had been absolutely correct in diagnosing the cause of Mendoza's depression. How could I have called the police or have him committed? He was perfectly lucid. Yet, despite his extended treatment and all my knowledge in the field, I could never understand the reason for his suicide."

"Mysteries are only solved in detective stories. I'm afraid that in real life cases of unsolved murders, suicides, and medical puzzles exist, but not the perfect solution." Enough talk about the human soul as an enigma, I added silently.

"And now, your phone call yesterday makes me reconsider the case..."

"I'm sorry."

"Please don't apologize. On the contrary, I now believe that I finally understand what happened to Humberto Mendoza."

"Have you gone over your notes again?"

"No. My time is so limited that not even the desire to help out a colleague would allow me this luxury. But I began to remember, to torment myself once more. All of us, including Freud, agree that dreams reflect one's daytime experience."

"Ah, so my poor student has appeared in your dreams to reveal the truth..."

"No, not at all. Apparently my dream had nothing to do with the patient, but it was related to your phone call. A fellow doctor who studied in Vienna represents the voice of the hidden conscience.

. . .Are you Jewish?"

"Of course, I am. I went to South America to escape persecution, not to enjoy the pleasant climate."

"Well, I'm neither a practicing Jew nor a Zionist. In fact, I dislike any kind of nationalism and often ask myself why we even bother to remain Jews. It's probably out of loyalty precisely because we've been persecuted and discredited for so many thousands of years. To abandon such an oppressed group would lack courage and sincerity. I'm not sure what your opinions are in the matter, but I repeat that although I have no ties to the Jewish faith and community, I. . ."

"Well," I said, "Hitler showed us that not even those who wished to assimilate could escape the Jewish fate."

"Yes, that's true. . ."

"But I agree with you on many points. You believe that only pride. . .!"

"If we start discussing the Jewish problem now, you'll never catch your plane tomorrow morning."

"I have a luncheon engagement today. . . ."

"Don't worry. I only wanted to show you how insignificantly I'm connected to the Jewish community. One might say that psychiatry itself is bad Judaism."

I remembered that Wagner-Jauregg did not have any Jewish blood.

"I don't know why I feel this way. . . .I never did. I'm not at all nationalistic. I'm just a purely atheistic American citizen. Perhaps some of these ideas were in my mind as I tossed and turned in my bed one night. I was perspiring. In August it is extremely difficult to sleep in this city with its infernal heat; and I can't use air conditioning because I find it impossible to sleep with it on. Thus, that night poor Humberto Mendoza pursued me and in order to drive away his ghost, I remembered you; the culprit who resurrected his spirit. I remembered your voice, and although you spoke English over the telephone, I recognized the voice of a Viennese. Naturally, I knew that you were a Jew as well and thus, I began to reflect on the Jewish fate to free me from the shadow of the stutterer, or the man who preferred to stutter . . .meaning that he preferred to die rather than live without stuttering."

Psychiatrists are bound to be crazy, I thought. No wonder they live in asylums, although this one is in a clinic on 74th Street.

"I didn't want to be a Jew, but I am. I didn't want to be born Jewish, but I was. My father tried to give us a modern education that didn't belong to the ghetto, and during World War I we moved to Vienna. Afterwards my father chose the Austrian Republic. You know how things were. We were always the 'outsiders from the East,' who had come because we were Jewish. We were always different in their eyes. At school I was the 'Jew.' Since I was a good student, they copied my homework, but they never wanted me around. In high school my peers accepted me only because I ingratiated myself to them by being helpful. I truly felt the need to distinguish myself by surpassing everyone else. 'Or is this my nature?' I wondered. 'Must I always be Number One?'

"I never became Number One. I was a good student and tried to establish friendships, but I always felt left out. I just didn't belong. Nor did they give me the best grades. I was a good student, but without a doubt, not the best.

" 'It's because I'm Jewish,' I told myself. 'If I were a gentile like the others, I'd get better grades and my peers would respect me. They wouldn't hit me in the nose with a ball and knock off my glasses. They wouldn't laugh at my clumsiness.' "

Only then did I realize that those "Freudian eyes" hidden by bifocals were just like my own.

"Finally, I entered the university. You remember how the antisemites dominated there. Ten times worse that the Triple Entente... Once again I pushed myself to excel academically."

Not me. I never had such ambition to succeed, I thought. But I shouldn't interrupt him. I wondered why he was telling me his strange little tale. A psychiatrist with his vulgar, ordinary, boring Jewish experiences...he's got something all right, he's a lonely person who needs to unburden his heart, I concluded. Victims of neuroses pay him to listen to their small, psychic sufferings, so I should be grateful to him for his time and lose my precious hours in New York City? I didn't exactly come here to bury myself in the life of Dr. A. E. Lewison!

Luckily I hadn't scheduled appointments with my friends for an earlier hour. While they work, I lounge around here, instead of strolling through this grand city, Central Park or the Metropolitan Museum.

"At least you were born in Vienna," he mentioned, "but I was always considered the Polish Jew. All Jews need ten times more publications than anyone else in order to become a member of the faculty. That had been my hope, but Mr. Hitler interrupted my career. You've known some professors...well in spite of everything, I completed my studies so successfully that they accepted me as an intern in the Department of Psychiatry at the University. Despite my Jewish origin, I accomplished the incredible feat of becoming a member of an institution of higher learning."

I also achieved this, I thought, but I listened silently to the confessions of this psychopathic psychiatrist instead of...!

"I became somewhat of a resident, an assistant doctor...."

"I too...," I broke my self-imposed silence.

"Yes, I was very proud, but although they honored me with a post, as a Jew they did not give me a paid position. I remained an assistant physician, ad honorem. And later, when the post for the head of the clinic opened up, of course a gentile colleague was promoted. ...We Jews never make it."

He was partially correct. Generally it was impossible for Jews to achieve anything. But just between you and me, anything is possible in the Psychiatric Clinic. In fact, the clinic chief under Wagner-Jauregg, who subsequently became his successor, was a Jew.

"But in the end, what did it matter; not going anywhere, being Jewish. You know, the German invasion and occupation swallowed all our hopes. Of course, had I become a full-fledged doctor, my reputation would have been better. As it was, I sought refuge wherever I could. Fortunately I have relatives in the United States who gave me an affidavit. But there was no one around waiting to offer me a job."

"You know, there's antisemitism. . . ."

"Of course, one feels it here at times, but in my case it wasn't even really antisemitism, just being Jewish. With the increasing flow of refugees, there was a tremendous selection of intelligent, already well-known people. No one would pay attention to an insignificant Jew with no more than five publications. I had to chose a more modest path like psychotherapy. But I must confess that deep down I hated this denomination, this emblem, this factory label of psychotherapist. After a while my patients arrived, but by then my career had been ruined without purpose and through no fault of my own, because I am Jewish."

"Weren't the majority of your patients Jewish?" I asked.

"A good percentage. . .but almost all my colleagues, all my competition is Jewish. And I never succeeded in getting an important post . . .well, I have deviated from the subject without intending to burden you, grumbling about my failures."

"We all have failures. If we were to hang our failures on our waiting room walls instead of diplomas, there wouldn't be enough space for all of them."

"Ah, how true," he assented. "Now, let me continue. I was lying awake in bed one night, perspiring. Ruminating over and reiterating the series of deceptions I had suffered, I thought of all the failures of my career and the misfortunes that destroyed the lives of all our generation—those of Jewish descent. I told you that now and then I can't fall asleep. Well, finally I must have done so. You are familiar, are you not, with the curious experience when one does not believe he has slept until he awakes from a dream? Only by dreaming can one be assured of having slept, although the actual passage of time is quite minimal. The dream may take place in a split second. In this way I had the following dream.

"I awoke suddenly and realized that it was the next morning. Besides that, I knew another very important fact. I was no longer Jewish. Yes, yes I knew it.

"When I said to my wife, 'That's the way it goes with us Jews,' she replied, 'What a boob you are, what's happened to you? Us, JEWS? NEVER!' I went to my office and everyone treated me differently. My Jewish patients—of course there are some—treated me with a new distance. I particularly recall Mr. Aron—he treated me with the same care with which we approach gentiles, fearing they will be disagreeable, or not accept us. In the meantime, my non-Jewish patients, Mr. Hart for example, showed me a new cordiality. We understood one another perfectly. I don't know what happened.

"I began to doubt everything. Could my own wife substantiate it?—she should know. I went to the bathroom and saw with great surprise that the sign of the pact between God and Abraham had disappeared—I possessed a foreskin. I returned to my desk.

"I immediately resolved to request a post as professor at Harvard University since it was the most renowned, and there was no longer any reason not to. They responded that not only did they already have a head psychiatrist, but he was a Viennese Jew. But—damnit, I thought—I'm not Jewish and the other guy got the post, he's sitting in my chair. I should become antisemitic.

"The nightmare continued. In it I returned to my youth. In general, we dream that we are younger, as if to confirm the Freudian theory that dreams fulfill our desires, especially those that are absolutely impossible, such as returning to childhood.

"My early years were unpleasant, and curiously, one always notices this when one returns to them in dreams. In the next phase of the dream I looked for jobs, for a career. . .always failing. There was always someone else more capable and better connected than I.

"Finally I resolved to return to my old age. Once again I was my actual age and found myself in bed. But since my wife had reassured me that I was not Jewish, that I had never been Jewish, I had no recourse. My disgrace was irreparable, I had no excuse for my failures. I returned to the bathroom, this time at home. After once again convincing myself that I was not Jewish, what do you think I did? I took my razor and cut my throat. When the blood began to spurt, I awoke.

"My first thought was that everything happened as though I hadn't slept at all. It had been a nightmare. Afterwards, in order to reassure myself that I hadn't tried the 'other thing,' I remembered that I don't even own a straight razor. I had always used a Gillette safety razor in the past, and for years now I've used an electric razor exclusively. Now you see!"

Great, I'm profoundly happy, I thought, that you didn't cut your throat—but why tell all this to me?

"Understand, colleague, my dream completely clarified the case of the unfortunate Humberto Mendoza. Now I understand perfectly. When I ceased being Jewish, when I had been freed from the stigma that embittered my existence, I found that I was left without an excuse for my failures. I felt guilty. And I realized that I was truly worthless."

"But it was only a nightmare. I also suffer from nightmares occasionally."

"You don't understand, doctor. Mr. Mendoza used his defect,

his sharp voice and stuttering to excuse all his failures; his ineptitude for medicine, probably his inability to run an important business, his inferiority in various fields.

"Cure him! Cure him!" he suddenly burst out in bitter hysterical laughter, unbecoming to a doctor. "That which *we* understand as a cure. I cured him! We have cured him! To cure Mr. Mendoza's stuttering was like taking the crutches from a legless man; he could no longer find excuses. Don't you see? We took away the crutches of his pride, stole the excuses. Unfortunately, he wasn't dreaming as I was. He had lost his defense, the protective defect; he was left vulnerable. He could only flee, so he escaped through the door of alcohol and barbiturates.

"Good—well not exactly—but thank you anyway, for your visit. I now know what happened to my patient and your ex-student. I truly doubt that this will help his bereaved parents. Doubtless it will not be a solace or lighten their souls in any way. But I will try to tell them. At least I know now. . .!"

And so the end of the case of Humberto Mendoza, as explained by Dr. Lewison.

In the streets were Jews, Blacks, Puerto Ricans—the others who will have other excuses. Maybe stuttering should not be taken from the people. Or it would probably be better to take the excuse from them and teach them how to live without crutches or escapes; teach them to confront life.

Mendoza fled because he couldn't deal with life.

I'm a doctor as well as a professor, which requires me to be optimistic in the face of wind and sea. I want to share this moral lesson with you, from an old teacher of young people. Perhaps I will begin to use old age as my crutch. It is probably the most secure defect, as it is inevitable and absolutely incurable.

Later on that day, I met my friends and we reminisced about school in Vienna and our behavior of the past. . .as if in a dream.

Trans. by Susan Riva Greenberg

Diego Viga *is the pseudonym for* Paul Engel *who is a doctor as well as a writer. Holding degrees in biology, anthropology, psychology and pharmacology, he is now professor emeritus at Universidad Central del Ecuador in Quito. His background in these disciplines, as well as his humanitarianism and humor is clear from these three stories. He has had published 15 novels, 12 of them in German, and three volumes of stories in Spanish. Born in Vienna in 1907, he makes his home in Ecuador.*

Benno Weiser Varon

The Diplomat and Dr. Mengele

In Ira Levin's best-selling thriller, *The Boys from Brazil*, Dr. Josef Mengele clones 94 Hitlers in Brazil. The film based on the book starts out in Paraguay, however, and Dr. Mengele is Levin's one non-fictional character. Because it is fiction, it may be unfair to take exception to its improbabilities. I am not referring to the plot, in which, from some blood and tissue given by Hitler, the "Angel of Auschwitz" produces 94 blue-eyed boys who are eventually adopted by unsuspecting families in various continents. What I call improbable, even impossible, is a procession of brownshirts through a Paraguayan town, and a ball in Paraguay in which nazis appear in full regalia.

When I set out for Paraguay in 1968, neither I, nor anybody in Israel's Foreign Ministry, gave it a thought that I was being sent to Mengele country. I spoke with several Israeli diplomats who had been non-resident ambassadors to Paraguay. None of them mentioned Dr. Mengele.

Not that I was unfamiliar with the history of the monster who received transports at Auschwitz. I had read about his pseudo-scientific research programs performed on human guinea pigs and his obsession with experiments with twins. I knew that Mengele was supposed to be somewhere in South America. But nobody mentioned the matter to me when I got the scant guidelines for my mission in Paraguay. I was to inaugurate an Israeli embassy in Asuncion. My assignment was to make friends and influence people. Paraguay had just joined the U.N. Security Council; for the next two years, Paraguay was a most important Latin American country to Israel.

The first mention of the nazi criminal's connection with Paraguay occurred on my way to Asuncion. As I was standing with my family at the Buenos Aires airport, we met a young Jew married to a Paraguayan. She introduced us to her father, who was puzzled that Paraguay, with its tiny Jewish community, rated an Israeli ambassador. Suddenly he had an illumination. "I know why you're going there," he said with a wink, and as I stared at him uncomprehendingly, he whispered into my ear: "Dr. M."

I was not yet installed in Asuncion when a Paraguayan asked to be received. I let him come to our hotel suite. He acted mysteriously, lowered his voice and said: "I know where you can find Dr. Mengele."

I did not know how to react. I suspected that the man had mercenary motives and did not encourage him to go on. He assured me he was not out for money, he just wanted to see justice done. He described a setting near the Brazilian border where, behind a wire fence surrounding his hideout, I could see the doctor take his daily walk. I thanked my informer and took his name.

After the embassy offices were inaugurated, hardly a week passed without somebody dropping by to offer me Dr. Mengele's whereabouts. The visitors were old and young, simple and educated, idealists and reward-hunters. But not two tips I received throughout the years coincided. Dr. Mengele seemed to be a ubiquitous fellow. He was in the north, east and west. He was an army doctor, a cobbler, a farmer, an idler.

I listened with interest to the first few informers. Later, I developed a standard answer: The Israeli government was not searching for Dr. Mengele; the Federal Republic of Germany sought him. Thus the appropriate recipient of their information was the German Embassy. This claim was valid although in 1968 the German Embassy in Asuncion was no longer keen on catching Dr. Mengele. My German colleague, Ambassador Hubert Krier, told me that his predecessor, Eckhard Briest, had, on instructions from Bonn, asked President Alfredo Stroessner for extradition. President Stroessner replied that since Mengele had acquired Paraguayan citizenship he could not be extradited. Ambassador Briest suggested that Mengele be stripped of his citizenship, since he had received it on the basis of false testimony to the effect that he had resided in Paraguay for five years. This infuriated President Stroessner, who had banged his fist on the desk and said, "Once he is a Paraguayan, he is a Paraguayan." The ambassador felt that he had outlived his usefulness in Paraguay and was soon replaced.

I must confess that I was not too eager to find Dr. Mengele. He presented a dilemma. Israel had less of a claim for his extradition than Germany. He was, after all, a German citizen who had committed his crimes in the name of the German Reich. Then there was no reason to expect that the Paraguayans would be more forthcoming with Israel than they had been with Germany, from which they were receiving foreign aid. I found it highly improbable that Israel could afford an operation similar to the one that spirited Adolf Eichmann out of Argentina. And 1968 was not 1960. In 1960, Israel enjoyed a relative honeymoon with the world. In the Security Council's debate on Eichmann's abduction—a debate demanded by Argentina—the Soviet Union had come out in favor of what undoubtedly was an infringement of Argentina's sovereignty. For once, hatred of the nazis outweighed Soviet hostility to Israel. And President Frondizi, who was presiding over a short democratic interlude in Argentina was not upset personally; he expressed anger for the benefit of the country's nationalistic army. But in 1968, Israel had just weathered a Soviet attempt to brand it an aggressor in the six-day war.

Nevertheless, I would have gladly shared the fate of my colleague, Arieh Levavi, who was declared *persona non grata* by the Argentine government after the abduction of Eichmann (in which he had no part and of which he had not been informed in advance). Perhaps to catch the most monstrous of all nazi criminals was worth the price of losing Paraguay's vote in the Security Council.

But Paraguay is not Argentina. It is much smaller. It is a police state with an effective secret service. It is landlocked. A *bungled* abduction would not have been worth the penalties.

Besides, bringing Eichmann to justice was a one-time operation. David Ben-Gurion wanted to make the world—and Israel's younger generation—relive the horrors of the Holocaust. I did not believe a replay of the Eichmann trial would add anything.

Yet I could not help but get excited when one day I received a call from the U.S. ambassador. He recommended that I see one of his compatriots who told me the following story:

He had married a Paraguayan woman and followed her to Asuncion where she had a business in partnership with an older sister. The two had a younger sister who had fallen in love with a German physician and was going to marry him. Though she had met the man in Paraguay, she never introduced him to her family and she disappeared one day from Asuncion. But the older sister ran into the younger sister in Buenos Aires, was invited to her home, and met the German doctor. Without the slightest provocation, he went into a vicious diatribe against Jews. There were hints that he did not feel safe and rarely left his home. Later, when an item on Dr. Mengele appeared in the newspaper and mentioned that he alternated among residences in Paraguay, Brazil and Argentina, it suddenly occurred to the American's wife that all the clues—German, doctor, anti-Semite, recluse—fit the image of the famous nazi. When the American's wife mentioned the similarities to her older sister, the latter became upset: What, after all, was more important, family solidarity or punishment for alleged crimes committed a quarter of a century before?

The genuine emotion of the American, as well as the story itself, and the fact that he had gone first to the U.S. ambassador, impressed me. He asked what he could do, and I told him that the best would be to procure a picture of the brother-in-law. I expressed one doubt: As far as I knew, Dr. Mengele was married to a German woman. But I did not exclude the possibility that the German wife was living in Europe, and that Mengele had taken up with a Paraguayan.

The encounter was serious enough to warrant a coded cable to Jerusalem. I never got a reply.

I saw the American again. First he informed me that his sister-in-law was carrying a snapshot of her sister's husband in her handbag. The American and his wife were trying to get hold of the picture without the sister noticing. The second time he called me, he asked to have a photographer handy. I called a photographer I trusted. The American arrived, out of breath: His wife had managed to snatch the picture while her sister went to the toilet. He wanted the snapshot photographed on the spot.

I took one look at it and said: "Your wife can put it back this very moment. I don't know Dr. Mengele. But I have seen some pictures of him. This man is at least 6'4". Mengele is 5'7". No amount of plastic surgery could have performed this miracle. There exists not the slightest resemblance in the shape of the head, nor in the body build. Your wife's kid sister has married another nazi doctor. Mengele wasn't the only one."

It seemed almost impossible to avoid Mengele, or, rather, the tracks he left behind. When I signed the contract for the embassy residence, the owner's lawyer, Cesar Augusto Sanabria, volunteered the information that he had transacted the naturalization of the nazi doctor. Of course, he added, he had not known at the time—in 1959—who his client was. (Mengele received worldwide notoriety only after Eichmann's abduction.) He got the case through a well-known member of the German community, and it was a routine affair for a lawyer. Every foreigner who resides in Paraguay for five years in entitled to Paraguayan citizenship. There were two German gentlemen—he gave me their names—who testified under oath that Mengele had been in the country five years.

I did not try to learn more. I was not sent to Paraguay as a nazi hunter. But Mr. Sanabria volunteered another piece of information. In Asuncion there was a podiatrist who looked just like the Auschwitz doctor.

I made an appointment for my wife and myself. We got a very competent pedicure and became clients of the murderer's look-alike. On our last visit we confessed what had brought us to him. He was surprised. He had never heard about the resemblance before.

There was someone else who was absolutely certain of having seen the doctor in Asuncion. We were friendly with a family who owned a jewelry shop downtown. The owner's wife was an Auschwitz survivor. She told us that one day two gentlemen entered her shop. They spoke English. As she looked at the face of one of them, she lost her speech. No doubt, this was the man who with one movement of his thumb had spared her life. Over twenty years had passed, but there could be no mistake. One remembers such a face. She was unable to utter a word while the two customers were in the shop. After they left, she beckoned to her husband and managed to stammer: "Dr. Mengele, that was Dr. Mengele."

All this had happened in the past: the naturalization in 1959, the incident in the jewelry store in 1965. It was now 1968.

Yet every few months an item would appear in the world's press about Dr. Mengele being sheltered in Paraguay. The government was annoyed. And Dr. Raul Sapena Pastor, the foreign minister, would call me to his office and complain. The basis of his complaint was that the news originated in Israel. There was a gentleman in Haifa, Tuvia Friedmann, who would make statements about Mengele and Paraguay.

Hardly a week passed without my having to ask the foreign minister for a vote in Israel's favor at the U.N. He was, theoretically, entitled to demand *quid pro quo*. Thus, I had to convince him that he had no leg to stand on. "*Senor Canciller*," I said the first time the matter came up, "I hope you will understand the handicaps of a democratic regime. It is utterly beside the point that from government to government the relations between our two countries could not be better. You can believe me that Paraguay's gallant stand at the U.N. is fully appreciated. But Israel is a democracy. We have a free press which is allowed to say whatever it likes about our prime minister, our cabinet members, everybody. If tomorrow one of our papers were to say that Mr. Eshkol is a scoundrel and Mrs. Meir a fool, nothing could be done about it. Now in Israel there are half a million survivors from the concentration camps. For you, *Senor Canciller,* the existence of Dr. Mengele may be a nuisance. For this half million survivors it's an outrage, a provocation, an abomination. There is absolutely no way to shut up Mr. Friedmann."

There were variations on the theme on subsequent meetings. I was never apologetic. Once a call from the ministry came while I was on vacation. A young first secretary served as charge d'affaires. The young man was so impressed by the foreign minister—who was indeed an impressive man—that he sent an alarmed telex to Jerusalem. (I did not report on these routine complaints.) Whereupon the Foreign Ministry of Israel made a statement that it had at no time accused Paraguay of sheltering Dr. Mengele. I don't know what distribution the statement received. But its text was telexed to Asuncion. I would never have suggested, nor agreed to such a statement.

President Stroessner and his foreign minister continued to be upset by reports of Mengele's presence in Paraguay. But they never went so far as to deny them.

On one occasion, Dr. Pastor asked me: "Why do they always pick on Paraguay? Whatever Mengele did, he did as a German, in the name of Germany. You know our country. Do you believe anybody can hide here without people knowing who he is and where he is? This is not a matter for diplomats. This is a matter for commandos."

I pricked up my ears. "May I take this as a hint?" I asked.

There was no reply. Possibly it was a hint of Dr. Pastor's feelings: Take him away, take him out of our hands. But he did not speak for the President. And in Paraguay the President has the first and the last word.

I have frequently wondered why Paraguay protects this criminal. When Mengele was naturalized, the Paraguayans did not know who he was. (There are other ways to do things for an alien if one wants to help him. I once saw a document in which Argentine President Juan Peron ordered 8,000 blank Argentine passports for an organization that helped nazis escape from Europe.)

When the West German government demanded Dr. Mengele's extradition, it touched several raw nerves. First, the matter of sovereignty: "Nobody is going to tell us whom we can naturalize and whom we can keep in our country." Then there was the Latin American attitude *vis-a-vis* political asylum: Few major Latin American political figures have not at one time or another availed themselves of political asylum. Whether one calls it chauvinism, over-sensitivity, or pride in sovereignty, one fact emerges: The protection granted to nazis is not a phenomenon *sui generis*.

But once this point is established, it has to be said that the southern countries of South America are a preferred shelter for nazis whom Catholic charities helped spirit out of Europe. When I met Colonel Hans Ulrich Rudel, Hitler's most decorated combat flyer, in the antechamber of President Stroessner's office, he introduced himself (believing that I was the Austrian ambassador) as the representative of the Siemens manufacturing firm. He was trying to sell a new telephone system to Paraguay. (Apparently, Siemens was cashing in on his war record to sell costly equipment to sympathetic heads of state.) I later learned that he was the head of the notorious *Kameradenwerk*, the nazi organization which helped find safe havens for nazis. I would not be surprised if Mengele's stay in Paraguay had been arranged under the auspices of *Kameradenwerk.*

I was told that a French dope smuggler had to bribe half of Asuncion for every day his extradition to the United States was delayed. I believe that in Mengele's case there was a waiver of bribes.

Toward the end of my mission to Paraguay, in 1972, I received Ladislas Farago. He pushed three heavy volumes—all written by him—into my hand: *Patton*, which I had seen in its stunning film version with George C. Scott, *The Broken Seal*, which had been filmed under the title *Tora! Tora! Tora!*, and a then-current best seller, *The Game of the Foxes*. An impressive calling card. Mr. Farago was from Budapest, downstream from Vienna, where I grew up. He arrived for tea at 4 p.m. and left at midnight.

Mr. Farago was researching a book, *Aftermath*. I had read none of his books, but the reviews were full of praise for his research. His prey was Martin Bormann, but he had an interest in Dr. Mengele. I told him what I had learned. My tour of duty ended before Farago's second visit to Asuncion. In Europe, I read an article in which Farago implied that he had found Mengele. In Jerusalem, I received a letter from him. He wrote that he had located the nazi doctor in a Paraguayan town near the Brazilian border.

Farago had asked for an interview through a go-between, and Mengele demanded $30,000. Farago sent him a message: "You are not worth that much, Dr. Mengele." The go-between brought Farago a second offer from the nazi doctor: a book he had written about twin research. For this, he wanted $100,000.

Two years later, in New York, my wife and I attended a publication party for *Aftermath*. Farago took me aside and showed me the complimentary lines he had written about my contribution. But when I read the book at home, I was stunned by the way he changed one of the episodes in which he had quoted me, and deeply upset by the twist he had given a second incident. Still, I liked the man too much to be angry. More than two years had passed since he had interviewed me in Asuncion. His memory must have failed him.

There were contradictions. In the din of the party, Farago told me about his encounter with Mengele. "But you wrote me that you sent him a message, 'You're not worth that much, Dr. Mengele,' " I said. "Did you shell out thirty grand?"

"Of course I didn't," Farago replied. "It was my fake interest in his twins book that made him receive me."

I searched in the book for the historic encounter between Mr. Farago and Dr. Mengele. There was a description of Dr. Mengele: "Now in his sixties, Mengele is not as 'beautiful' as he used to be . . . his hair is graying . . . his little mustache has been trimmed. . . . When confronted, he blossoms into a compulsive talker . . . his 'Big Mistake' in life . . . [is] that he went on the run . . . instead of staying in Germany to face the music. He points out that he was only one of scores of 'Auschwitz doctors.' Yet he has been singled out as the worst . . . and became one of the world's most hunted men."

It goes on: Dr. Mengele confesses to guilt feelings, cannot rationally account for his deeds.

I couldn't help asking myself: To whom did he reveal all this? If to Mr. Farago, why didn't Mr. Farago say so? Why did he remain in the background, vivacious storyteller that he is? In the book, he describes a meeting with Bormann, whom nearly everyone believes dead. Why this vagueness about an encounter with Mengele who, no doubt, is alive?

I called Mr. Farago and expressed my bewilderment. He gave me the following explanation: "I wrote you that Mengele demanded $30,000 for an interview. Had I quoted him directly, he could have sued me for payment."

Again, my liking for the man made me accept his answer. For the moment, at least. But the more I thought about it, the more puzzling the answer appeared. Where and how would Dr. Josef Mengele, international outlaw, sue Mr. Ladislas Farago? And what proof did Dr. Mengele have of an agreement that he would get $30,000 for an interview?

The hunt for Dr. Mengele is a diversion in Farago's 480-page book. Its critics have concentrated on Farago's claim to have found Martin Bormann, alive, in a monastery high up in the Bolivian Andes. I abstain from judgment on the Bormann chapters. But I am convinced that Mengele is alive. Whether Farago has actually seen him can only be an issue between him and me. He did not stake that claim in front of his readers.

In June 1978, Mr. John Ware called me and asked whether he could visit me to ask a few questions about Dr. Mengele. He told me that the firm he worked for, Granada Television Ltd., wanted to shoot a film, *The Hunt for Dr. Mengele*, and to send a crew to Paraguay. He was eager to see me before the trip. (Part of the interview was shown on *60 Minutes*, on March 11, this year.)

In Germany, Ware interviewed Judge Horst von Glasenapp, the official in charge of Germany's search for Mengele, and in Israel, Isser Harel, the former chief of Israel's secret service who directed Eichmann's abduction. In his book, *The House on Garibaldi Street*, Mr. Harel mentions that while he was holding Eichmann prisoner in Buenos Aires, awaiting the departure of the plane to Israel, he realized as an afterthought, that this might also be an opportunity to get Dr. Mengele. Mr. Harel got Dr. Mengele's Buenos Aires address from Eichmann. But he was two weeks late: Mengele had moved.

The Ware interviews broke new ground: Harel disclosed that after the abduction of Eichmann there was a plan to kidnap Mengele. The nazi doctor had taken up lodging in Hohenau, Paraguay, in the home of a German, Alban Krugg. Harel's agents reported that Mengele was protected by bodyguards, lookouts and dogs, and he lived in a stronghold within the nazi enclave of Hohenau. To storm the house would have required a military operation, practically in the jungle, far away from the airport.

The most valuable member of Ware's team was a German woman who infiltrated the German community in Asuncion and won the confidence of important nazis. While she interviewed Krugg with a hidden camera and microphone, the man who had sheltered Dr. Mengele for two years after the abduction of Eichmann said, "I wouldn't advise anyone to start anything with me. I can tell you that. Anyone who laid hands on me wouldn't get out of here alive. He wouldn't get out of here alive."

This was in 1978 and he was not bragging. Mr. Harel told Ware that in 1961 he either had to abandon his hunt or have Mengele assassinated. Infiltrating a killer into Mengele's circle of friends was contemplated, but then Harel resigned as chief of Israel's secret service and this was the end of Israel's hunt for Dr. Mengele. According to Ware's script, by 1963 the Germans had traced the doctor to the same Hohenau region where the Israelis spotted him.

Mengele had returned to his practice of medicine. His patients were mainly nazis or Germans, but as "Dr. Jose" he occasionally treated Paraguayans. He lived close to the Parana river—across the river lies Argentina. Then came the extradition request by Germany, and its rebuff by President Stroessner.

While in the early 1960s Dr. Mengele made forays into Asuncion —such as his visit to the jewelry store—news about his presence in Paraguay embarrassed the government, and he was apparently told to keep out of sight.

In 1974, Dr. Mengele's brother died in Germany. Judge von Glasenapp thought Dr. Mengele might attend the funeral because his brother had been his benefactor. Police watched the funeral, and the family telephones were tapped. But Dr. Mengele was too smart to show up.

In 1977, another top nazi criminal, Eduard Roschmann, "the Butcher of Riga," died under an assumed name in a public hospital in Asuncion. Ware's television crew interviewed Emilio Wolff, an Auschwitz survivor who had identified Roschmann's body. Wolff said that the night following this identification gunmen sprayed his apartment from a passing car. The incidents provoked a circulation battle between two Asuncion dailies, *ABC-Color* and *Hoy*, the latter owned by President Stroessner's son-in-law, Humberto Dominiguez Dibb. While *ABC-Color* published the Roschmann story, *Hoy* printed a center spread on Dr. Mengele. A follow-up story on the locations where Dr. Mengele sometimes hid was suppressed.

The mention of Dr. Mengele in a paper owned by the President's son-in-law encouraged the German Embassy to renew the request for Mengele's extradition. Minister of Interior Montanaro replied that he did not know Dr. Mengele's whereabouts. (Dr. Montanaro frequently invited my family for yachting. If there was one thing he was even prouder of than his yacht, it was the efficiency of his police. Paraguay was a crimeless country, he said, his secret police knew *everything*.)

The German woman in Ware's TV team managed to have lunch with Enrique Mueller, known in Asuncion as "Nazi Mueller." This was in the summer of 1978. Mueller was filmed in the restaurant with a hidden camera and the conversation was picked up by a hidden microphone. Mueller, who in the conversation came through as an unregegenerate nazi, acknowledged that he saw Dr. Mengele every four weeks. They had a friendly card game.

"Everybody knows Mengele [is] here," Mueller said.

"Would you hide him in your house?" the woman asked him.

"Hide him?" Mueller replied. "Well, now, I wouldn't need to hide him. The President says he is a Paraguayan citizen. I needn't say any more."

"You mean Stroessner is helping him?"

"Stroessner helps him? There is no need for Stroessner to help him. Listen, everything here is run by different laws."

Farago in *Aftermath* tells of twelve young Brazilian Jews who banded together to kidnap Dr. Mengele. Two who went to reconnoiter the terrain were found with their throats cut from ear to ear. Simon Wiesenthal, in his book, *The Murderers Among Us*, tells of an Israeli concentration camp survivor who met Dr. Mengele by chance in Bariloche, the beautiful spa in the Argentine Andes. Perhaps she could not suppress a gasp of recognition; he might have noticed the tattoo on her arm. Her bruised body was discovered some time later near a crevasse. There exist more stories of this kind, as well as innumerable accounts of traps set for the Auschwitz doctor and his last-minute escapes.

At this writing, Dr. Mengele is still alive. He is about 70, and has not the slightest resemblance to Gregory Peck. He does not live in the splendor which the book and the film attribute to him. He pays the price for his past by not living in the style which his means permit—he is heir to a Bavarian empire of agricultural machinery. He moves from Brazil to Argentina to Paraguay. Dr. Mengele might have had some nervous times, but for the last few years, nobody has thought of catching or killing him. Chances are he will die in bed.

It is this thought which sours many otherwise pleasant memories I have of Paraguay, a country of jasmine and orange blossom fragrances, of the most beautiful trees in the world, and of a kind and pleasant people.

But the kind and the pleasant are not in power.

Benno Weiser Varon *is cited in the* Encyclopedia Judaica *for his role in rounding up the decisive Latin American vote for the U.N.'s Palestine Partition Resolution of 1947. Born in Germany, he became an Israeli Ambassador to several Latin American countries, including Paraguay. A poet in his native German, he writes in three languages, is a prolific journalist in Spanish and has contributed to every major Latin American daily. He has published three books in Spanish, and in English has contributed to* Commentary, Midstream, The New York Times, The Boston Globe, The Christian Science Monitor *and elsewhere. He presently lives in Brookline, Massachusetts, where he is working on his memoirs.*

Julio Ricci

The Shoyhet

To all the Jewish friends of my youth
who still live in my memories

I don't know why, but it's a fact that just before I turned 70, I started to think about the days of my childhood and my early youth —I did more than think about them. Digging into the past became an addiction. It was summer and mornings I would sit in the backyard and sip maté. I'd be sipping quietly and without a worry in the world. I would look at the geraniums that I had planted two years ago, and, without really wanting to, bit by bit, I'd be back in the past. I was going through a 'nostalgia' phase. "Is that what old age is like?" I asked myself. "Is it nothing but nostalgia, reliving the past?" Come to think of it, this was nothing new. For years I'd had this habit of sitting and remembering, of wanting to reconstruct the past, of finding something there that I could not find in the present and which no doubt the future would not bring.

Lately, it was the same memory which plagued me. I was carried back to my childhood and I saw in my mind the image of Lazaro Doron. As a child, I had spent many hours with him. We played "statues" and marbles and "catch;" we fought and argued, but we remained friends. Very good friends.

I admired not only his character and his intelligence, but also his background. Lazaro was not like my other friends in the neighborhood; he came from Europe, from Russia; from a small town, where it was cold and there was snow almost all year long—it was just the thing to stimulate my imagination. He was not like Juan, nor like Alvaro or Gastonito, the other neighborhood kids. And because of this mystery which surrounded his person, I was always ready to drop the others and play with him. My childish mind seethed with curiosity. I wanted to unravel the secrets of this European world which he—willy-nilly—represented and which were hidden in his gestures, his looks and even in his smile, which to me seemed mysterious and sometimes inexplicable.

One day—I don't know why—I asked him in which language he talked to his parents, and he told me that they spoke Yiddish. At once, I wanted to learn this language, but he stopped me. "If you want to learn an important language, learn Hebrew," he said. "I went to Hebrew School and I can teach you." I still remember the first lesson, the first letters of the alphabet, and the first sentences he taught me to speak: aleph, beth, gimmel. Hine hashicun shelanu. Dina ovedet baguina.—This is our housing development. Dina is working in the garden.

Winter evenings—those rainy gray evenings of winter in Montevideo—we used to sit around in our front parlor. He'd bring his Hebrew textbook and would teach me with great enthusiasm. We'd interrupt our studies to play for a while. Once, I don't know how it came about, we happened to get hold of a motion picture projector. It was the most primitive device imaginable. It was hand operated and the light came from a little kerosene lamp. I remember how we turned the lights in the room off and tried feverishly to project a film with Charlie Chaplin which we had obtained through a friend. For hours we would try—but never succeeded in seeing more then a few images, some shot of Charlie, immobile. And yet, strange as this may seem, we felt triumphant. Breathing the strong odor of kerosene, we stared in ecstasy at the frozen picture of Chaplin on the wall. Since then, kerosene has haunted me. Whenever I smell kerosene at home or wherever, I cannot help being carried back to the days of my childhood with Lazaro.

Within a few months, I managed to learn quite a few sentences in Hebrew and whenever I said something in Hebrew to Lazaro, I felt elated. I had the feeling that I had gotten hold of something essential, a piece out of this world of strange ideas and values which he represented. Sometimes I would go to his house. There too there was a different atmosphere. His mother was very warm and would offer me cookies which she said were a specialty of her native country, or she'd give me a slice of some scrumptious cake. His father, however, was rather sullen and seldom opened his mouth. I had the impression that he disapproved of his son's friendship with a "goy," what they called Christians, as I found out later.

One day I met an old man who used to come to Lazaro's home every Monday. He was very odd. He was severely dressed in black, wore a very wide-brimmed round hat and did not shave: he had a long pointed beard which made him look like a medieval knight. If I had then been asked to describe him, I would have said that the old man had come from some sacred place, some shrine, a place of serenity, dignity and austerity; from a place where greatness of spirit and love for all the unknown reigned supreme. I would have said that he had come from a mysterious region, to spend a few perhaps painful hours with people of flesh and blood—those people who were never able to live together in harmony. I soon found out that he was Lazaro's grandfather and was the Rabbi of one section of the Ashkenazi community of the town, which is what gave him his serious mien and his solemn ways. Lazaro explained that he dressed according to the customs of the Mizrahis and that he was a very austere man.

One morning—I can hardly remember it—the Dorons left the neighborhood. They left—and there is a gap in my memory which I am unable to fill. What I do remember is that a few days before moving, Lazaro's parents gave a big party for him. It was a family party, one that seemed to me full of secrets and mysteries, and it had a name that sounded to me like magic: Bar Mitzvah. He tried to explain it to me. He told me that from that day his parents considered him to be a man in all respects, and that was it. And he apologized for not having invited me.

Inevitably, our lives drifted apart. Life leads us along different roads and moves at a speed that is always too fast; it turns a child into a grownup, a grownup into an old man before he is ready—and so on. . .

When, last year, I felt an obsession to find this old friend again, I thought that there must be something wrong with me. Why this obsession? What's past is past—what else can be said of the past? I could not understand my own intensive eagerness to revive it in the person of Lazaro Doron, whose image, remaining in my memory for so many years, began to feel non-existent. Obviously, he had played the role of childhood friend in my past, but something mysterious about our friendship clung to this memory, something intangible—so that now, more than half a century later—I felt compelled to seek him. I could not resist this urge to find him again, to speak to him, to talk about "our" past and I made plans to relieve my feelings: I began to search for him, first by checking the names in the telephone directory, an obvious beginning, but a disappointment. There was not a single Doron listed in it. I searched an old Almanac, in vain. No Dorons. But I have willpower and I am a good strategist, so I set out to organize my approach: I would talk with the rabbis in town and find out if they had his name registered in their books. If this failed, I would search more thoroughly. I would call on the oldest Jews of the community, I would search in the Old City and in Villa Munoz, where Jews lived. Someone must surely have known the old man and would remember him, the old rabbi of the Mizrahis, and would be able to tell me of the family's whereabouts.

I covered a lot of mileage through these neighborhoods. I visited all the synagogues. When I had to wait, I was glad of the opportunity to look about. These temples are not like the Catholic churches. The interiors of these old synagogues have an austerity and quietness which impressed me. At the front is the "heyhal" with its scrolls of sacred scripture imparting an air of the grandeur of history to the surroundings. And on a side, the purity of the "tevah" reflecting the mystery of meditation. And on the walls the lights recreating the stylized shape of the Menorah in memory of the Maccabeans. I would wait, then a rabbi would come in to see me, and the answer to my question was always the same: Doron was unknown.

Once I even had come to the conclusion that Lazaro perhaps was not Jewish, that perhaps my memories were playing me tricks. But I dismissed my failures and renewed my search. Obsessed, I didn't know what else to do. I looked into the Jewish stores, talked to the shopkeepers, and always asked the same question: whether they'd ever heard the name Doron. The result was always the same. Nobody knew Doron, not the Mizrahi Rabbi, nor his grandson, my old friend.

One day I had an inspiration. It occurred to me that Lazaro and his family had moved to Buenos Aires. One afternoon in the Fall I took off with an Austral flight and installed myself in the capital on the shores of the Rio Plata. I found a place to stay in what was to be the nerve center of my search—perhaps the solution to my problem: I took a room in the hotel Wertheim, a Jewish hotel in Tucumán Street. It was incredible, how well I felt there. I heard Yiddish spoken all around me, and if it wasn't Yiddish, it was Spanish with a Yiddish accent. I was overwhelmed listening to so many adult Jews talking about their past in Europe and about their trials and tribulations when they settled in Argentina.

Practically all of them were elderly Jews; towards evening, when it started to get dark, they'd set up something like a "circle"; each one of them would bring his chair into the lobby and they would gather there among friends, eager to hear and be heard for two hours or more. One of them was ancient—he must have been close to 90, and his feeble, cracked voice made it almost impossible to understand what he was saying, especially when he spoke Yiddish. The others, who spoke much more clearly, would often intersperse whole sentences in Spanish, which helped me to understand them. There was a Sefardic Jew among them, a "turco," who joined the group from time to time. Then they would all speak Spanish and I would pick up my ears and fully enjoy the stories. One of the men would speak of his childhood in Poland, another of his youth in Russia, another again of his grandparents in Lithuania. Sitting in my chair on the fringe, I would play dumb, while I would listen to them for hours. It was like attending a secret rite, where the mysteries of man and creation might be revealed—because for me, these people were impenetrable creatures who had come from another world.

In their presence I almost forgot about Lazaro himself, and why in fact I had come to Buenos Aires; as if settling myself into the hotel lobby, into this atmosphere and listening to the inevitable stories, was the reason I had come, after all. Even an autumn mood lent the proper tone to the setting. Outside the hotel, a grey April, passersby in Tucumán Street; inside, the warmth of a hotel lobby and old Jews who drifted in there to form their circle.

One evening, however, I forced myself out of this mood. "You are crazy," I said sternly to myself. "Didn't you come here to look for Lazaro?" But I could not intrude into this circle and ask these old Jews about him. I preferred to wander by myself through the neighborhoods, go into the shops on Tucumán Street and on the side streets, Junin, Paso, Larrea—the streets of the "ghetto," where the names above these shops brought back to my mind exotic things, imaginary towns, story-book countries: Koldonski Buttons, Malamud Clothing, Bazaar

Goldberg, Chicurel Modes. I searched these windows, trying to read the atmosphere inside the stores, and when I felt familiar enough, I began to go into them. Always, merchandise and variety, activity and vitality, people carrying bolts and stacks, piles of colorful towels and shiny fabrics. It seemed to me like a good life, anchored in the stability of business and things, in packages and colors and perfumes and wares, and I imagined the Jewish proprietor combining, with old knowledgeability, business and religion, traits from the east joined without friction. I felt as if I were returning to antiquity, to Oriental marketplaces filled with their marvels and their mysteries, and I was struck by the contrast with what now seemed to me like the cruder way of life of the Galician shopkeepers of little shops full of stale foodstuffs, smelly codfish, semi putrid sausages, rancid cheese!

The Jews were cultured, sophisticated, but also mysterious to me. I believed they knew how to live among the signs of luxury like gentlemen. That was because they had come originally from the Orient; they were the people of the Thousand and One Nights; they knew and were masters of the secrets of life. I envied them this dimension of mystery, their intimate circles, and felt estranged and had to summon a courage to enter their stores. One day I went into a notion store and bought a spool of thread, making use of this opportunity to ask, offhandedly: "Would you know a furniture dealer around here by the name of Doron?" I gave my question a business aspect, for I did not wish to be inquiring without a purpose. But the answer was "no." No Doron on that street.

The next day I visited the other stores and soon I became accustomed to the atmosphere in them and felt less estranged. So much so that I wandered everywhere through the ghetto, treating myself to cakes in a cruller shop from which fabulous odors emanated—but I found no Doron.

Finally, I must leave. I had come to the end of my stategy and my wanderings. The past was coming to an end, and I felt depressed on my flight home. My old friend might have gone anywhere, to any big city in the world, to New York or Los Angeles, perhaps even to live in Israel.

When I returned home I moved into a new apartment, one on the corner of Brasil and Chucarro. Naturally, I noticed the names of the other tenants here to see who my neighbors would be. Almost all had foreign names. Instinctively, I looked for "Doron," but there was none. My neighbors on the floor were pleasant, but our relationship was limited to exchanging greetings. From their names, "Levinski," I concluded that they were Jewish. Again, memories of Lazaro were stirred pleasureably. Only a single couple seemed to be occupying this apartment, with a maid, a young girl with an Indian-looking face who passed me every morning on her way to pick up the milk. But one day, that fall, to my surprise, I noticed an old man emerge from that apartment. I saw only his back, but it made a sufficient impression upon me which I could not explain. I could not understand why I had not noticed him before—though he obviously lived in the apartment next door and was no doubt the father of one of the spouses. I looked out the window onto the avenue below, and the dead autumn leaves piling up on the sidewalk. Looking, without seeing, my imagination wandered and I made up my mind to find out who this old man was, who he was and how he was.

A day later, even at the same hour, I waited for him in the recess of the stairway. At last, the front door of the Levinski apartment opened and his dark figure emerged: a man of about my age, but more fragile. It was obvious that he was not in good health. He was bald and the big ears that stuck out from the side of his head were noticeable, the ears Lazaro had had. He went downstairs, but I remained where I was, thinking. A human face changes so much in fifty or sixty years. Time can change any fresh and youthful face into an unrecognizable combination of wrinkles. This could be Lazaro, aged.

Of course, I immediately set to work on a plan to find out who he was, but in the meantime an unexpected event happened. One evening Mrs. Levinski herself came to my apartment to discuss a matter regarding the terrace of our building. She had the vivacity and the charm of a Jewish lady. As she was leaving, she herself mentioned the old man who lived with her, that he had worked hard all his life, that he was now not well. She left her calling card, a gesture of friendship. It read: Salomon Levinski
Rosa D. de Levinski

I could not miss the "D." The pull of the past went through me, for that it stood for "Doron" leaped at my imagination, and the irony that I had wandered far afield to look for him, when he was now living next door to me as my neighbor. For that it was him struck me with total conviction.

I needed only to know my neighbor's maiden name, but how ask such a personal question, for no seeming reason? I could not resolve this diplomatic problem. Then, at the depths of this frustration, a small miracle happened. Mrs. Levinski again called on me to talk about the dampness of the terrace and, one word leading to another, I managed to ask her:

"Are you by any chance a Dubinski? I am asking because I noticed that your maiden name begins with a D. and I knew a Dubinski at school."

I felt more comfortable, somehow, with a circuitous approach. It would have been presumptuous to ask her straightforwardly what her name was. And I could see at once that I had been right. Mrs. Levinski looked at me with the kind of expression that showed how pleased she was that I was interested in her and in spite of that sixth sense which the Jews have, she fell for my ruse, a victim of her vanity.

"No, I am a Doron," she said, emphatically and with a tone of pride.

I felt dizzy; everything turned around me; and I did not dare open my mouth.

"Are you tired?" she asked; perhaps she had noticed something strange.

"No," I managed to reply, as I tried to recover from the shock. "I'll be all right. If you don't mind, perhaps we'll talk again about the terrace tomorrow."

As soon as Mrs. Levinski, née Doron, had gone, I let myself drop into the old chair of dark green velvet which had come from the house of my parents, and I began to think. My mind started to operate at an incredible speed. Without meaning to, I went back to my childhood and to those days with Lazaro. Fate was now offering me the chance which I had been looking for. My friend Lazaro—for it had to be he—was within my reach. Soon I would be able to talk to him!

Next day, when I had recovered from the happy shock, and when Mrs. Levinski had finished talking about dampness on the terrace and stood up to go, I returned to the attack between a phony cough and an inaudible mumble.

"Pardon me—the whitehaired gentleman who always goes for a walk about noon—is he your father?"

"That's right. He's rather old—prematurely old. His memory is almost gone," she said.

All night long I planned my encounter with Lazaro; I had no longer any doubts whatsoever that this was Lazaro. The following evening, according to my plan, I rang the bell next door. Mrs. Levinski herself opened and asked me in at once. She was most cordial.

"Now it's my turn—I'd like to talk to you," I said, to get the conversation going.

"Go ahead," she answered.

"I was thinking that there is a very good firm that could perhaps take care of the terrace for us," I explained.

The pretext worked. We talked for a while and exchanged ideas about the problem of dampness. Then the old man came into the living room. I looked at him closely and was almost completely convinced that it was Lazaro. Time had left its inevitable traces on this face, and especially on this mind. It was obvious that he did not recognize people very well. He greeted me pleasantly and sat down in a dark leather chair.

"He's exhausted," whispered the daughter. "But he loves meeting new people. Do you mind if he stays here with us?"

"By all means," I said.

"Father, this is our next-door neighbor, Mr. Lopez." She raised her voice so that the old man could hear. And in the same breath she said to me: "Mr. Lopez, this is my father, Lazaro Doron."

The conversation about the damp terrace came to an end and we started to make small talk, the kind of small talk people always fall back on when they don't want to or are not able to take up a serious subject. How expensive life had become, how miserable the weather was, that the summer would be rainy, etc. Mrs. Levinski excused herself to get me a glass of brandy. I again looked intensely at Lazaro and believe I said a few trivial words. I did not dare approach the main subject. I was trembling as one trembles in the presence of one's first love.

"Have you been staying here long?" I finally managed to break the silence.

Lazaro did not hear well. He answered that he never felt well in the winter. I vibrated with emotion in my innermost heart. Here I had Lazaro right in front of me and I was unable to say anything, unable to talk about the past, this past we had shared like brothers when we were children. The happiest scenes of my life crossed my mind: the movie projector, with the kerosene lamp, the little ball made of old stockings; I saw us sitting around the table in his house, the lamp lit, and the two of us studying Hebrew—and other memories.

Mrs. Levinski still had not come back. The minutes went by and I had not made use of the heaven-sent opportunity to make myself known to him. He looked at me and said again: "I don't feel well in winter."

At last, the daughter returned with a tray and two glasses of brandy.

I rarely drink brandy. Never have indulged and especially not now. But I was so depressed, so anxious, that I accepted without hesitation and drained the glass in one swallow.

I stayed only a little while longer. Then I got up, shook hands with her and then with Lazaro. My friend's hand was cold and sweaty. I looked again into his eyes, and then I left.

That night I heard a lot of goings-on in the Levinski apartment. At half past twelve Levinski himself came over to use the telephone. He apologized for putting me to the trouble but their telephone was out of order and he needed to make an urgent call. The old man had suffered a partial stroke and was unable to move.

Several weeks went by. The old man pulled through, but he was not in good shape. At night he would moan and groan like an animal in pain. Since we were now on more familiar terms, I decided to look in on him as soon as he was a bit better. I felt that now I would be able to talk to him and reminisce about the past.

One day, it was almost summer, they let me see him and I sat with him for quite a while. He stammered badly, but he made himself understood. Once he looked at me and said:

"You look familiar to me."

I was deeply moved and could not say a word. I wanted to tell him who I was and talk about the past, but I was unable to. After a few moments, I managed to say:

"Could be—" and then said no more.

He died a few days later. I went to the funeral. There were not many people. The coffin was placed on two low trestles. It was all very austere. There were two simple candlesticks and the Star of David. And on a ribbon around the coffin the name: Lazaro Doron.

And so I had indeed met Lazaro. But it was too late. I remained alone with my memories of the past.

In a corner of the room there was a middle-aged gentleman who was deeply saddened by this death.

"Our beloved shoyhet is gone," he suddenly said, looking at me.

I managed to answer: "Yes, he's gone."

Trans. by Miriam Varon

Julio Ricci *is a professor of Linguistics, Philology, and Spanish Linguistics at el Instituto Nacional de Docencia, de Montevideo. He is a friend of many Jewish writers in Latin America, and has been the subject of articles by such authors as Bernardo Verbitsky.* El Grongo, *which included "el Shoijet" won first prize in the Municipal Contest of Literature, 1976-1977. Professor Ricci recently participated in a symposium on The Contemporary Latin American Short Story, at Montclair State College, New Jersey.*

Teresa Porzecanski

Parricide

It was when my father, Mr. Pimpirimpum, changed into a bottle, that I saw clearly the essence of the matter. I got up from my chair: the shadowy room was full of magic, spirals of strange vapors festooned the air, the wizards, squatting, rocked back and forth. Everything was charged with import, and it felt powerful to know those rivers flowing sleepily, to light a hundred candles of fire and delirium and illuminate these final crossroads. To know, in short, to know the intricate compass points, which might be that better way I didn't take, we didn't take, to recover the many things that today are dead: the tick-tock of the old grandfather clock which anyway wasn't the rhythm that could change essences.

"Funerals for the dead," I wrote him mentally in a letter dated the twenty-second of the fifth month of the year, "make my eyes droop the same as other fairy tales. One must invert the contents of the letters, and suddenly reverse the meanings; one must overthrow the meticulous education those precious dictionaries built up." It was a long, dizzy letter whose meaning could be anything, whatever one gave it depending on when and where he read it.

Mr. Pimpirimpum, I was saying, turned himself into a bottle one Saturday at four in the afternoon. We all saw him, in that vanished room, unfold in reflections, shrink away. He had fervently, earnestly, assured us he could turn the process around again, drinking no more than two drops of that green sweet-smelling liquid. We all saw him, in that vanished room, silence humanity's password, disappear, transform, alongside the green receptacle engendered by his new birth.

Gentlemen, I repeat, it was that day when my questions were calmed, when I did no more than get up and look around the room full of twisting broken spirals, appearing and disappearing at intervals.

Later, I thought of writing him that letter; it seemed important to me, urgent, that he know the cause of the heartless course of action, as everyone says, that I took. Therefore, I took special pains, trying to draw near to those rivers forever teeming with life, intending to spread myself open and stand naked, as at the end or maybe the beginning. "Forgive me," I began, searching for words, "if I consider irreversible all transformations occurring while we still exist. Just as the crude, inviolable birth cannot be postponed, neither can the magical unmerited change of shape, size and matter be restored." "Forgive me, but one must X out all maps and forget geography, because if one can manage to be there, what do we care about exact location." "I always believed it was indecent to claim for oneself someone else's fantasy, to create ends, goals, that will always be foreign to ourselves."

"You will say—and I'm sure your new crystal form will help you see things better—that I was hasty, that you miss your members, the brief heart beating, but the important thing is that you keep the essence, the minute, impossible attribute of the essence."

"You will say, we all will say, that only thought, the great invincible Reason, can save us. In this dark room, nothing is left, nothing but the always unfinished Inquisition, the fruit torn from so many religions. There's nothing left in this room but our own unbridled sweat, the hydrogen bomb, perhaps, and in recent times, the solar system. We can no longer care about the past, having longed for the worshipped works of other peoples and other men, having classified in order and reverence the data of so many destructions. We can no longer care about discovering today or tomorrow that something will give us more courage—some pill, or a wave teletransmitter—since no matter how long the years stretch, the fear is one and hard all the time."

"What else can I tell you in this letter? I always loved you: you were my father. But now that I have no cemetery to go to and cry over your bones, this bottle to which you will always be reduced represents my first biological freedom. Maybe now, I can stop eating all day long, let myself die at will or make love with no other responsibility than giving birth to men apart from men, exquisitely clean, liberated."

After which—everyone who was there will confirm it—I got out of my chair and walked towards the receptacle that contained the improper possibility of life. Next to it stood the resplendent crystal bottle that that liquid could turn into a person, and make it explode into the form of Mr. Pimpirimpum. But then, with one precise gesture, I swept the receptacle to the floor, the liquid spreading into a green gurgling pool and seeping, little by little, into the cracks between the old paving stones.

Trans. by David Pritchard

Teresa Porzecanski

from
This Red Apple

1. Identification

I could invent the characters: you, her, Mr. Gregory, but the problem is that the scissors which cuts them out snips them in half. This Mr. Gregory, for example, has his legs off to one side and his body won't match up. Besides, on flat paper he lacks volume, and to tell the truth, he suffers for it. We might rather say he feels confined, barely able to catch his breath. He makes a rough and uncertain surface on the paper, you understand.

Which is to say, his surface can be calculated by using a complex formula derived from E equals mc^2. Applying Euclidean tables with all recent and tested modifications, you can arrive at this gentleman's surface, I assure you. Though the true problem is not on the surface, you understand: he has failed to sink roots into space.

Now then, let us concentrate: two raised to the third power is the volume of a two-by-two cube, wouldn't you say. But this Mr. Gregory is not a cube.

Let us pass on, then, to linear dimensions; let us suppose that the being in question resembles a circle with a radius of three point five. Thus it should be quite simple to get to know him. But look, he's skewed off to the east and has lost his symmetry. So, in conclusion, it is impossible to know him: his finity-infinity baffles our measuring his birth. For this reason, and considering the abovementioned data, this Mr. Gregory has not been born; clearly he never came into the world.

But I, I who am he and am us, was definitely born one day in November far from here, unseasonably, in one supreme effort by my mother: genes, acids and convolutions all jumbled up, my frightful mutation arrived in glory to give birth to my skeleton. Identification: the eastern meridian over the median base of north latitude and directly above, occipitals and cranial measurements normal, thought to be descended from pithecanthropus erectus, Lombrosian stigmas type A, average intelligence quotient, blood pressure eleven, pulse to sixty, respiratory capacity nine, able to move the hands, make desperate gestures.

Identification: five fingers on each hand, blood color red, height and other statistics within the average for his size as found in tables of measurement available to anyone on request, skin color, number of leukocytes in the urine, daily and hourly temperature, infections and contagious diseases—the stray staphylococcus—oxygen capacity, glands, life systems functioning with no outside control. IDENTIFICATION: which is the precise location on the map of the image of God on Earth.

3. First Apology

This grand home, gentlemen, this nursing home which in its infamy has erected immortal human monuments, is represented by the ironic voice of the Director: "I understand you have objections to going back home, is that correct?"

I am gratuitously blessed with the wonderful gift of forgetfulness, though I still maintain a vigorous contempt. Gradually my family disappears, as if my birth were some arbitrary test tube soup. The unbreakable chains of foolish misplaced love, misspent love deprived of madness, of hope and fear, fall away before the unique odor of beans warmed over on the tiles, that pungent signal of the invariable meal times. The corridors begin stretching along the walls.

"Still, they've paid your stay. That is, they worry for you."

But I, presumably, am a crazy woman. I see his body growing until it assumes a rigid structure. Today is Friday, I think, time, I think, for breakfast. "The people we lodge here are impeccably..." I think: the cots lined up against the walls, the cracked toilets in the bathrooms, the embroidery I'll never finish, stretched tight on its innocent frame.

The doors come at me from across the room and I know that in a moment their well-oiled hinges will swing in silence and behind them, the street will swallow my footsteps.

Or else I was paranoid, after all, that's how I had been diagnosed. The examinations they put me through showed something like a sluggish beast who imagined spies in the ventilators and worms twisting in the food. Or rather, I was an animal feigning madness, a monster burning daily at the stake, and if they decided to lead me to the grave of a decorous life it was because benevolence had triumphed over the discussions of the experts in relation to my misguided interpretations of Rorschach, over my being and my conscience and my morality and my habits. I mean that time had passed through my bones leaving its fantastic flight, and the morning suns had found me painless in my madness. Or maybe I had lived witnessing things.

In my Aunt Azucena's gloomy trunk, purchased in giggles for her honeymoon, all my belongings float like desparate sailboats: nostalgic coats, musty-smelling clothes, my cousin Flor Luz's faded dress, too tight for her mighty bosom, the Bible, useless in there, cut off from its destiny as companion to final convulsions and agonies.

The corridors, empty and soothing: currents of air glide sweetly where the halls cross. On the back stairs you don't smell the beans anymore or the dampness creeping through the walls. At the bottom, the great marble doorway throws a burst of light on the last step, which Doña Lila scrubs on her knees.

"You're going?" she says. "So soon?" The years erase her madness: fifteen ago she arrived at this same door and the only charity she found was that spot on the stairs, those hands on the marble every winter day, her skin withered, huge knots crippling her fingers. "Goodby and good luck." Doña Lila scrubs stairs in a state home every morning, escaping from age up distant stairways, frozen, harsh stairways separating her more and more from her grandchildren.

Son of a bitch: the wide muddy street exposes the poor shacks across the gullies, in front of darkened houses, clothes spill from a wire. The shopkeeper has filled out his lottery ticket and on his concrete patio there is nothing left but a loose cash drawer.

Ah, the mysterious orphaning of my life, black light straining my childhood of faraway parents, of schools and games, of lyric debris. Maybe I wasn't born in a test tube, maybe they died ordinarily of some modern sickness that wasn't poverty, nor hunger, nor the bomb, nor murder, torture, grief. What was it that killed them, how did it suddenly come about, their simple disappearance, their search, their anxious fluttering through a world preserving them from other deaths.

The first bus is an old lumbering hulk with six people and a guard chewing the few teeth left inside his shapeless hole of a mouth.

"How far." His glance slides up that woman's stockings, stretched tight over the first varicose veins. In this seat an old man in blue dozes and nods his head against his chest. There comes the guard shaking him: "Pay the fare, no freeloaders here." A woman with a basket of greens is engrossed in the final chapter of The Abducted Bride. "Hey, freeloader," said the guard, "for free you can get out and walk." Two kids get on shivering, their hands squeezing the coins counted out for their fare. The old man opens his eyes: his coat hangs in rags from his neck, his face is a blank in the shapeless mass of his body. "I already paid, stop bothering me."

We have left behind, gentlemen, the country roads, the tall buildings begin to close in on us like enormous shoe boxes, their balconies over the little world. "OK, wiseguy, off here." It's going to start raining any minute, puddles will shine on the pavement.

My stomach is feeling sicker and sicker: maybe the warmed over food has left me strangely disposed to madness. "Give me one ticket," I say. "Let him pay, lady, you keep out." The woman with the basket is forcing herself to memorize details for her neighbors, to entertain them on the broken sidewalk tomorrow morning, also to console herself with during half an hour's house cleaning. Jury of men, institutions of faith and democracy, the activity behind the window is silent.

Let us repeat once again, if it is possible. The churches are choked with alms, with confessing sinners getting absolved. In the portals the blind sell holy pills. Funerals of nameless murder victims block traffic at an intersection and the weeping, in respective coffins, is buried along with the body. At sterile formica lunch counters the sandwiches gleam in the big windows like gems, but mister, you better hide your days-old hunger in a wave of vague nausea and by superhuman effort hold off the digestion of your own insides.

That same morning, then, I decided to annihilate order, to throw my most prosaic ends to the wind, to sniff the distance in search of frozen scattered pieces of a unique unity forever incomplete. That morning, I saw, like corpses, the leaves of the sycamores and realized that I was radiating death with renewed love. Walking past the enormous streaming plate glass windows, the mannikins looked to me like icons. I understood the agony of standing there forever waiting to be dressed. Down interminable blocks I saw that there was no such thing as genuine adoration of the sacred; at a clean table in a fussy luncheonette I cried out my rage for joy. It must have been eleven o'clock, the pungent smell of food crept over me, silverware clattered and the custards trembled on their trays. A fly measured the window with arbitrary innocence, and I suppose the noon crowd was hurrying down the street.

One by one I went over the detestable myths, I discovered shameful details in them, I dragged all the symbols down the stairs of my esteem and the images stood naked. In one minute I grew twenty years, fell out of love; all that mattered was to survive in repeated cycles until the lone unexplored end. But that was no great problem: the light from the sun fell with the noise of air and the minutes. The most intense pain and pleasure are the same praise for life: that morning, time disappeared down a growing hole in space and I slowly crossed an endless passage and, on the other side, I kept crossing.

Trans. by David Pritchard

Teresa Porzecanski: *self description: "I was born in 1945, in Montevideo, Uruguay, in the heart of a Jewish family. My father came from Latvia in 1923, and my mother is Uruguayan born from Syrian Jewish parents who came to Uruguay in 1920." In 1962, she was awarded a scholarship of The American Field Service to live and study in the United States for a year. She has done research at Indian communities in Mexico, Paraguay and Peru, has written books on community development, and recently was named Consultant Assistant and Professor of Community Development, by the Ministry of Education of Brazil. She has written four books of fiction.* The Puzzle and Other Stories *(1967), was awarded the first prize for Poetic Prose by the Ministry of Education of Uruguay, and her book of poetry,* The Heart Untouched *(1976) also received the first prize for poetry.*

Clarice Lispector

Love

Feeling a little tired, with her purchases bulging her new string bag, Anna boarded the tram. She placed the bag on her lap and the tram started off. Settling back in her seat she tried to find a comfortable position, with a sigh of mild satisfaction.

Anna had nice children, she reflected with certainty and pleasure. They were growing up, bathing themselves and misbehaving; they were demanding more and more of her time. The kitchen, after all, was spacious with its old stove that made explosive noises. The heat was oppressive in the apartment, which they were paying off in installments, and the wind, playing against the curtains she had made herself, reminded her that if she wanted to she could pause to wipe her forehead, and contemplate the calm horizon. Like a farmer. She had planted the seeds she held in her hand, no others, but only those. And they were growing into trees. Her brisk conversations with the electricity man were growing, the water filling the tank was growing, her children were growing, the table was growing with food, her husband arriving with the newspapers and smiling with hunger, the irritating singing of the maids resounding through the block. Anna tranquilly put her small, strong hand, her life current to everything. Certain times of the afternoon struck her as being critical. At a certain hour of the afternoon the trees she had planted laughed at her. And when nothing more required her strength, she became anxious. Meanwhile she felt herself more solid than ever, her body become a little thicker, and it was worth seeing the manner in which she cut out blouses for the children, the large scissors snapping into the material. All her vaguely artistic aspirations had for some time been channeled into making her days fulfilled and beautiful; with time, her taste for the decorative had developed and supplanted intimate disorder. She seemed to have discovered that everything was capable of being perfected, that each thing could be given a harmonious appearance; life itself could be created by Man.

Deep down, Anna had always found it necessary to feel the firm roots of things. And this is what a home had surprisingly provided. Through torturous paths, she had achieved a woman's destiny, with the surprise of conforming to it almost as if she had invented that destiny herself. The man whom she had married was a real man, the children she mothered were real children. Her previous youth now seemed alien to her, like one of life's illnesses. She had gradually emerged to discover that life could be lived without happiness: by abolishing it she had found a legion of persons, previously invisible, who lived as one works—with perseverance, persistence, and contentment. What had happened to Anna before possessing a home of her own stood forever beyond her reach: that disturbing exaltation she had often confused with unbearable happiness. In exchange she had created something ultimately comprehensible, the life of an adult. This was what she had wanted and chosen.

Her precautions were now reduced to alertness during the dangerous part of the afternoon, when the house was empty and she was no longer needed; when the sun reached its zenith, and each member of the family went about his separate duties. Looking at the polished furniture, she felt her heart contract a little with fear. But in her life there was no opportunity to cherish her fears—she suppressed them with that same ingenuity she had acquired from domestic struggles. Then she would go out shopping or take things to be mended, unobtrusively looking after her home and her family. When she returned it would already be late afternoon and the children back from school would absorb her attention. Until the evening descended with its quiet excitement. In the morning she would awaken surrounded by her calm domestic duties. She would find the furniture dusty and dirty once more, as if it had returned repentant. As for herself, she mysteriously formed part of the soft, dark roots of the earth. And anonymously she nourished life. It was pleasant like this. This was what she had wanted and chosen.

The tram swayed on its rails and turned into the main road. Suddenly the wind became more humid, announcing not only the passing of the afternoon but the end of that uncertain hour. Anna sighed with relief and a deep sense of acceptance gave her face an air of womanhood.

The tram would drag along and then suddenly jolt to a halt. As far as Humaitá she could relax. Suddenly she saw the man stationary at the tram stop. The difference between him and others was that he was really stationary. He stood with his hands held out in front of him—blind.

But what else was there about him that made Anna sit up in distrust? Something disquieting was happening. Then she discovered what it was: the blind man was chewing gum. . .a blind man chewing gum. Anna still had time to reflect for a second that her brothers were coming to dinner—her heart pounding at regular intervals. Leaning forward, she studied the blind man intently, as one observes something incapable of returning our gaze. Relaxed, and with open eyes, he was chewing gum in the failing light. The facial movements of his chewing made him appear to smile then suddenly stop smiling, to smile and stop smiling. Anna stared at him as if he had insulted her. And anyone watching would have received the impression of a woman filled with hatred. She continued to stare at him, leaning more and more forward—until the tram gave a sudden jerk, throwing her unexpectedly backward. The heavy string bag toppled from her lap and landed on the floor. Anna cried out, the conductor gave the signal to stop before realizing what was happening, and the tram came to an abrupt halt. The other passengers looked on in amazement. Too paralyzed to gather up her shopping, Anna sat upright, her face suddenly pale. An expression, long since forgotten, awkwardly reappeared, unexpected and inexplicable. The Negro newsboy smiled as he handed over her bundle. The eggs had broken in their newspaper wrapping. Yellow sticky yolks dripped between the strands of the bag. The blind man had interrupted his chewing and held out his unsteady hands, trying in vain to grasp what had happened. She removed the parcel of eggs from the string bag accompanied by the smiles of the passengers. A second signal from the conductor and the tram moved off with another jerk.

A few moments later people were no longer staring at her. The tram was rattling on the rails and the blind man chewing gum had remained behind forever. But the damage had been done.

The string bag felt rough between her fingers, not soft and familiar as when she had knitted it. The bag had lost its meaning; to find herself on that tram was a broken thread; she did not know what to do with the purchases on her lap. Like some strange music, the world started up again around her. The damage had been done. But why? Had she forgotten that there were blind people? Compassion choked her. Anna's breathing became heavy. Even those things which had existed before the episode were now on the alert, more hostile, and even perishable. The world had once more become a nightmare. Several years fell away, the yellow yolks trickled. Exiled from her own days, it seemed to her that the people in the streets were vulnerable, that they barely maintained their equilibrium on the surface of the darkness— and for a moment they appeared to lack any sense of direction. The perception of an absence of law came so unexpectedly that Anna clutched the seat in front of her, as if she might fall off the tram, as if things might be overturned with the same calm they had possessed when order reigned.

What she called a crisis had come at last. And its sign was the intense pleasure with which she now looked at things, suffering and alarmed. The heat had become more oppressive, everything had gained new power and a stronger voice. In the Rua Voluntários da Pátria, revolution seemed imminent, the grids of the gutter were dry, the air dusty. A blind man chewing gum had plunged the world into a mysterious excitement. In every strong person there was a lack of compassion for the blind man, and their strength terrified her. Beside her sat a woman in blue with an expression which made Anna avert her gaze rapidly. On the pavement a mother shook her little boy. Two lovers held hands smiling. . . .And the blind man? Anna had lapsed into a mood of compassion which greatly distressed her.

She had skillfully pacified life; she had taken so much care to avoid upheavals. She had cultivated an atmosphere of serene understanding, separating each person from the others. Her clothes were clearly designed to be practical, and she could choose the evening's film from the newspaper—and everything was done in such a manner that each day should smoothly succeed the previous one. And a blind man chewing gum was destroying all this. Through her compassion Anna felt that life was filled to the brim with a sickening nausea.

Only then did she realize that she had passed her stop ages ago. In her weak state everything touched her with alarm. She got off the tram, her legs shaking, and looked around her, clutching the string bag stained with egg. For a moment she was unable to get her bearings. She seemed to have plunged into the middle of the night.

It was a long road, with high yellow walls. Her heart beat with fear as she tried in vain to recognize her surroundings; while the life she had discovered continued to pulsate, a gentler, more mysterious wind caressed her face. She stood quietly observing the wall. At last she recognized it. Advancing a little further alongside a hedge, she passed through the gates of the botanical garden.

She strolled wearily up the central avenue, between the palm trees. There was no one in the garden. She put her parcels down on the ground and sat down on the bench of a side path where she remained for some time.

The wilderness seemed to calm her, the silence regulating her breathing and soothing her senses.

From afar she saw the avenue where the evening was round and clear. But the shadows of the branches covered the side path.

Around her there were tranquil noises, the scent of trees, chance encounters among the creeping plants. The entire garden fragmented by the ever more fleeting moments of the evening. From whence came the drowsiness with which she was surrounded? As if induced by the drone of birds and bees. Everything seemed strange, much too gentle, much too great.

A gentle, familiar movement startled her and she turned round rapidly. Nothing appeared to have stirred. But in the central lane there stood, immobile, an enormous cat. Its fur was soft. With another silent movement, it disappeared.

Agitated, she looked about her. The branches swayed, their shadows wavering on the ground. A sparrow foraged in the soil. And suddenly, in terror, she imagined that she had fallen into an ambush. In the garden there was a secret activity in progress which she was beginning to penetrate.

On the trees, the fruits were black and sweet as honey. On the ground there lay dry fruit stones full of circumvolutions like small rotted cerebrums. The bench was stained with purple sap. With gentle persistence the waters murmured. On the tree trunk the luxurious feelers of parasites fastened themselves. The rawness of the world was peaceful. The murder was deep. And death was not what one had imagined.

As well as being imaginary, this was a world to be devoured with one's teeth, a world of voluminous dahlias and tulips. The trunks were pervaded with leafy parasites, their embrace soft and clinging. Like the resistance that precedes surrender, it was fascinating; the woman felt disgusted, and it was fascinating.

The trees were laden, and the world was so rich that it was rotting. When Anna reflected that there were children and grown men suffering hunger, the nausea reached her throat as if she were pregnant and abandoned. The moral of the garden was something different. Now that the blind man had guided her to it, she trembled on the threshold of a dark, fascinating world where monstrous water lilies floated. The small flowers scattered on the grass did not appear to be yellow or pink, but the color of inferior gold and scarlet. Their decay was profound, perfumed. But all these oppressive things she watched, her head surrounded by a swarm of insects, sent by some more refined life in the world. The breeze penetrated between the flowers. Anna imagined rather than felt its sweetened scent. The garden was so beautiful that she feared hell.

It was almost night now and everything seemed replete and heavy; a squirrel leapt in the darkness. Under her feet the earth was soft. Anna inhaled its odor with delight. It was both fascinating and repulsive.

But when she remembered the children, before whom she now felt guilty, she straightened up with a cry of pain. She clutched the package, advanced through the dark side path, and reached the avenue. She was almost running, and she saw the garden all around her aloof and impersonal. She shook the locked gates, and went on shaking them, gripping the rough timber. The watchman appeared, alarmed at not having seen her.

Until she reached the entrance of the building, she seemed to be on the brink of disaster. She ran with the string bag to the elevator, her heart beating in her breast—what was happening? Her compassion for the blind man was as fierce as anguish but the world seemed hers, dirty, perishable, hers. She opened the door of her flat. The room was large, square, the polished knobs were shining, the window panes were shining, the lamp shone brightly—what new land was this? And for a moment that wholesome life she had led until today seemed morally crazy. The little boy who came running up to embrace her was a creature with long legs and a face resembling her own. She pressed him firmly to her in anxiety and fear. Trembling, she protected herself. Life was vulnerable. She loved the world, she loved all things created, she loved with loathing. In the same way as she had always been fascinated by oysters, with that vague sentiment of revulsion which the approach of truth provoked, admonishing her. She embraced her son, almost hurting him. Almost as if she knew of some evil—the blind man or the beautiful botanical garden—she was clinging to him, to him whom she loved above all things. She had been touched by the demon of faith.

"Life is horrible," she said to him in a low voice, as if famished. What would she do if she answered the blind man's call? She would go alone. . . .There were poor and rich places that needed her. She needed them. "I am afraid," she said. She felt the delicate ribs of the child between her arms, she heard his frightened weeping.

"Mummy," the child called. She held him away from her, she studied his face and her heart shrank.

"Don't let Mummy forget you," she said. No sooner had the child felt her embrace weaken than he escaped and ran to the door of the room, from where he watched her more safely. It was the worst look that she had ever received. The blood rose hot to her cheeks.

She sank into a chair, with her fingers still clasping the string bag. What was she ashamed of? There was no way of escaping. The very crust of the days she had forged had broken and the water was escaping. She stood before the oysters. And there was no way of averting her gaze. What was she ashamed of? Certainly it was no longer pity, it was more than pity: her heart had filled with the worst will to live.

She no longer knew if she was on the side of the blind man or of the thick plants. The man little by little had moved away, and in her torment she appeared to have passed over to the side of those who had injured his eyes. The botanical garden, tranquil and high, had been a revelation. With horror, she discovered that she belonged to the strong part of the world, and what name should she give to her fierce compassion? Would she be obliged to kiss the leper, since she would never be just a sister. "A blind man has drawn me to the worst of myself," she thought, amazed. She felt herself banished because no pauper would drink water from her burning hands. Ah! It was easier to be a saint than a person! Good heavens, then it was not real, that pity which had fathomed the deepest waters in her heart? But it was the compassion of a lion.

Humiliated, she knew that the blind man would prefer a poorer love. And, trembling, she also knew why. The life of the botanical garden summoned her as a werewolf is summoned by the moonlight. "Oh! but she loved the blind man," she thought with tears in her eyes. Meanwhile it was not with this sentiment that one would go to church. "I am frightened," she whispered alone in the room. She got up and went to the kitchen to help the maid prepare dinner.

But life made her shiver like the cold of winter. She heard the school bell pealing, distant and constant. The small horror of the dust gathering in threads around the bottom of the stove, where she had discovered a small spider. Lifting a vase to change the water—there was the horror of the flower submitting itself, languid and loathsome, to her hands. The same secret activity was going on here in the kitchen. Near the waste bin, she crushed an ant with her foot. The small murder of the ant. Its minute body trembled. Drops of water fell on the stagnant water in the pool.

The summer beetles. The horror of those expressionless beetles.

All around there was a silent, slow, insistent life. Horror upon horror. She went from one side of the kitchen to the other, cutting the steaks, mixing the cream. Circling around her head, around the light, the flies of a warm summer's evening. A night in which compassion was as crude as false love. Sweat trickled between her breasts. Faith broke her; the heat of the oven burned in her eyes.

Then her husband arrived, followed by her brothers and their wives, and her brothers' children.

They dined with all the windows open, on the ninth floor. An airplane shuddered menacingly in the heat of the sky. Although she had used few eggs, the dinner was good. The children stayed up, playing on the carpet with their cousins. It was summer and it would be useless to force them to go to sleep. Anna was a little pale and laughed gently with the others.

After dinner, the first cool breeze finally entered the room. The family was seated round the table, tired after their day, happy in the absence of any discord, eager not to find fault. They laughed at everything, with warmth and humanity. The children grew up admirably around them. Anna took the moment like a butterfly, between her fingers before it might escape forever.

Later, when they had all left and the children were in bed, she was just a woman looking out of the window. The city was asleep and warm. Would the experience unleashed by the blind man fill her days? How many years would it take before she once more grew old? The slightest movement on her part and she would trample one of her children. But with the ill-will of a lover, she seemed to accept that the fly would emerge from the flower, and the giant water lilies would float in the darkness of the lake. The blind man was hanging among the fruits of the botanical garden.

What if that were the stove exploding with the fire spreading through the house, she thought to herself as she ran to the kitchen where she found her husband in front of the spilt coffee.

"What happened?" she cried, shaking from head to foot. He was taken aback by his wife's alarm. And suddenly understanding, he laughed.

"It was nothing," he said, "I am just a clumsy fellow." He looked tired, with dark circles under his eyes.

But, confronted by the strange expression on Anna's face, he studied her more closely. Then he drew her to him in a sudden caress.

"I don't want anything ever to happen to you!" she said.

"You can't prevent the stove from having its little explosions," he replied, smiling. She remained limp in his arms. This afternoon, something tranquil had exploded, and in the house everything struck a tragicomic note.

"It's time to go to bed," he said, "it's late." In a gesture which was not his, but which seemed natural, he held his wife's hand, taking her with him, without looking back, removing her from the danger of living.

The giddiness of compassion had spent itself. And if she had crossed love and its hell, she was now combing her hair before the mirror, without any world for the moment in her heart. Before getting into bed, as if she were snuffing a candle, she blew out that day's tiny flame.

Trans. by Giovanni Pontiero

Clarice Lispector

The Chicken

It was the chicken for Sunday's lunch. Still alive, because it was only nine o'clock in the morning. She seemed placid enough. Since Saturday she had huddled in a corner of the kitchen. She looked at no one and no one paid any attention to her. Even when they had chosen the chicken, feeling the intimacy of her body with indifference, they could not tell if she was plump or thin. No one would ever have guessed that the chicken felt anxious.

It was a surprise, therefore, when they saw her spread open her stubby wings, puff out her breast, and in two or three attempts, fly to the backyard wall. She still hesitated for a second—sufficient time for the cook to cry out—and soon she was on their neighbor's terrace, from which, in another awkward flight, she reached the roof. There the chicken remained, like a displaced ornament, perched hesitantly now on one foot, now on the other. The family was hastily summoned and in consternation saw their lunch outlined against a chimney. The master of the house, reminding himself of the twofold necessity of sporadically engaging in sport and of getting the family some lunch, appeared resplendent in a pair of swimming trunks and resolved to follow the path traced by the chicken: in cautious leaps and bounds, he scaled the roof where the chicken, hesitant and tremulous, urgently decided on another route. The chase now intensified. From roof to roof, more than a block along the road was covered. Little accustomed to such a savage struggle for survival, the chicken had to decide for herself the paths she must follow without any assistance from her race. The man, however, was a natural hunter. And no matter how abject the prey, the cry of victory was in the air.

Alone in the world, without father or mother, the chicken was running and panting, dumb and intent. At times during her escape she hovered on some roof edge, gasping for breath and, while the man strenuously clambered up somewhere else, she had time to rest for a moment. And she seemed so free. Stupid, timid, and free. Not victorious as a cock would be in flight. What was it in the chicken's entrails that made her a *being*? The chicken is, in fact, a *being*. It is true that one would not be able to rely upon her for anything. Nor was she even self-reliant like the cock who believes in his crest. Her only advantage was that there were so many chickens that when one died, another automatically appeared, so similar in appearance that it might well be the same chicken.

Finally, on one of those occasions when she paused to enjoy her bid for freedom, the man reached her. Amid shrieks and feathers, she was caught. She was immediately carried off in triumph by one wing across the roof tiles and dumped somewhat violently on the kitchen floor. Still giddy, she shook herself a little with raucous and uncertain cackles.

It was then that it happened. Positively flustered, the chicken laid an egg. She was surprised and exhausted. Perhaps it was premature. But from the moment she was born, as if destined for motherhood, the chicken had shown all the signs of being instinctively maternal. She settled on the egg and there she remained, breathing as her eyes buttoned and unbuttoned. Her heart, which looked so tiny on a plate, raised and lowered her feathers, warming that egg which would never be anything else. Only the little girl of the house was on the scene, and she assisted at the event in utter dismay. No sooner had she disengaged herself from the event than she jumped up from the floor and ran out shouting.

"Mummy! Mummy! Don't kill the chicken, she's laid an egg! The chicken loves us!"

They all ran back into the kitchen and stood round the young mother in silence. Warming her offspring, she was neither gentle nor cross, neither happy nor sad; she was nothing, she was simply a chicken—a fact that did not suggest any particular feeling. The father, mother, and daughter had been standing there for some time now, without thinking about anything in particular. No one was known to have caressed a chicken on the head. Finally, the father decided, with a certain brusqueness, "If you have this chicken killed, I will never again eat a fowl as long as I live!"

"Nor me!" the little girl promised with passion.

The mother, feeling weary, shrugged her shoulders. Unconscious of the life that had been spared her, the chicken became part of the family. The little girl, upon returning from school, would toss her school bag down without disturbing the chicken's wanderings across the kitchen. The father, from time to time, still remembered. "And to think that I made her run in that state!"

The chicken became the queen of the household. Everybody, except her, knew it. She ran to and fro, from the kitchen to the terrace at the back of the house, exploiting her two sources of power: apathy and fear.

But when everyone was quiet in the house and seemed to have forgotten her, she puffed up with modest courage, the last traces of her great escape. She circled the tile floor, her body advancing behind her head, as unhurried as if in an open field, although her small head betrayed her, darting back and forth in rapid vibrant movements, with the age-old fear of her species now ingrained. Once in a while, but ever more infrequently, she remembered how she had stood out against the sky on the roof edge ready to cry out. At such moments, she filled her lungs with the stuffy atmosphere of the kitchen and, had females been given the power to crow, she would not have crowed but would have felt much happier. Not even at those moments, however, did the expression on her empty head alter. In flight or in repose, when she gave birth or while pecking grain, hers was a chicken's head, identical to that drawn at the beginning of time. Until one day they killed her and ate her, and the years rolled on.

Trans. by Giovanni Pontiero

Clarise Lispector *recently died, at a time when her reputation in the United States amd elsewhere is growing. The stories in this volume are from her collection,* Family Ties, *published by the University of Texas Press, 1972. She was born in the Ukraine and was brought to Brazil at the age of two months. She became a journalist and a lawyer, traveled widely and spent eight years in the United States. In addition to her stories, she has written six novels, none of which have been translated into English. Her stories were written mainly during the 1940s and 1950s.*

Poetry by Jorge Plescoff

from
Exercises in Comprehension Number Seven

I'm a leaf
shaking in panic
on a trembling branch.

Dew
weary of sweat
before the enormity
          of oblivion.

A man who grows
          in his limits
driving his shoulders
into the stars.

I'm a great question
and the emptiness of its answer.

Tell me, Lord, who do you want
                    me to be!

I walk the steps of time
wearing dust and skins
                    suffering
among delicate daybreaks
and late afternoons of grief.

I contemplate the shadows
of the fallen brothers,
the surprise in their eyes
at losing the definitive,
and I see myself preceded.

Why did you create us!
Aren't your own eyes
          enough applause

that you need ours
to confound you?

Is not the weeping of the earth
enough
that you provoke our seed?

Weak,
you need our weakness
for you to feel strong.

My soul
a taut rope
interwoven in sorrow,
a silent lament
of summer flowers
without more sky
than he who waters its roots,
wanting to guess a promise
in the thin texture
of the absurd universe
the falling of the tender leaves
of premature age.

Trans. by Yishai Tobin

from
Exercises in Comprehension

My knee against the ground
        the left one
in order to recite dead prayers
        our age
over a bed of rock
        a veil
the tenuous veil of anxious reason.

The ladder has no steps
        nor dreams
Jacob only wanted to play.
In front of my house a smiling slide
        and the children
their knees on the ground.

Whoever prays creates mist
        without incense
without churches there are no prologues
        nor zeros
a process is misplaced in the sun
the sun repeating
its tender warmth

Trans. by Yishai Tobin

from
Exercises in Comprehension Number Forty

Tongues of fire, I say
I say white moon, waiting.
I call out wheat,
a rocky projection of wit,
a foreign reef of the cry.
I look at the sky weeping
in the damp eyes of the stream.

The painted desert, I live
painting whole shadows, I live
frames from dyed carob wood,
a background of indigo, almost blind.

I say moon, I see white,
a foam of sea of sky
over fire, consumed.

Trans. by Yishai Tobin

from

The Mist of Dawn
The Agony of Being

When I believe I'm me
I'm another
and I'm many,
I'm everyone of these
without realizing
that I'm no one.
How can I accept not being
if I am,
one by one,
joy,
sorrow,
love,
success,
thousands of forms
that enslave
and convince
to be this one
or that one.
But to be so many
is not to be none;
this is known,
at least,
by one of the many.

Trans. by Yishai Tobin

Jorge Plescoff, *born in Santiago de Chile in 1940, is now an oral surgeon in Israel, where he has been living since 1969. He is the editor of two magazines,* Mabat *and* Cuadernos De Jerusalem. *He has had two books published in Chile:* Sonrisas De Luna Verde *(1976); and* The Mist of Dawn, *translated into Hebrew and published in Israel as well.*

Poetry by José Kozer

from
Este Judío De Números y Letras

I never see my father, still living,
but I know he has gotten smaller,
he has a family of brothers turned to ashes in Poland,
he never saw them, he found out by telegram about his mother's death,
he inherited nothing, not even a button from his father,
god knows if he inherited his nature.
My father who was a tailor and a Communist,
my father who said little and sat down on the terrace,
not to believe in God,
not to have anything to do with people,
just mumbling against Hitler, mumbling against Stalin,
my father who once a year took a shot of whiskey,
my father sitting up in a neighbor's tree eating his apples
on the day the Reds came into his village
and set my grandfather dancing like a bear on a Saturday
making him light and smoke a cigarette on a Saturday,
and my father left the village never to come back,
he went off never to stop grumbling against the October Revolution,
hammering over and over that Trotsky was a dreamer
and Beria a criminal;
hating books, he sat hunched up on the terrace
and told me that mankind's dreams are nothing but empty words,
that history books lie because paper can put up with anything.
My father who was a tailor and a Communist.

Thirteen years and thirty days in New York City,
but I still follow the multiplication rules in Spanish,
and eight times eight is *sesenticuatro*,
and when I add I still carry numbers in Spanish,
and if it weren't for that, I'd have already settled into
the American kingdom of indifference,
and the sugar cane's lively juice wouldn't make me so serious
and the sound of the shofar wouldn't make me happy
when it prophesizes a hundred years of lamb and barley.
I probably wouldn't even hear the clear, distressing blasts

of boleros conspiring together,
whose whiny trumpets full of one last burst of pain
fan the exiled feelings of all Cubans.

But I go back to my writing, unnoticed,
I scribble with deceit, blood, and curses,
I say what's on my mind, I grind my heels,
and like an ox hardened by duty
I know that three women want to throw away my verses,
there was hatred, decrees, even murder in my own house
but I, like an annointed ox, keep regurgitating, I plot
in some other corner, I rise above the tribes of Levi
and cut loose this flock of minor poems
to face the harsh rule of women, kings, and nations.
Yes, I recharge my poem, I provoke devotion and rebellion,
and I won't bend my knees, alone I become corrupted
by echoing and repeating the obscure cry
of this poem that won't repent.
I'm the poet, in the throes of death,
a nation of rumbas that bring back pain,
I'm Joseph, Benjamin, the young victim of these events,
Judith holding a giant's grisly head between her straight
lady-like fingers.

Trans. by David Unger

José Kozer *was born in Havana, Cuba in 1940, and has been living in New York since 1960, and teaching Spanish at Queens College since 1965. His book,* Este Judío de Números y Letras *won the Julio Tovar Poetry Prize in 1974, and has been translated into English, Portuguese and Greek. Two more books of poetry by him will appear shortly, one published by the University of Mexico City, the other in Spain.*

Samuel Rovinski

from the novel
Ceremonia de Casta

Knock

....

Knock Knock

....

Knock Knock Knock

....

The doorbell lies useless under a coat of rust. Since his return from Paradise, things have been deteriorating. The doorbell doesn't work. There are leaks in the gutters. Their boards have warped. A coat of slime covers the tin drainpipes. The bell doesn't work. The porcelain is cracked like old skin, like bark splintered by the sun, the dust, the wind, like the very core of death.

More knuckles.

"Harder, man!"

Knock. Knock. Knock.

No answer.

"Could I be mistaken?"

Gray facade, flat columns, Doric capital. Gigantic dwarves supporting a toy roof. Bas-relief roses in crumbling stucco. Shattered red tile floor.

"Do you think it's the other one, across town?"

Yellow clapboard walls. The patio gone to seed, with night-blooming cactus in the middle and bougainvillas on the walls. Harelip grin of the rotting wood veranda.

"The devil roast me if this isn't the same house!"

The Greek temple front, designed by an architect who left his sense of proportions behind at graduation. Stealing the idea from "A History of Art," from Barcelona: The volume the old man wasted all his hours over. The volume with which the old man ordered his submissive architect to wall up the original Andalusian facade, to disguise the narrow corridor leading to the replica of a Moorish patio, overlooked by whitewashed rooms with windows flung wide onto a horizon hung with enormous pots of cool ferns and blazing red begonias. The volume responsible for the prostyle columns of a temple of Athene with cottage windows. A bizarre jumble: a peasant half enlightened, between Paradise and Paris.

It won't help them to hide. History doesn't stop. Today for you, tomorrow for me. It won't help them to hold their ears. It won't help them that the bell doesn't work anymore. My voice pierces everything. My voice reaches to the darkest corner. My voice catches on the silver threads of the cobweb. My voice, in the fragrance of the begonias. My voice in the foul breath of the black well. My voice in the air, in the brain, in the wingbeats of nocturnal apparitions, in the omens that tell of ruin, of full life, of lusty life, of frivolous, superficial, complacent, empty life. It won't do them any good because they're all used up, because time is no longer theirs. Because I'm coming in, by the door of their eyes, by the taste of their spit, by the caked wax of their ears, by their pores, by their wasted touch, by their acid sweat, by their worn out step, by the portal-stone festooned with ladies-of-the-night.

"Preservation of national traditions will safeguard our country from the triumph of alien doctrines right or left," concluded Fernando, and likewise the conversation, once the elderly travel agent, an occasional companion of his philosophical rambles through the streets, had the fortuitous tact to agree with Fernando's energetic opinion.

"Nicetalkingtoyouandregardstoyourfamily, Don Fernando."

"Mypleasureandrespectstoyourhousehold, Don Malaquías."

The elderly travel agent walked heavily on, stooped under the afternoon heat, treading his customary path over paving stones that for more than fifty years had endured his weight.

Fernando climbed to the landing, cast a brief glance over the sagging portico, the worn red tile of the terraza, the roman baluster whose stone had recently been chalked white (defining the limit of the progressively narrowing walk), and, in a movement repeated many times, took out his key, attached to his waist by a silver chain, and opened the front door to the old Matías mansion, one of those mansions that recalled the old-time coffee planters' fanaticism for imposing an air of Spanish nobility on this district of the capital, choked now with office buildings, department stores, parking lots and supermarkets.

Viewed from the bottom of the hill, at an oblique angle, a few feet from the pepper tree with its decorative wicker of long thorns, no one could guess that this was the facade of a one-story house. A row of Doric columns, the shafts soaring over the windows another third their height, resting on square pedestals of inordinate measure, supported, on their capitals decorated with geometric motifs, the voluminous architrave of a cornice whose frieze sloped just in proportion to the pitched roof.

As you climb the street, the facade begins to flatten against the rising line of the horizon, until, standing in front of it, you regain a proper sense of its true proportions.

In the middle of the open spaces between each pair of columns, a terracotta urn marks the position of a white casement window flanked on either side by green folding shutters, fixed to the wall, outlined against the gray brick.

Nor does the facade offer any clear idea of the space the property occupies. Two carved wood doors divide the six windows into three perfectly equal spaces. The cornice serves the function of determining the position of the main entrance, though access to the other door is equally distinguished by the projection of a horizontal eave that begins at the inferior angle of the cornice.

When you walk towards the main entrance, the columns seem to grow flat, you can make out more clearly the roses carved into the stucco, and there is the impression that the dimensions have suffered a distortion, as if gigantic dwarves were bearing, on their backs, a toy roof. It takes an expert eye to discover that the facade has been superimposed on a house originally of Granadan design, in the country cottage style.

The red tile roof of the portico has a hexagonal pattern. It preserves the luster of floors that have been well cared for, oiled and waxed, in spite of the coat of dust that collects on it daily and that, by the end of the afternoon, gives the appearance of the first stage of ruin.

Two wrought iron lamps with ocher-tinted panes of scalloped glass watch over the porch, imparting a pleasant warmth to the brick facade.

On a level with the keyhole, a knocker with a golden tongue in the shape of a roaring lion offers itself instead of the bell whose white button on a blue glass plaque is set into the cornerstone on the left.

The windows are protected by iron grills wrought in delicate traces of birds, flowers and spiders, forming a cage out in front of the embrasure with enough room for the casements to swing open and let in the morning air.

The ferns and geraniums in the urns look fresh, as if they had just this moment sprung up. Nobody seems inclined to pick them. In fact, you would think there is a general conspiracy to keep them forever fresh just where they stand.

A few steps from the door, your hand hovering at the knocker and your eyes turned, for the last time, toward the street, all communication is lost with passersby, vehicles, stray animals, shops, words.

It starts raining. The wind blows the drops almost horizontally and most of the porch is soon soaked. The brick facade darkens. The gutters turn to rivers that scrape away all the refuse in the streets. People run to shelter under the eaves of nearby houses. No one seems to notice the existence of this house, of this ample porch, of this toy roof that could easily take in twenty people.

You pull at the knocker but it doesn't work.

Then, the bell.

A stifled moan came from under the wrinkled comforter, rocking gently at the center of a nightmare that only the bright tinkle of two wineglasses knocking against each other in Ana Lucia's hands could dispel.

Don Juan opened his tiny eyes, lost amid the wrinkles of his eyelids, and fixed a yellow gaze on the far side of the patio, next to the dining room, where the women were bustling about preparing the meal. He felt the heavy hand of his son Fernando bear down on his shoulder in greeting. He paid thanks, with a broad grin, to the two events whose chance coincidence had succeeded in waking him from the nightmare that had been tormenting him with the hateful image of that already fading face.

"Why does he have to take it out on me? Because I didn't recognize him legally, which was only proper for a man of honor? I was always generous with him, and her too, as long as they kept the prudent distance that circumstances regarding his good name obliged. Why won't he leave me alone? What's he want with me now?"

Stealthily, on those oppressive summer afternoons, just at dusk, when the family would begin to draw closer, perhaps from the terror of losing everything, being left poor, the familiar nightmare would take shape, in brief flashes, of his return, the return of the one they never spoke of in the Matías household.

No one ever mentioned him. Not even his son Fernando, who was always with him at dinner time, even after he married; always, like a religious act. No one was to speak of him. Not even the daughters: María del Carmen, Beatriz (like her mother), Anabelle (a name from those happy carefree days at Chevalier) and Ana Lucía. No one. Not even the sons-in-law, nor the grandchildren, nor any of their friends. Because his was the forbidden patronym. Because his name, repeated on everyone's lips, could plunge them in shame, awaken suspicion, stir hatred.

Don Juan imposed the secret on the house.

Liar. . .! Cheater. . .! Cur. . .!

With your well pressed suit and your shirt so white (like the milk you left unmilked in your cows when you finagled a notary certificate, when you hammered out that strict regime of work and pleasure and then crammed it down your dutiful dimwit family's throats, with that deep self-important voice of the ignoramus who knows everything about every facet of human knowledge), you made up some ancestors, invented a reputation, a golden limpid halo of respectability around your name.

Old hypocrite!

I found you out. I showed them who you were. I showed your naked hide to the world. That's why you kicked me into the gutter, why you sent me away. That's why you bought up the air I breathe and the ground I walk on. Knock! Knock!

Another squint.

"Is this really the right house?"

Near the door is a porcelain bell, on the right the old dilapidated house. The walls are flaking, revealing festering sores. In the middle, the stone staircase, with several loose or broken-off blocks. The pedestals along the gallery are crumbling to gray dust, with clay-colored stains where the rain blows in all along the street when the wind shifts around to the northeast.

"We must have a closer look."

Was this urn always here on the portico, resting on spider legs of wrought iron? There are no roses or begonias or geraniums or ferns. No tree cactus either. The urn is clogged with dried up cigar butts, orange and banana peels, a couple of crumpled pages of newspaper and a *pejibaye* palm nut.

"Flowers of the city, of my street, of my house, of my favorite retreats."

"Carry me down to the depths!
Lewd goat, carry me!
Caught over your horns.
In the rainbow's fire.
Piercing my heart."

Old Matías shook off the ominous shadow, with a sudden jerk that disturbed two flies resting on his sweaty neck. This brief dream brought back others, more pleasant, from his childhood. Dreams of fairies, but different from the ones they told children stories about. Exciting dreams, that invariably ended in the bathroom.

He sighed.

At that moment he started dreaming awake. Or rather remembering one of his favorite dreams—that dream he used to burrow happily into bed for, that dream that had stayed with him through every year of his life, from the time he started being a man, as his father had put it. That dream that made up for his unfortunate experiences in brothels.

He smiled at Beatriz, who was watching him from the kitchen, letting his eyelids droop until he sank back into the drowsiness of the air rarefied by the smells escaping from the kitchen and the fragrance of flowers and the penetrating stench of mildew and the dank wood of the furniture on the terraza, which were all growing heavy with the past.

But it shouldn't be imagined that Don Juan lived in dreams. He was the able administrator of La Llorona and El Poró estates, of the Las Delicias works in Turrialba, of extensive coffee plantations at San Antonio de Belén and of the Depot Warehouse, which he leased to commercial importers behind in their payments of customs duties. He was also owner of the Queen Pharmacy, now under the charge of Remigio Corrales, husband to Ana Lucía, his youngest daughter.

His father had always praised him and held him up to the family and outsiders. Now Don Juan, in turn, with grave patriarchal gestures, lauded children, in-laws and grandchildren alike, everyone who helped spin the web of his extensive fortune.

Thanks to Raúl, his favorite grandson, Fernando's son, with his degree in economics specializing in business administration, the Belén coffee plantations had been turned into luxurious new developments, taking advantage of the re-evaluation brought about by the routing of the General Cañas Freeway straight through the middle of this considerable property. Also thanks to Raúl, he had consolidated his holdings, passing control into the hands of directors of corporations in charge of the operations of buying and selling lots and dwellings and of making short and long term loans to industries, businesses and individuals, charging excessive interest and choice collateral, and of leasing the Depot, of running the Queen Pharmacy, of the rental of a large office building and of a fishing venture in a working class neighborhood, of a warehouse of building materials, and more.

And it was this same Raulito, this bright, restless, enterprising boy, formed in the school of the North American promoters, who was always prodding his grandfather with the question that haunted everyone's mind but that no one dared to ask:

"Grandfather, why in the world are you so stubborn about staying on in this tumble-down house? You ought to sell it—with what this property is worth today, you could build yourself a grand little palace on one of the best lots in Belén. Why in the world do you keep putting up with the noise on this busy street, the crude talk of the trash collectors and cart pushers and deliverymen and newsboys and the drunks outside El Sol de Barcelona cantina? Why in the world does a family with a lineage like the Matías family shut themselves up in this old ramshackle dump stuck in between two modern buildings like this, oblivious to the progress of the world and of Costa Rican society?"

The old man clapped his hands at his beloved grandson's questions, humoring him like a precocious child:

"So we want to know why we don't abandon this relic and move out like all the other rich families to the modern suburbs, do we? Well, I'll tell you: Because it would spell the end of the Matías—quite simply, the end!"

And he never went on to interpret this statement. He never went on to describe the fears that haunted his mind. He couldn't tell them that, on selling the house, the shadow would become human and the Nameless would at last achieve his end: to come back and tear down everything that had been built.

Don Juan, in his will, had left clear instructions for his family. The house must always be left standing and the property was not to be sold by any member of the family. Furthermore, the evening gathering, at the sunset hour, when the people of San José were beginning to return to their homes, must be preserved as an inviolable rite, as a renunion of all the Matías for the purpose of sticking together, remembering all their names, fixing the images of their past, of seeing themselves in the nodules of the ferns, of breathing themselves in with the fragrance of the geraniums, azaleas and roses, of engraving themselves into the stone masonry walls, the wood of the roof, the carved cedar of their furniture.

Fernando gave his mother his excuses for Margarita's absence. His wife had a migraine and had been in bed since the night before.

Fernando excused his wife almost mechanically, because he knew no one paid any attention to it anymore. Because it was no secret that Margarita Rutheford González de Matías hated these family gatherings. Because she didn't want to submit, like her husband, to the head of the clan's wishes. She had her own pride, born of the double lineage of her surnames, and she did not like standing in the shade of the Matías tree. So, instead of the clan supper, she preferred to stay with her youngest son and give the gardener instructions about where to root the gladiola cuttings, pruning the dwarf cypress that bordered the property, cutting the roses that would fill the vases in the living room, dining room, drawing room and study.

Doña Beatriz listened to her son with a complacent disinterest. She was accustomed by now to the absence of a daughter-in-law she had never much cared for anyway. She was satisfied to see Fernando, Raulito and María del Rosario.

Doña Beatriz remembered, among the whispers of conversation, her childhood in Alajuela.

The country house, the lazy summer evenings after classes at the Institute, the blue pleated skirt and starched blouse of her uniform, smoothing the hint of plumpness around her belly and the beginning of her hips, while the eyes of the whole town followed her, savoring her lovely bosom that looked like it was straining to burst through her tight blouse.

When the young Matías came to the graduation ball at the Institute, with a group of college boys from San José, the engagement became official and it was only a matter of waiting a few years to tie the knot.

Beatriz Rodríguez moved her maiden name into Matías territory. The marriage was the culmination of a lengthy engagement spent on sighs and words of love stolen from Bécquer, Darío or Nervo. Furtive kisses, languid looks and repressed desires, their hands, interlaced on the Rodríguez parlor divan, tirelessly stroking each other, always under the vigilance of one of the Rodríguez, in that humble wooden house tilting crazily over the sidewalk that hid the modest and jealously guarded fortune of Don Desiderio: pharmacist, planter, newspaperman and politician.

When Beatriz looked at her fiancé, her thoughts dissolved in the mists of a future rich in surprises, in which every moment would seem foreign to the last, in which every step would anticipate the sundered veils of mystery.

"What is love?"

Every sigh torn from Beatriz's virtuous bosom moved Juan to the deepest fibers of his soul.

The simple contact of her fiancé's fingertips brought to Beatriz's mind the images in the forbidden books, those images that had been so deeply etched ever since the first time she saw them at her cousin Albertina's house.

Her cousin was an expert in erotic novels and oriental love manuals. She got the books from Uncle Manuel's secret library and brought them to look through with Beatriz.

Page after page, image after image, Albertina and Beatriz were immersed in the fiery ambience of eroticism.

And Beatriz sighed, and Juan's eyes swam with ardent affection for this blossom that would soon be his wife, his life's companion, the mother of his children.

And Juan throbbed to imagine Beatriz naked, her big breasts offered like a fountain to quench his thirst, her legs. . .But he couldn't keep his imagination fevered for too long for fear of reproach, for fear of offending the symbol of his adoration, for fear of besmirching the name of a future wife to whom he owed all his respect and chivalrous honor.

The afternoons wore on, and when it became dark, Juan made ready for the trip back to San José.

The kiss, their lips tight and sweating in agony, would be interrupted by the severe gaze of Beatriz's mother, who sat knitting in the green velvet armchair, underneath the portrait of herself in her wedding gown.

Then night would be there to cover Beatriz's sighs, when the images from the books began to stir and the sheets grew unbearably hot.

Grandmother Matías blinked back those hazy memories and busied herself with giving orders to the servants to begin bringing the food to the members of the clan, most of whom were present.

Beatriz and María del Carmen arranged the centerpieces with freshly cut roses. Ana Lucía sorted the baccarat deck quickly and expertly. A long Swiss tablecloth, embroidered with tiny white flowers, heightened the luster of the dinner service at each member's place, with blank spaces left for Antonio and Anabelle, who were in Europe on their annual visit.

Fernando left the kitchen to go talk to his father, rocking monotonously on the terraza.

He started to tell him, in a voice low enough that it wouldn't carry to Doña Beatriz's ears, the latest version of the story about Uncle Manuel and the reasons behind his avoidance of the marriage bed.

Old Matías choked on a laugh. His chest seized, trying to catch at some air to keep the laugh going. He begged his son to tell him, sparing no details, the story that had scandalized Alajuela back then and and forced the Rodríguez family to shut their doors and windows in hopes that time would blot out the shame that had settled over their heads.

Fernando. . .! Fernando. . .! You dutiful little clam! How could you ever hope to explain all the truth of Uncle Manuel's case when in reality no one is in a position to deliver the details Don Juan craves?

The old man thinks it's funny to imagine Uncle Manuel in a turban, burned black under the merciless sun of India, squatting on some wide filthy sidewalk, looking for a little room in the crowd of human misery, trying to coax a cobra out of a wicker basket with the flute he bought at the Llobet Bazaar. Naturally he can laugh his head off all he wants to, since the honor of the Matías isn't in question, since the Rodríguez are no relations of the Matías, since, after marriage, Beatriz watched her maiden name sink into oblivion, since the ties that bound her to Alajuela were broken by jewelry, children, high walls and azaleas. . .Of course he can laugh at the Rodríguez! Of course he can smack his lips over the delicious sweets of scandal!

Fernando, papa's little pet! Fernando, plodding old turtle eating scraps off the family rock! I'm warning you: don't start snooping, don't nose around, don't pry! Because to bring Uncle Manuel's story to light would be like opening Doña Beatriz's chest of memories.

You ask yourself about that decisive night in the old sea wolf's life?

The answer is locked away in the musty library, where the pages of books have been gnawed by termites, where the smell of mildew impregnates the damp corners, stained a dirty white.

You'd have to know that Uncle Manuel received his pupils beginning at dusk, when the cicadas still painted hypnotic melodies on the air; when, coming from the watchmaker's, the road would still be lit by thousands of fireflies; when all along the banks of the stream that ran by the side of the dirt road, white ladies-of-the-night were spreading their vainglorious petals; when the orange blossom perfume from the nearby groves hoisted the anchor on Uncle Manuel's ship of thought and sent it off towards the Canaries, sailing in search of the fragrant canebrakes of Montego Bay and the steaming jungles of Malaysia; when the dome of sunset cast reflections on a tranquil sea, announcing the approach of a great starry spectacle: Orion, the Great Bear, Andromeda, and then steering for the North Pole, towards the sea of sirens.

Rest assured, Fernando! You could never, from here, in the middle of a city that will soon look like any other city, imagine the twilight world of Uncle Manuel.

You would have to hear his anxious breathing again. You would have to see the trembling of his nostrils. You'd have to touch the sweat on his gaunt hands, his long sharp bony fingers, that skin softened by years of idleness, of not lashing ropes, of not untying knots, of not scrubbing the deck of his young manhood.

Ah Fernando, your eyes couldn't see him if he were standing in front of you!

Uncle Manuel was a kind of clipper stranded out in the harbor roads, rotting with the years, becalmed in the middle of a sleepy village. Only the gentle tug of that tide of youth, flooding the sofa in the library, could stir the ship's belly, like a sign of good weather to cast off moorings.

You'd have to get up pretty early in the morning, conformist clam!, to understand the reason prompting Uncle Manuel to pull up anchor, to escape Paradise, to lose himself in the streets of Bombay.

The gossipmongers say Uncle Manuel had always been an odd case. A sailor from age sixteen to thirty, in love with every skirt that happened to cross his path, he had been the carnal mentor of all the young girls who dared to enter his house at sunset, when the clouds were turning colors. And the gossips affirmed that he had also been teacher to his nieces Beatriz and Albertina, and to Sonia Vargas, the most beautiful girl in Llano de Alajuela.

They say he taught them all the secrets of the human body, how to get children and how to avoid them so as to safely prolong an affair, how to catch a man and keep a husband, and all the rules of conduct currently fashionable in sohpisticated societies.

They say only Albertina ever learned to make full use of these instructions, citing the many and various romances she indulged in, finally to launch herself into the upper regions of Mexican society, where she got hold of a millionaire who built her a Moorish palace in Coyoacán.

They say only the teacher himself and Beatriz ever failed in applying the infallible systems: she substituted dreams for reality and he betrayed his own principles to marry Sonia, his most ardent pupil.

"Teachers should never practice their teachings, like the priest who instructs Christian couples in matrimony but who in turn is barred from taking a wife; or like the captain who trains his sailors without feeling obliged himself to work the engines or hoist the sails," he always affirmed in front of his students.

Why had he broken his word? Why didn't he remain celibate until death? Why had the monk abandoned his miraculous cave to go down and share the material poverty of this world with the beautiful Sonia?

All the malicious gossips in the city had created a mosaic of contradictory hypotheses, most of them deceitfully fabricated to destroy Uncle Manuel's and the whole Rodríguez family's honor.

And now Fernando was coming with a brand new theory that was apparently on the verge of being accepted by the new generation of Alajuela and that promised to dust off the old legend.

Trans. by David Pritchard

Samuel Rovinski *is a civil engineer by profession, whose plays and fiction both have won awards. He was born in San José, Costa Rica in 1932, and belongs to the Association of Costarican Authors, the only Jewish member among 230. His fiction,* La hora de los vencidos, *won the Premio Aquileo J. Echeverría in 1963; and his two act play,* Un modelo para Rosaura, *won the Premio Editorial Costa Rica de Teatro in 1974.*

Esther Seligson

A Wind of Dry Leaves

Tomás could not remember the first time it happened. It had taken shape little by little, not so much a nightmare or vision as an image growing steadily stronger, so that each time the dream would be different, though the pattern, the background, stayed the same. The details multiplied and sharpened as Tomás grew older: the dream developed to the rhythm of his body, of his discoveries and experiences.

From early childhood he had slept alone in the room overlooking the garden, on the other side of the hall. Mornings it was full of sunlight, and by afternoon, from the front room where he read or played with his sisters, he could feel it slowly fill with night, slowly empty of reflections. While he was gone from his room, at school, in the park, or in any other part of the house, its presence gave him the assurance and serenity of someone guarding a deep and important secret. A slight tremor always shook him before he went into the room, as if he were afraid that the scrupulous order which reigned inside—an order he had imposed himself and that was respected so thoroughly that no one except his mother ever came in—might have been altered by the same imperceptible process that altered his dream. Not that there was anything special about the room itself: a bed, a night table, a bookcase, a desk, a wastebasket, one straightbacked chair and a small blue cozy armchair. There were white walls with no pictures or photographs, white shutters, curtains of fine transparent tulle. Nor was he a nervous child, prey to fantasies or a fear of the dark. A little quiet, perhaps, and rather withdrawn. That is, he was becoming so little by little—distant, like someone who spends all his time working puzzles.

Tomás lived for dreaming, for that dream he was never sure would be there, the one that would stand apart from the day's events, surging from among the other images clear and sharp and unbroken. When he had learned to distinguish it on waking from his other dreams, without yet trying to penetrate its meaning—he was eight or nine years old and rather enjoyed the idea that he was piecing together a puzzle—he decided to describe it in a special notebook, or sketch it, in cases where words seemed too vague or he didn't know the exact terms.

From whatever he read, overheard or discovered in some picture, during class, while out walking around, he brought back just that word, that color, the feeling or the shape he needed for the world he was weaving little by little into his notebooks. Any external detail capable of shaping the vagueness, drawing the fragments together, filling in the gaps left in his dream, Tomás hunted down with morbid eagerness. He was like an insect collector attuned to the slightest buzz. He also turned his attention to the light, observed it closely at dawn and on moonlight nights, making note of the changes it went through during the day, because sometimes his dream would be dominated by light, and then he would wake feeling even weaker, more confused.

When he was about twelve the images began to take shape, completing the pattern. He would find himself in an old three-story house quite different in architecture from the homes of that region. The house smelled dank. The only light from it was a dusty shaft from a high round window. He was about to push open a door when he saw a troop of girls in ballet costumes and slippers making a great clatter as they came down the staircase. Their sudden appearance lit up the ceilings and walls in gold. Tomás followed them through the hallway to the garden. There the moldy smell was intensified by a countless number of half-rotten trunks and vines, and the decay all around seemed centered in the enormous unvaulted apse, in ruins, with its double row of high gaping windows set randomly one on top of another, into whose hollows the ballerinas were now crawling. The light surrounding them remained amber, but down in the semicircle and among the arches and limbs it was greenish, nearly black. It seemed that they were about to perform something, and Tomás was startled to find that in fact he was holding a text in his hand and that he was standing up in front of what he now saw as a stage. Suddenly a cold wind stirred. The girls' dresses began to unravel in long white threads and their flesh began to disappear, as though someone were peeling their skin down from head to foot. The wind, stronger, brought Tomás the sound of rustling paper and a murmur of words. One of the women was coming toward him rattling her skeleton loudly under her rags. Seized by panic, Tomás stared at the page in his hand. At that instant the wind blew through his now empty skull. His fingers were losing their flesh:

"Death, a wind of dry leaves, enters by the sockets of the eyes."

At that age, the features of the woman floating among the clouds were always blurred in the violent amber light, but Tomás knew that she was, like him, a child, perhaps a little older, like his sisters. Sometimes her hair would get caught in the branches of the tree, and when he climbed up to help her there would soon be such a drop beneath his feet that he could make out, far away, the spires of the cathedral and the dark cluster of roofs, chimneys and weathervanes. Trapped, his eyes searched in vain for the girl who had disappeared but whose laughter he still thought he heard. The light and the setting wouldn't always be the same; the tree might be a willow, an oak, a cottonwood or a combination of all three, broad and leafy, with long and intricate branches. It might be midnight, a full moon, amethyst and topaz, in open fields among furrows perfectly traced as in a drawing; or late in the day, on a bridge over the city bathed in gold or aquamarine. Nothing in these visions was sinister, but he could sense the hardness of stone, the cold transparency of glass. And, at the center was Tomás, like a toy, a shuttlecock the girl was blowing, that struggled among the branches or went whirling out over the city. Nor was fear the predominant sensation. The impulse to soar aloft into an ecstatic brilliance would be followed by exhaustion, an unconquerable lethargy, release.

That summer, when he turned thirteen, Tomás went with his family to the seashore. He had never been before, and as he neared the beach, from the top of the slope, he realized that this expanse of silver scales sparkling under the midday sun was his dream. He undressed and ran toward the water. Shimmering delirium, deluge of nameless pleasures. . .for the first time his body experienced sensuality free of images, a total abandonment. All day long, until night was already falling, Tomás lived the sand, sun and water, the noise of the sea, the textures of earth, the intensities of heat, the awakenings of his skin. He came away with fever, and his sunstroke kept him off the beach for the rest of the vacation. From his window, however, he learned to recognize the clamor of gulls and pelicans, the silences of the breeze, the perfume of so many flowers in full bloom, and the passing hours in the light changing on the clouds.

Soon after, the sea worked its way into his visions. At first it would appear at the least expected moment in the dream, upon turning a street corner, behind a door, alongside his desk in the classroom, and its presence was always a slap of light across his eyes. One night, Tomás was sucked into the waters, seized by the same panic as in the dream of dry leaves. He was flying low over the city when a strong gust swept him towards a mud and rock beach strewn with broken shells. A wave licked his feet; receding, it opened a smooth glistening path, maroon and copper colored, extending to the edge of the foam. At last he thought he could see the girl and he advanced, sensing the cold thick swirl on all sides. His own body bathed in semen woke him.

During that period, until he broke his leg, Tomás's attitude towards the world outside underwent a total change. He stayed on the street all day long. During classes he joined the pranks the boys played, the mischief and disruption they caused, even the soccer team. At home he was scornful with his sisters and grew defiantly coarse in his manners, careless in what he wore. He adopted the speech and gestures of a gang of young neighborhood boys with whom he and some other friends from school spent their afternoons. They had bicycles, roller skates, cigarettes. The violence of his daytime habits would be followed by long hours of sleeplessness, which Tomás consumed reading books about pirates and adventurers. When at last he went to sleep, dizzy with fatigue, no dreams rose to his consciousness. Until bicycling when he broke his leg and had to stay in bed. Then Tomás's room began to recover its old air of impenetrable mystery, and soon he stopped letting visitors come. His hours were regulated by the changing play of lights and shadows from the garden on the walls, the ceiling, the floor, the furniture. With his black crayons, charcoal shading stumps and gum erasers, his dreams too returned to his notebook. Still, his insomnia did not go away, and a kind of anguish, like an impetuous longing, bathed his body in sweat and inflamed his nightmares.

Looking over his notes and drawings, Tomás began searching for the possible meanings of that dream whose pieces still hadn't formed a coherent whole. He read poetry and volumes where death seemed to speak in the language of his visions, but something essential, vivid, still escaped him. The time came to study for exams and to exercise his leg. Tomás left the bed. In the mornings he hobbled outside into the garden on his cane, and afternoons he studied the lessons he had missed. His convalescence coincided with the blossoming of spring: the new shoots, the twittering of birds in their nests, the flowers spreading open, the impulse that seemed to push everything towards light and life, stirred too in Tomás's body, equally restless, eager for air and sap.

He did not want to go to the seashore again. They decided on a hot springs resort in the mountains, in a semi-wilderness area of forests and sudden cliffs. Here the land had been tamed only around the swimming pools, the tennis courts and the hotel grounds that stretched down through meadows and ponds to the edge of a gorge where the river tumbled. Footpaths and stairsteps wandered here and there, and from the terrace the scenery offered an ingenious collage of orchards, lawns, hot springs, flower boxes, jardinieres, mountain slopes and crags. Tomás hardly knew enough tones for the variety of greens, for the shades of light, or had names for the flowers, trees and butterflies. The first few days he limited himself to exploring the gardens and footpaths that ventured farthest from the resort. Next he skirted the paths down along the river gorge. Finally, one morning, he plunged into the forest, up the mountainside behind the playing fields.

If his encounter with the sea the year before had been instantaneous and total, the sensations he now felt from the mountain, in contrast, seemed little by little to merge from the outside in, with Tomás's interior landscape, smoothly, with no apparent change. He himself believed he was discovering everything: in reality, he was recognizing it, it was a re-encounter. That was the reason behind his almost painful excitement and the alertness of his senses. From the cover of dead leaves rose a moist, warm odor. The shouts and noises from the resort faded as he climbed, until there was only the trilling of birds, the swaying of boughs, the creaking of tree trunks and of sunlight through the needles. A cold breeze sprang up. Tomás headed for a bright clearing. In the middle of it—tennis shoes, socks, white tennis dress and racket—a girl was twisting and leaping. Her hair tossed against the light with the same airy grace as her clothing, her legs and arms. She didn't stop when she saw Tomás, and only after a while, visibly tired, she threw down her racket and stretched out face down on the grass. Tomás came closer. She rolled over, suddenly.

"What are you doing here?" she asked.

At the same time she motioned him with her hand to sit down next to her. Feeling strange, Tomás crouched down.

"I'm Alicia. How about you?"

She was no more than a year or two older than he was, blonde, her amber eyes smiling and mischievously watching him. A moment went by. Not more. Then she took his hand and audaciously guided it to her breast.

"Know what to do?" she asked.

He shook his head, unable to get a word out. She sat up and pulled off her blouse. Facing each other, on their knees, he surrendered to the caresses that flooded his body, and to his hands that returned her touch with unexpected boldness and passion. Eyes, lips, fingers, thighs, buttocks, breasts, their necks and arms, rushed at each other, drenched with sunlight, heat, with desire.

"Are you going to be here for very long?" he asked.

"God no, what a horrible thought! I can't stand any more of this place. At last, after a whole month, we're getting out tomorrow."

Tomás saw her body which the sun had turned gold, her agile movements, and that lack of modesty in everything about her, in her smile, her small breasts, her wide hips under her skirt, the idle swinging of her racket through the air as they walked. He still felt the tide pulling inside him, and a tension that was exasperated by every word and move of this girl enshrined in distant voluptuousness. A noise of waters drew them to the edge of the gorge. Shining rainbows drifted in and out of the falls, a fine mist that the noon sun dispelled against the seagreen background of the cliff. Tomás knew this was his dream, and he felt afraid. Alicia smiled at his paleness.

"Yes, maybe it's too bad I'm leaving. You could learn a lot of things. Come here."

She hugged him around the waist and tried to kiss him. He stepped back: first he had to explain to her, tell her about his dream, about his encounter, and about his fear, above all about his fear. He struggled to free himself from her. She thought he was being playful and held him all the tighter. He was seized by a panic, felt breathless, and pushed against her.

She fell, like the shadow in his dream, she disappeared among the white tops of the shining trees; when a sudden wind parted the luminous veil of water, he thought he saw her hands stretched up to him, playfully, still calling him. . .

Trans. by David Pritchard

Esther Seligson

Luz de Dos

iv.

It begins in Cuenca. Do you know that city? The story is the story of three days, their image, a church's: Santa Clara-a-Velha. Or it might start at the other end: it might be Coimbra, one night in front of San Nicholas. In a letter you said it was so lovely, so passionately beautiful, I went to see for myself. You were waiting for me on the platform. I trudged roads of rock and stubble, the land dry and hard along the straw-colored paths. And now here we were, near dusk, at the river bank, sullen, saying nothing. We both watched the same scene—the violet sky, the washerwomen in the middle of that enormous streambed, a thread of water barely trickling through—but looking at it in different ways: you, lost in clouds, in the memory of the presence you so badly wanted near you; me, more to earth, surrounded by everything your letters had spoken of, but beside me only your absence. At that moment, under the giant acacias—or were they chestnuts?—that bordered the walk above the dying river, we hated each other with fierce conviction.

Unlike you I have no craving for precision, so it does not matter if it all gets mixed up, if I confuse churches, names, legends and even our own story with the history surrounding that couple from the banks of the Mondego.

Lovers' whispers, dreams, among the stones of the river, of a wedding: That was this city. The other, ocher and ash, a land of olive groves and windmills. And above both cities, the mountain, a blue sun, the rectangular tower, the sharp spire: tile roofs climbing hillsides while the streets wind down to the water.

"In the 9th Century, *Conca* was an Arab fortress belonging to the Sultan of Valencia. It was conquered by Alfonso VIII in 1177. Following the expulsion of the Moors, toward the middle of the 17th Century, the population dwindled to 1,500 inhabitants. Today Cuenca is a city of 36,000 people perched along an outcrop of the small Serranía range, hemmed on either side by the deep gorges of the Júcar and Huécar rivers. The climate is harsh in winter, with temperatures to 9 below zero celsius. The late spring, the beginning of autumn and especially the summer, are the best times to visit. In the old quarter of the city are found the Cathedral (an example of Norman Gothic style), the Episcopal Palace, and the churches of San Pedro and San Pablo."

The guidebook, long out of date, says nothing more. The rest, what was ours, we were in fact discovering during the first cool days of autumn. Clearly separations are no good. It's hard to guess which knots, imperceptibly, a life not shared will undo. Nor is absence always a staggering blow that wrenches every fiber of body and soul; its real erosion begins when, one morning, we wake up and the light in the room is changed, the noises and surrounding silences are different. Maybe our habits, feelings and thoughts haven't changed, but everything around is moving, drawing us apart, distracting us, taking our time, separating us. So to let you go or to go myself—is there any difference?—was to open the crack through which the weeks and hours would begin to filter, the little outside trifles that cling to the change brought about by living someone's absence day after day. Reality then becomes a struggle against an emptiness which, little by little, no poem, no song, no memory can fill.

Unless, of course what matters isn't "reality." For Inés, for example, what mattered was presence, the smell of the lilies by the spring, the warblers' song, the lively gossip of the washerwomen at the edge of the river. The rest, the letters, the separations, merely confirmed what was missing, and she sought escape by rending time. Foreign by origin and religion, taught not to bind herself to anything or anybody, she would not, with her spirit, accept a material security which all the voices of her race opposed as fictitious. And it wasn't that she was ashamed of being a Jew. On the contrary, in those times the most devoted servants to the Court were Jews. Her father and her grandfather had been faithful counselors to their Majesties, but—as they told her so often—unless asked directly it was advisable not to mention one's origin or to make a public display of one's beliefs and ceremonies. Distrust is as ancestral (and hadn't this attitude just been confirmed by the recent expulsion of the French Jews?) as respect for tradition: "Who keeps the Law saves his life," her grandfather repeated, Ecclesiastes in hand.

Then too there was no ignoring the rumors of outbreaks of violence against other Jewish communities, especially during Easter week when it was declared that Jews kneaded their unleavened bread with the blood of new-born Christians. The problem would not be solved by arguing with popular ignorance and superstition. One must maintain a reserve, show oneself to be conciliatory and, whenever possible, try to go unnoticed. This latter was the hardest, mostly because a great many of the conflicts were brought on by the Jews themselves, the result of quarrels among powerful families, or over economic interests, or from envy surrounding some favorite of the Court. They quarrelled, too, over questions of orthodoxy. Her grandfather was one of these. Inés went to the discussions—her father was considered a renegade—conscious that it was not her place to be listening to such subtleties (that was for her brothers), but rather, being only a woman, to concern herself with what was feminine. Nothing was more alien to her than submission, but she broke down under the ritual of words, the figure of her grandfather, his sternness, the trembling ecstasy with which he led the service, and his awesome remoteness. Her father was a tax-collector, her grandfather a provincial governor, and the children too would be destined to the King's service.

en él, pues, reposa toda mi pena
Tal es el cautivo que me tiene cautiva,
y puesto que en él vivo,
menester es que yo viva.

And so, with exodus her only patrimony and assurance, that first separation and the exile Don Alfonso later imposed on her merely strengthened Inés's eagerness to exhaust each day, and sharpened her awareness of impermanence. When there were letters, she lived the letters, but in each new encounter the pages were torn to pieces and burned in order to live in the presence, in the touch, the smell, the sound, the taste and the sight of Don Pedro. Can you believe this lasted a full ten years after the death of Costanza, the legitimate wife, in whose retinue Inés had originally come? What was her life like before Coimbra? Mountains where jagged rocks cut shapes against the green, dizzy stairstep trails where goats leap, houses clinging to outcrops, and below, the river, the rivers, a gray fringe, a thin thread that towards evening gives off vapors. Streets, cramped plazas, hermitages and convents: a city with two slopes rising toward the Serranía, and the town itself closed off, hermetic, with high walls and thick studded doors.

"No use telling—you already know—how from every wall your face emerges, how from every corner, every streetlamp, every timber holding a balcony to a house, your eyes appear, your lips, your breasts, your caresses, the taste of your tongue and the smell of your body. In this way I can dream, in this way I can see you. Tonight I will love this pleasure of loving you, and in waiting, the agony of knowing how painful this long, this wounding time is between dreaming of you and having you with me. Sleep in peace, if peace ever comes to love and to two who love each other..."

By daybreak we were in Coimbra, that white luminous city overlooking the fields along the Mondego. In the *Quinta de las Lagrimas*, murmurs still cling to the trees. If you wander through the garden near the pool, along the path that disappears above the spring, or if you pause under some chestnut, at midday, when the light is so strong and the willows look most languid, when the shade under the cedars feels coolest and the insects are laziest, you can hear the drawn-out lament, the voices gathered around the *Fonte Dos Amores.* From the palace, along the narrow canal—they say—the letters were sent down every day, every night, to the fountain, right here where Inés's severed head fell: sheet after sheet, sentence after sentence,

y mientras escribía,
un alma en cada lágrima cabía,

siendo en tantos renglones
las almas mucho más que las razones.

However, neither of these two was made for sorrow, but rather for the joy of life. From Castillian reserve to Portuguese *saudade*—melancholy—the cool skin, the wide eyes, the glossy hair, the eager hands: they were all these; Inés, the "heron-necked," Don Pedro, "muito guapo e grande monteiro," as the chronicles tell us.

Swift, thirsty, the river tumbles, boring down to carve pools where the women wash, soak, scrub. The air fills the lungs, bitter-sweet, cool. Streets take us in, allow themselves to be taken. The greediness of our senses, an eternity where nothing stands still. Yesterday, toward midmorning, the woman brought her flowerpots out into the sun, one by one, along the window ledge. Then, one by one again, she started watering them. Below, in the inner courtyard—you and I, elbows along the rail on one of the steep roads down the mountain, watched, fascinated by this rhythmic, meticulous labor—three men in heavy work clothes pounded a bar of metal on an anvil. And above all of us the mountain, the gypsy caves, the yellowish peaks. And still higher, the white sky, so luminous, so liquid.

Today, only a little later, we didn't find the woman at the window, and the men were gone; but the flowerpots, the anvil and the morning with its vibrations were still there. Asking ourselves what it is that gives each of those daily chores its solidity—watering, forging, sweeping, cooking, hauling—that makes these people real who fill a narrow unvarying place within the village monotony, we envied that fierce security of those who know what part they play: bakers, carpenters, laborers, drovers, shopkeepers, signalmen, nuns, sextons, druggists, churchgoers, beggars or simply old women. . .women like the one who, if you stop to draw her out, will tell you her stale stories, of when she was keeper of the priest's keys and why now she's only the doorkeeper at the church of San Nicolas. And it must not have been so hard to get used to the tolling of the bells, the nightwatchman's cry, and the passing of the seasons, to the tension and weariness of a body in which every part has been hard at work. To learn a skill was an obligation first before any other endeavor: "God didn't make man with his own hands for nothing," her grandfather grew tired of repeating over the rash exploits of his grandsons, who thought only of hunting, riding and challenging the other equally idle young noblemen. And no one ever changed her mind that this idleness, this leisure, this excessive ease, was a punishment, a sign of God's abandonment and of evil times that were beginning to be evident in Spain itself.

Though not extraordinary, the vigilance over Inés del Castro was strict, as was proper for the only daughter of a family of good descent; none of the domestic skills—weaving, embroidering, spinning, darning, baking—nor anything touching on tradition, had been overlooked.

What life could Inés have had before coming to Portugal? An infatuation whispered behind Moorish screens at the Synagogue? And doesn't it seem absurd to have fled from one confinement to fall into another? *Répandre sa vie dans les embrassements de l'amour, c'est jeter des racines dans la tombe,* warned a proverb of the time. But is there any other way of making radiant contact with the mysterious? Not that daily life in itself is so shallow, but plainly there are better means of arriving at knowledge, and when one has lived in the delirium of the senses, in full possession of oneself, in the vertigo of being one with the world, it is difficult, painful, to see how the days end up blunting the edge of passion, how shared habits can eventually domesticate even the divine rage. Still, we can't deny that it is in the fabric of daily living that knowledge ripens and ages. Those people we've just been envying would tell us that life is to be found in simplicity, that it's enough to have faith in the inherent meaning and justification of the smallest of our actions, and that (watch out!) it's for madmen and fools to rush in where angels fear to tread. And we would laugh, and agree with that good woman who grieved because her son had gone away to study rather than stay on the land as everyone had always done, and who, tapping her finger significantly against her temple, concluded that "too much thinking's bad for you." Here we stood, at dusk, desiring each other with all the ardor our words had poured into our letters. Where, then, did this tension come from, this scrutiny of each other with so much hatred? What madness made us deny our bodies, cheat them of the only moment possible, stifle and turn away the joy of this new meeting? The poet says happiness strikes fear, that by waiting so hard for joy, tense and sleepless, its imminent arrival goes unnoticed. Loyal to what loneliness, what fear, did we let that silence go unbroken?

Ate a fim do mundo reads the inscription in solid granite: foot to foot so that, according to legend, they will be face to face, their eyes meeting, on Resurrection Day. When Pedro learned of Inés's death, he rose in arms against his father and for two years, "in a burst of madness, he set out to ravage and destroy the entire region between the Duero and the Mino." But the murder was kind to them both: only by perpetuating themselves in the popular imagination, through art and history, could they attain their destiny as lovers and redeem their inability, despite all effort and desire, to live the present moment. Ten years do not pass for nothing, and if she refused to accept the position Costanza left when she died—the *Quinta* on the banks of the Mondego was a secret from no one—it was because she already knew that nothing was ever going to change between them.

There were also, I don't deny, reasons of politics, the jealousies among courtesans, the desire for power among the Castro brothers, for whom the religious obstacle was never of the slightest consideration. And there was Don Pedro's fear of opposing his father Don Alfonso, much firmer and more decisive than his son. That much the poet called

Destiny. Most of all, there are the personalities with all their masks and turnings, the contradictory, the unforeseeable. Still, transience can last forever, and when we allow the moment to hold us, the only reality is to let our steps be drawn toward the celebration of the senses. In this way, unprotected against the vertigo of being alive—(at times we might wish not to love in order not to ache for the loved one, or to blot the other from our minds, and be blotted, in order to hold off loneliness) —but embracing the moment, not shutting the present out, in this way spring and summer and the exuberance all around us is merely the reflection of our own urge for expansion and bounty. Nostalgia, then, that case of bittersweet anxiety, that desire to belong to other times and take part in other lives, becomes the blithe certainty of a flow sweeping us with it. Surely we are not best suited to mourning, nor to withdrawal, nor to weeping. Why run from pleasure to find refuge in affliction?

"Better grief than laughter, for with a countenance of sorrow the heart will be healed." Where could her grandfather have gotten the idea that only with a grave and serious face could one stay good? Yes, the old seemed too serious and had little patience for the uproar of children and the rashness of youth. Life was subject to a law on whose obedience depended the entire meaning of this brief lapse between birth and death. Escape was impossible, at least that was what Inés believed until she discovered that to know herself, to feel herself alive, passionately alive, was the only risk worth running.

Some chronicles say she had four children, others three, and in the dramatic works only two are mentioned. I don't know whether certain times more than others favor a spirit of lyrical pantheistic exaltation, but what is clear is that the world had just left behind a gruesome plague, and this need for renewal, this turning toward man and the mundane, was a means of conjuring the fear of death and the suspicion that God, in fact, was now merely the stuff of theologists and charlatans. In this light it cannot seem strange that Don Pedro crowned Inés two years after her death in 1375, removing her from the sepulcher at Santa-Clara-a-Velha to carry her to the monastery at Alcobaça, and demanding, not posthumous homage but, on the contrary, all the honors due a living queen: "and there to make his vassals kiss those bones that had been beauteous hands." The ephemeral had been conjured, and the power of life over death affirmed.

Once the Mondego was broad and full; it ran between groves of pine to the sea, and its waters lapped the hill where houses climbed upwards, dominated by the tower of the University. Today the church of Santa Clara is drowning under sands that have been flooding it over the centuries. Surrounded by chestnuts, it guards between its naves the remains of the river: pools, mud, the play of light and wind, echoes of the ancient splendor among the columns of what once was its upper gallery, in the gaps of the rose window where now the wild grasses stick out, and in the great empty windows behind the choir. Whose story had we come here for? In reality we were running away, protecting ourselves again from memory and nostalgia. And all for what? To end up regretting even more sharply what was done and what undone, hating this separation and accepting it. . . The same spring, they say, feeds the *Fonta Dos Amores* and the convent of Santa Clara. . .

How can one hope to draw an inner map, which by its nature never follows accounts, no matter how precise? Cuenca, Coimbre: two plain, solid names: streets withdrawing toward the higher, older quarters. Two cities that look nothing alike but are linked by the same tragedy. Dazzled by the huge variety of greens, the trees and wooded land, by the warmth of the sand, the profusion of bachelor-buttons, everything brimming with *saudade*, Inés, who came from the rocks and crags, from austerity, from blacks and ochers, from swift muted outbursts of spring, let herself be surrounded and rocked by the "sweet clear waters of the *saudosos* lands of the Mondego." Mingling inevitably with her intoxication was a melancholy, that emptiness that rises no one knows from where, aching, weighing, gnawing, no one knows why. . .a strange disconsolation in the midst of euphoria, binding the two together—this feeling was no stranger to him either—with the same force and the same impetus. Amid the hydrangeas, carnations and roses, her embroidery, verses and love letters, Inés spent what Don Pedro called

ausencias inexcusables
solamente acompañada
a ratos de mi firmeza
y siempre de mi esperanza.

It was there, in this isolation, that Inés understood the cult among her people of physical uprooting, that insistence that "the true roots are found in matters of the spirit," and the consequent determination to keep the traditions, to concentrate all hope on one alone, the messianic, endlessly and without repose. She began to understand the sense of those prayers, half lament, half song, that filled the Synagogue like hands lifted in attitudes of praise, at once joyous and frightened, from which might burst either supplication or reproach. And she felt a longing for those chants, those feasts on which the Lord's service bathed the atmosphere with that light, that odor, so intimate, so high above individual cares. A longing caused her to ask, in her letters, not so much after each member of the family as about what they did and how they felt on Friday nights, for example, or during some festival: had they lighted the candles, blessed the bread, observed this or that fast? The nearest community was at Leiria, but, given her personal circumstances at the Court, she felt hesitant to go very far from her confinement at the *Quinta.*

I don't conceive of Inés begging for her life and the lives of her children, asking mercy of a mortal driven solely by political concerns. Crimes by "reason of state" were as common then as now, and they knew it. It wasn't death that obsessed them, but what lay after. It was a question of finding solace in present happiness and of perpetuating their being, their appetite for life. She was seventeen when they met, he was sixteen, and at no moment, in all the twelve years that make up their story, did their adolescent passion diminish, neither in their quarrels nor in their fits of remorse and reconciliations. Neither, then, was there anything "ferocious and terrible" in what Don Pedro did to Alvar Gonçalves and Egas Cohelo, the noblemen murderers: first cutting out their hearts, live, biting each one through in rage, and then ordering the bodies burnt. Everything was thought out with an eye for posterity. The two of them encouraged the pretensions of the Castro brothers and other rebels to the king, who promised Don Pedro they would recognize his expected marriage to Inés and give him the crown of Castille. This, and the advantages that would come from marrying his son to the Infanta de Navarra, determined Don Alfonso to order the execution. And Inés, broken down by melancholy and longing, out of her religious context, and doubting her lover's faithfulness, accepted

– Quién contigo se quedara!
– Quién se partiera contigo!
–Muerta quedo.
– Voy sin alma!

Seven gates and eight bridges link the city to the outside. Tired by all our walking, still lost in the reverberations of all the events we'd been hearing about, all the stories we'd been imagining, we returned, in no particular hurry, to the train station. A few peasants with big baskets on their heads emerge from a gateway and set off down the steep San Miguel road, while in the red and black dusk the mist rises off the river and lights go on all over the skirts of the mountain. Doña Inés and Don Pedro got their wish, and here they lie, white marble statues, united under the vaults of the Alcobaça monastery. No magnificent sepulcher awaits you and me, nor the consolation of the Resurrection, nor the eternity of legend. . . For you and me all that's left is the word, these lines I write, as the poet said, "to speak with your absence."

Trans. by David Pritchard

Esther Seligson's *literary activities are extensive, embracing philosophy, history, criticism, translation, and fiction. Beginning with her early schooling at la Escuela Israelita Yavne in Mexico (1948-1959), she has studied at the University of Paris, The Institute for Hebraic, Sephardic and Oriental Studies in Madrid, the Martin Buber Center at the Free University in Brussels, and the University Center for Jewish Studies in Paris. She has conducted seminars on such diverse subjects as Samuel Beckett, Jewish Traditional Thought, and The Art and History of the Middle Ages. She has translated E.M. Cioran into Spanish, and has written philosophical fiction. Her novel,* Otros son los sueños *won the Premio Nacional de Literatura "Xavier Villaurrutia" in 1973.*

Poetry by Isaac Goldemberg

Staraya Ushitza's Rabbi

Someone asked him for the meaning of time one day.
He wanted forty days to think it over.
He took to the woods and camped out in a cave.
Ideas swirled in his head.
He undressed from head to toe.
He purified himself in the water running over the rocks.
He made the darkness his bed.
He crawled down endless tunnels till his hands bled.
He recited passages from the Bible under his breath.
And he sometimes wondered if he had died.
Meanwhile circles got deeper around his eyes.
His memory started slipping.
Bats had swarmed into the cave.
He could hear them copulating in the silence.
Gradually he was losing his patience.
He went deeper into the cave.
He figured his children might be out looking for him.
He answered in a voice like thunder:
Time is in the Cabbalah.
Time is an ostrich's egg.
Time is a devil with a thousand horns.
He tried to think but mirages ravaged his mind.

Trans. by David Unger

Epitaph

Here's a man who died on us:
His name was Javier Camilo Ernesto*
he died as he left our heart
to us, the deaf of this world,
he died screaming
Liberty or Death
he died
under the spell of a prison
he died
in the thick of the fighting
he died at the same time
in all four corners of the planet
because one day he had been born
with our hunger
and dragged his lovely sickness
up and down mountains
he was born one day
by the simple act of being born
he was born with a gentle corpse in his heart
he was born both kind and wicked
to look at us with an eye on every face
this man died in our womb
he pulled up our world by the roots
and left a deep hole all around us

this man died before our noses
and took his words somewhere else

Trans. by David Unger

---

* Javier Heraud—Peruvian poet and revolutionary, killed; Camilo Torres—revolutionary, killed; Ernesto "Che" Guevara, killed.

Chronicles

Then I set out on my journey through history
and now I remember that heroes—I mean those
who thought about life as they were dying—
flashed their ghostly claws

And it so happened that in the end
I couldn't forget Mariatequi's seven poems
that even though my head had been cut off
I still kept in my pocket
the left pocket
two cents worth of patriotism

Then I took the road that neither began
nor ended in Jerusalem or Cuzco
finally I discovered that confuciusjesuschristkarlmarx
were scheming to put out a new edition of the bible
and that the earth's navel
could be found inside a barren woman

Solomon ordered that the son of my conscience be cut in half
and that his head be handed over to the Western mother
and his ass with two legs to the Eastern mother
and that's how a lie the size of a nose
began growing on our culture

A parched, dying voice revealed to me that
civilization began when Cain committed his crime
who cared if Wiracocha was born in a Bethlehem manger
or if Jesus was Lake Titicaca's son
we didn't need sperm tests
but tests of conscience
in the end I, the offspring of Abraham's rape of Mama Ocllo
paternal step-brother of David the Hebrew Pachacutec
spun my roots in the Span-Jewish wool of Tahuantisuye

Poets: don't waste your words
today the word is no longer the prophet's sword
and reason, in this age, further removed than ever
from the mystery that the universe weaves around us
is only reflected in the stubborn silence of our dead

It's necessary, however, if you are looking for pseudonyms
to understand that it makes no difference to be called a lion
        a horse or a cat
that heroes' names already smell like parchments
it would be easier to look for a man with a name like Che
and that's why it's better to be called a ram than Abraham
a lamb instead of Jesus or llama instead of Manko.

Trans. by David Unger

Isaac Goldemberg

from
The Fragmented Life of Don Jacobo Lerner

The format of Isaac Goldemberg's *novel,* The Fragmented Life of Don Jacobo Lerner, *is narrative interspersed with articles from many sources. The following excerpts, from the beginning, middle, and end of the novel, are arranged to suggest the novel's structure.*

I

The night before he died, Jacobo Lerner thought of the mild catastrophes that would be occasioned by his passing. He imagined his sister-in-law living on, unable to love anyone else. His brother Moisés he imagined bankrupt, abandoned by his son, asking for help from friends. His mistress, doña Juana Paredes Ulloa, he imagined reviled by everyone because she had not known how to squeeze money out of him in payment for her love. He imagined his sister-in-law's sister, Miriam Abramowitz, in deep repentance because she had not married him, who was now dead and buried. His son, Efraín, he imagined at the task of reconstructing his father from what was said by others. And Efraín's mother, who continued to live in the village where Lerner had met her, he imagined a victim of her father's insults for not having married the Jew while it was still possible.

He thought, too, almost melancholically, that his last will and testament would not have any effect whatever on whether or not these things came to pass.

The frayed yarmulke from the days of his childhood in Staraya Ushitza, he left to Moisés. To doña Juana Paredes he left the Louis XVI bed (with the pink coverlet that she herself had made) on which for the last five years they had frolicked like adolescents, three times a week. To Miriam he left an invitation in black gothic script and gold filigree for the wedding that never took place. To Efraín he left a small sum of money obtained through fourteen years of work and privations, for the day when he became twenty-one. To his sister-in-law he left the complete works of Heine, in German, with a dedication in Yiddish on the flyleaf written three years before, when he thought of giving her the book for her birthday.

Jacobo Lerner also remembered that the last time he saw his old friend León Mitrani was in 1925, on the day that Jacobo left for Lima, nine years before Mitrani died, victim of carelessness on the part of the village druggist, who instead of selling him the fifty milligrams of bicarbonate of soda prescribed by Doctor Meneses, sold him the same quantity of stain remover. He imagined Mitrani in the half-darkness of the grocery store, sitting placidly in the same rocking chair, behind the same counter where he had spent the last years of his life, bounded by ramshackle half-empty shelves and the ceiling on which spiders had woven their complicated structures, imperfect tetrahedrons. It was Samuel Edelman who had told him Mitrani died in the first hours of the morning, invoking the name of Jacobo Lerner between spasms and memories of his childhood in Staraya Ushitza.

"If you come to Chepén, you will be rich in a very short time," Mitrani had assured him in one of his letters. And Jacobo had found him prematurely old, dragging a lame leg, which Mitrani explained was the result of a kick by the mule used by Serafín, the water-seller, in 1922. It was the middle of the winter when Jacobo Lerner arrived in Chepén with a suitcase full of trinkets on his shoulder, three years after his friend. He realized how much Mitrani had changed since the last time they had seen each other aboard the SS *Bremen* in Hamburg. Besides the lameness that Jacobo found intimidating because the man dragging his leg was the same age as he, Mitrani seemed to be weighed down by heavy premonitions of things to come.

One afternoon, as they sat in the café, Mitrani told Jacobo it would would not be long before the northern part of the country would be swept by a violent pogrom. Samuel Edelman, a salesman who came to town every other month to keep Mitrani supplied with merchandise and who brought all the news, both national and foreign, that did not reach Chepén, had reported that in Trujillo, a city about one hundred kilometers away, the army had been preparing for months to move against the Jews who had settled between Chimbote and Tumbes. The Jewish community of Lima had already been liquidated, and the government had decreed that Jews living in the provinces should suffer the same fate as soon as possible.

According to Mitrani, that was what Edelman, who was now fleeing toward the jungle where he was sure he would not be found, had communicated to him. It is quite possible that if Jacobo Lerner had not been at least partly successful in ridding him of these delusions, Mitrani would have carried out his own planned flight to Iquitos and left behind the woman with whom he had been living since a month after his arrival in the town. And even when he remained, Mitrani never completely stopped being afraid that there would be a pogrom in Chepén. The murder of his uncle by the Czarist soldiers, in 1911, had been burned into his brain and remained there no matter what happened to him.

Jewish Soul: No. 4—April, 1923

ON JEWS IN PERU

(Exclusive for *Jewish Soul*)

We have lately seen a commercial and industrial guide to Loreto, published in 1916, and were very surprised to discover the great number of Jewish establishments that exist in Iquitos.

In the aforementioned guide we found an article entitled "The Amazon River Was Navigated by Hebrews and Phoenicians," that begins thus:

"Onfroy de Toron, in his work, *Earliest Navigation of the Ocean: Voyages of King Solomon's Ships to the Amazon,* proves that Hebrews and Phoenicians took their ships up the Amazon River which they named the Solomon, after the great King."

Mauricio Gleizer

Iquitos, January, 1923

Jewish Soul: No. 4—April, 1923

THE WANDERING JEW

(Exclusive for *Jewish Soul*)

Those who have seen the Wandering Jew in his nocturnal walks say that he is a man over one hundred years old and at least seven feet tall. He is dressed in a black frock-coat and, at the end of a crook, he carries a lamp whose flame is eternal. The detail that most impresses those who have met the apparition, however, is the horrifying sound of his iron spurs.

Whenever he is seen, epidemics or droughts follow shortly after.

An anonymous chronicler recorded the following event, witnessed by the inhabitants of Huancavelica at the turn of the century:

"On that day, it became suddenly dark and then a mysterious light, a kind of Aurora Borealis, illuminated the village so that the terrified townspeople could see how their huts were lifted high in the air, whirling like feathers along with their chickens, ducks, and sheep. The earth shook and, finally, they saw the Wandering Jew rise on a ball of fire that flew into the distance until all that was left of his presence was a glow behind the hills."

FRAY FERNANDO,
Lay Brother of the Convent
of La Merced

. . . .

V

Whenever he went into León Mitrani's house, Jacobo Lerner felt that he had tumbled, arms flailing, into a world where everything was at once strange and familiar. Faded engravings of the Saint of Motupe, shiny chromos of the Sacred Heart of Jesus, and wooden crucifixes of all sizes were arranged side by side with bronze candelabra, a red philactery bag on which the star of David was embroidered in gold, and several *sidurim* with tooled leather covers that Mitrani had taken from his father's house.

The first time Jacobo Lerner saw these relics he thought about his own father who had died in Staraya Ushitza, in snow and loneliness, and wondered whether Abraham, his brother, still had the old man's things.

In that large old house of passageways, of closed rooms, of spacious interior gardens that appeared to float in rarefied air, where it seemed necessary to move in silence and with head bent as if marching in procession, Jacobo Lerner always felt oppressed by windows that were always closed, by narrow hallways that led nowhere; he felt locked in a world of armchairs worn by use and chests redolent of moths and mothballs.

Mitrani's wife, who had gradually gone blind in spite of the efforts of doctors and medical science, lived on the top floor of the house. There she had a room apart from her husband's, where she spent most of her time sewing throws and pillow covers, which he then sold at modest prices in his store.

Once, lost in the labyrinths of that old house, Jacobo went into her room by mistake, and stood by the door while, unaware of his presence, she recited a litany in a barely audible voice: "Lord, forgive me for not having followed your precepts; for having given my body to a heretic who blasphemes your name, forgive me. Lord, please try to understand, who will take pity on me, now, old and blind as I am? Who will take me into his house? Lord, I repent, I will always repent falling into temptation, Lord, repent having disobeyed my father, repent having not set foot in a church since I came to live in this house. Forgive me, oh God, I have even thought of killing him. I have stayed awake nights planning how to kill him. Forgive, oh Lord, and hear the prayer of this, your wayward sheep; take her unto your kingdom."

When Jacobo told Mitrani about the incident, he shrugged his shoulders and said he knew his wife was crazy. Later he warned Jacobo, in a threatening tone, not to meddle in what did not concern him. Jacobo was very disturbed, not so much because he had been told off in such an insulting manner, but because of the lackadaisical way in which his friend had received the news. That particular conversation confirmed the suspicions that had been taking shape in his mind since his arrival in Chepén. If it was true that the wife was not sound and sane, it was also true that León was not far behind. Lately, he had taken to getting up at the first glint of dawn to put on the philacteries that had been his father's and his grandfather's before him.

Absurd, thought Jacobo, how absurd that León, who had been publicly vilified by the rabbi of his village because he had not been present to say *kaddish* for his father after having renounced the religion of his ancestors, should now, an old man, become a punctilious observer of religious ritual. He had even begun to study the Torah again, and sometimes, no matter where he was, he spoke of Isaiah and his prophet's fury against the King of Judea for having bled his people, sacked the Temple of Solomon, abolished Hebrew as the kingdom's official language, and instituted the adoration of Assyrian gods, all for the sake of appeasing Tiglat, the invader.

As was to be expected, Mitrani's behavior not only frightened the people of the village but also required the intervention of Father Chirinos. The priest's admonitions, however, had little effect on the spirit of Mitrani, since they issued, he claimed, from an imposter. Did he not, after all, represent a god whose existence, both celestial and eternal, had been doubted as early as the thirteenth century by Abraham Ibn Ezra, the Judeo-Hispanic poet?

It was about this time that people stopped going to Mitrani's store, and gradually his friends abandoned him as well. Out of necessity, Mitrani's old customers ended up patronizing Jacobo Lerner's store, where, if it was true that they might not find what they needed, at least they were certain of not being accosted and insulted in the language of a cheap brothel.

After a while, Jacobo was the only one who dared speak to Mitrani. When they met each other in public, in the lobby of the hotel where Jacobo lived or on a bench in the little park across the street from the hotel, Jacobo tried as hard as he could to keep the conversations in Yiddish and in that way disappoint the expectations of all those who stopped to listen. But, invariably, Mitrani would end up speaking the impeccable Spanish that he had learned by assiduously reading the Spanish version of the New Testament. This command of the language, which now carried the meaning of his words to all those who were eagerly listening, had been the sole result of his wife's efforts to teach him the true doctrine.

No wonder, then, that Jacobo decided to limit his sporadic visits to either his own small hotel room or Mitrani's house. Even when it became almost impossible to deal with his friend, Jacobo still derived a certain satisfaction from going to see him in that big old house where the sun, instead of giving light, seemed to make all objects dark.

By then, most conversations were nothing more than incoherent perorations about Mitrani's frustrated career in the Bolshevik ranks in 1920, but Jacobo still liked to hear him speak of that period when they lived together in that distant Ukrainian village. There were many things that tied them one to the other. They had been born in the same year. Together they had gone to school at Rabbi Finkelstein's, and together they had their *bar-mitzvah* in the synagogue. They had left Russia together, crossing the police border on foot, and now, after a separation of three years, they were together again in the godforsaken town of Chepén.

But friendship was not the only reason Jacobo went to Mitrani's house. In a room that looked over an uncared-for garden that had become the domain of weeds, Mitrani kept a few books in Yiddish and Russian. While Mitrani slept in the afternoon, a habit that he had learned to keep religiously, Jacobo read novels by Isaac Peretz, Sholem Asch, and Sholem Aleichem. Among those volumes of yellowed, cracking sheets, he found a coverless edition of *The Eternal Jew,* a play by David Pinsky that had been performed in Moscow by the "habimah" company around 1916. But his favorites were the novels of Sholem Aleichem, especially *The Death of Yankel Brodsky* that told what happened to a Jewish family in Czarist Russia.

What he read those afternoons, reminiscing with León Mitrani, and an old portrait of his parents that he kept packed at the bottom of his suitcase were the only contacts Jacobo Lerner had with a past that was quickly breaking into small fragments as days went by in Chepén.

VI

The photograph showed a tall, thin man wearing a dark coat and a wide-brimmed hat. He was leaning on a cane, and a thick white beard fell, raddled, halfway down his chest. Next to him, sitting on the edge of an armchair covered in some flowered material, was a small woman with her hands crossed on her lap. Her face was drawn and her eyes were sad. Her hair was covered by a kerchief. The photograph had been taken in Minsk the day the whole family had gone to witness Aunt Natasha's marriage to Leopoldo Myshkin, a man of heavy limbs and disproportionately large head which was crowned by a shiny bald pate. The wedding took place in 1905, when Jacobo was only ten years old and incapable of imagining that ten years later he would begin to watch the progressive disintegration of his family.

First there was the mysterious disappearance of his sister Judith. Judith left the village with her six-year-old son in the middle of the war to look for her husband Mishka, who, according to the letter received from the military authorities, was convalescing in a hospital in a not too distant city. There was never any further news of either of them. Judith's husband, who had lost his right arm, crisscrossed the Ukraine on foot, trying to locate his wife and son. After several long months of futile search, he showed up one day at the Lerner house, completely defeated. His clothing was filthy and ragged, his face was sallow, his beard dirty, and his back bent. Hunger and desperation had driven him mad, and he spent the rest of his days in the asylum at Poltrava.

Jacobo's father died the following year. He had gone to a nearby village to sell a few bags of oats and was found frozen on the road where his wagon had lost a wheel. Two months later, his wife followed, dying in her sleep at the age of fifty-five.

Without any family ties to keep them there, the three Lerner brothers decided to go their own ways. Abraham, the eldest, ended up in New York where, in time, he opened a furrier's shop in Brooklyn, married, and had three children. Jacobo stayed in the village, living in the house of León Mitrani. Moisés, the youngest of the three, went to live in Minsk, where he was warmly received by Aunt Natasha.

Jacobo and Moisés saw each other again in 1922, in Lima. Until 1923 they worked as peddlers in the streets of the city, selling razor blades, cheap bracelets, necklaces made from glass beads, and other trinkets. During this time they lived in a rooming house in the quarter of Jesús María, run by Madame Chernigov, a Russian countess who had seen better days. It was toward the end of this period that Jacobo Lerner received the letter from León Mitrani. Since he had been able to save a modest amount of capital, and since Moisés was planning to marry a Jewish woman from Vienna, Jacobo decided to follow his friend's advice and move to Chepén.

After living in Chepén for a year, Jacobo Lerner met Bertila, a seventeen-year-old girl with a gypsy cast to her face. She was the second daughter of don Efraín Wilson Rebolledo, a tall, red-faced man of English and Spanish blood, and of doña Jesús Alvarado, a dark-skinned lady with a tendency to gain weight, whose ancestors had been Andalucian and Indian. Bertila, who had never set foot outside of Chepén, fell in love with Jacobo Lerner the first time she saw him. She would look at him from across the street while he worked in his store, half-hiding among the bags of peanuts piled in front of Chang's grocery.

Since Jacobo had become the topic of dinner conversation in most of the houses of the village, Bertila had already heard of him, particularly from Efraín Wilson, who used to refer to him as "the Jew" not without a certain admiration, because, as he said, he was a businessman himself and respected "men of enterprise." Besides, the old man considered himself an Anglo-Saxon, choosing to forget his Hispanic side, and imagined that between him and Jacobo Lerner there was a link: they were both foreigners and both had the firm intention of increasing their wealth as quickly as possible by abstaining from unnecessary luxuries.

Don Efraín Wilson Rebolledo had moved to Chepén after the death of his father from whom he inherited a considerable sum of money and a capacity for hard work. Married and already the father of a daughter, the first thing he did when he arrived in the village was to buy a house on the main street. With time, don Efraín acquired more children and more houses. He owned twenty-five by the time Jacobo began courting Bertila, and their combined rents were more than thirty-five hundred *soles.* If one added to this the income from his trips to nearby villages, where he sold basins, pots, paraffin stoves, kerosene lamps, china, and almost everything else that might be of use in the house, one might finally come to consider him a wealthy man.

The more León Mitrani neglected his business, the more Jacobo Lerner prospered. His financial success intensified the curiosity don Efraín had felt toward him, and one night don Efraín went to his store to ask him to dinner.

That same night, Jacobo was formally introduced to Bertila. Despite the natural shyness of the girl, they got along very well from the moment they met. As soon as she felt slightly more at ease, Bertila began to ask him question after question about his travels through the world and the people he had met. Since he did not think his life had been in any way exceptional, Jacobo Lerner seasoned his adventures with wholly invented incidents. After a while, he found he could make Bertila believe him without difficulty, and so he convinced her, among other things, that he had been a soldier in the world war, that he had gone on pilgrimage to the Holy Sepulcher, and that he had been present at the opening of the Panama Canal. Bertila had never received any kind of formal schooling as the village school had opened when she was in her early teens, and Jacobo had to explain to her what each of these names meant. Only religious topics required no explanation, because Bertila, who could read a little, loved to exercise this skill with the Bible. So, lying on the cot that he had set up in the back room of the store, Jacobo also told her a hundred times of the love of David and Bathsheba and of Samson and Delilah. Bertila listened, charmed by that voice that seemed to transport her to where all these marvelous events had taken place.

Jacobo, who had just turned twenty-nine, and whose sexuality had, until that moment, found satisfaction only in a few encounters with streetwalkers in Berlin, did not believe that a man could be so content.

° • • •

X

The day he decided to leave Chepén, Jacobo Lerner stopped opening the store. He imagined Bertila would keep her pregnancy a secret and that he would have to suffer neither the flattery of don Efraín nor the anger of doña Jesús. He had arranged to sell the store to don Manuel Polo Miranda and to be paid in cash. But before he had made his decision to leave the village, Jacobo had consulted León Mitrani, who spoke openly and directly: Jacobo had only two options, he said, either stay in Chepén, settle down and raise a family, or leave immediately for Lima, before it was too late.

Mitrani, who didn't want to lose the company of his friend, favored Jacobo's staying. Jacobo replied coldly that the idea of marrying Bertila Wilson and staying permanently in Chepén didn't appeal to him in the least. What he did not say, perhaps for fear of making Mitrani furious, was that he would not like to find himself one day in Mitrani's situation: tied to a superstitious, ignorant woman who had threatened to kill him, considered a circus freak by the townspeople, abandoned by those who formerly called themselves his friends, and constantly bothered by the priest to convert.

Jacobo Lerner had come to Chepén with only one goal, making money, and he was not going to permit blind luck to make him forego such a practical plan. After his second year in Chepén, even though his affair with Bertila was already underway, Jacobo wanted to follow in the footsteps of his brother Moisés. He wanted to marry a Jewish woman and have many children. He wanted to live in the capital surrounded by all the luxuries that money could give him. He wanted to go to the synagogue with his friends, to celebrate religious holidays surrounded by his family and to see the bar-mitzvah of his sons. This order of things in his mind was what he leaned on to survive in a country where the way people lived was extremely strange to him. To stay in Chepén now meant giving up all this, to break with the traditional order of his family and his race, in short, to be swirled up in chaos.

"I will die here," Mitrani said when Jacobo proposed they move to Lima together. Jacobo understood then that chaos had already become the master of his friend's spirit, whereas for him, Jacobo told himself in a convincing tone, Chepén was nothing more than a way-station in the travels of his life. He wrote to Moisés telling him he would arrive in July, after he had sold the store.

Don Efraín Wilson had demonstrated great interest in buying the store, but he was not ready to meet the asking price. Jacobo told him that no one would ever become a wealthy man by running a small-town store, which was why he was going to Lima to buy up the government lands next to the mill of Santa Fe and then plant enough sugar cane to supply the mill. He promised to make don Efraín a partner in the enterprise, and he insisted don Efraín keep his plans an absolute secret because the success or failure of the project depended entirely on discretion. Don Efraín swore solemnly, invoking his dead father's name; his lips would be as sealed as a grave.

Jacobo Lerner met Father Chirinos at the house of Mayor Pablo Morales Santiesteban when a small group of neighbors had gathered to celebrate the mayor's wife's birthday. Jacobo thought Chirinos' appearance corresponded exactly to his profession: he was a tall, thin man with drawn features, and his hands were also long and thin, like those of an old woman of good family. His cassock was always spotless and well starched, his face clean shaven. That night, Father Chirinos spoke in a low and convincing voice about several topics concerning the Old Testament in an attempt to impress Jacobo with his erudition. But the priest's words were replete with mistaken facts and baseless judgements and so did not have the desired effect on Jacobo. Because his father had taught him to respect both civil and religious authority, Jacobo chose not to interrupt while the rest of the guests listened raptly to the priest.

Father Chirinos turned his head this way and that, coquettishly pulled at his sleeves, and at the end of some sentences looked up as if toward the heavens, while an ecstatic expression invaded his face.

The priest stopped only when they began to serve dinner. For Jacobo's benefit, the mayor's wife recited the name of each dish as the serving girl brought them to the table.

Jacobo Lerner had never tasted food like this, because in his hotel he only ordered what appeared to be least harmful to his health and least offensive to his sense of what was proper for a Jew. But now he served himself a little from each dish so as not to slight his hostess. As they ate, they spoke of the climate and the customs of Chepén, of how and when the original clump of houses had been built, and by whom, as well as of the reconstruction of the village after the earthquake of 1920. Mrs. Morales, who came from Chiclayo, told them about that village, larding her conversation with references to one of her ancestors, a Spanish captain who had come to Peru with the troops of Pizarro. When dessert was served, Jacobo was asked to tell something about his life in Russia. And so he related his adventures during the war, describing along the way his own village with its quaint houses and its synagogue, and the Dnieper River, so deep and broad that big barges carried cargoes up and downstream, his father's mill by the side of the river, and the woods nearby which he once had to cross at night in order to evade the patrol. Then he told how he had to sweep streets to earn a living in Germany, and, finally, of how he had arrived in Peru on a rainy night in 1921, on board the steamer *Reina del Pacífico.* He was careful, as he spoke, not to mention León Mitrani's name, judging it unwise to let them know that they had been childhood friends. "I came to Chepén because Samuel Edelman advised me to do so," he said when Father Chirinos asked him if he had known Mitrani in Russia; "I met León here."

After dinner, the guests sat in the living room. Don Pablo Morales, a short man with bent back and a face that reminded Jacobo of an inquisitive rooster, continued the line of conversation that had been started by Father Chirinos. With the exception of the priest, who had studied in the seminary at Trujillo, don Pablo was considered the most erudite man in the village, and his greatest source of pride was a collection of the classics of Spanish literature. Jacobo Lerner, who had had never read anything in Spanish except the newspaper and the catalogues that were essential to his business, was very impressed by the man's conversation, but he did what he could to hide behind his own façade of man-of-the-world. The mayor told about the life of the Jews in Spain during the Middle Ages, of how they were banished in 1492 by order of the Catholic kings, and of the extraordinary contribution that the *marranos* had made to the political, cultural, and economic life of the nation. "The history of Spain would have been quite different," said don Pablo with an authoritative tone, "if the Jews had not been expelled and persecuted."

Wanting to show that he too had knowledge of what the mayor was talking about, Jacobo added that his teacher in Staraya Ushitza had maintained the selfsame thing, and that he had backed it with statistics, dates, and the names of people and places. The truth was that Jacobo knew little of anything that was not related to the Bible or the Talmud. His acquaintance with history went no further than a few events in Czarist Russia that he had gleaned from Yiddish novels and some discussions with León Mitrani. He could never have imagined that Jews had lived in Spain during the Middle Ages, and he had not the slightest idea of who the Catholic kings might have been or of what the meaning of the word *marrano* was.

"The people of your race always stick together," continued the mayor. "I know that from my own experience. A few years ago, in Chiclayo, I met a certain Mauricio Gleitzer. After another Jew had died, he took the widow and children into his own house. True, I heard later he married her, but that means nothing. What is really important is that instinct all members of your race have. Believe me, don Jacobo, the story I've just told you would never have taken place among Christians. It's not that we don't have the spirit of charity; it's just that we are not as used to helping one another."

After the mayor finished what he had to say, his wife sat at the piano and played "Clair de Lune," one of her favorite pieces, for the guests. Paying scant attention to the music, Jacobo settled in an armchair, and thought of Bertila's pregnancy, of the bent figure of León Mitrani, and of the plans he had made to start a new life in Lima.

. . . .

XVIII

The only person who visited Jacobo Lerner while he was at Orrantia del Mar Hospital was his sister-in-law. Moved by his misfortune, she had promised herself not to abandon him to his luck. She did not know she had assumed a responsibility she didn't really want, one that filled her with anxiety each time she went to the hospital, against her husband's wishes. She would arrive with a bunch of flowers, assuming an air of optimism to crush the disgust that Jacobo's wasted appearance produced within her. From the beginning, her visits were absurd little dramas played to the same conclusion. Shaken by the depths to which Jacobo had descended, she decided to resist all possibilities of getting close to him.

Once she found him resting in the shade of a fig tree. He was leaning against the trunk, his legs bent against his chest, his hands weakly clasping his knees, his head sunk, and his eyes fixed on nothing. He had been in that position for hours, imagining he was in León Mitrani's orchard, surrounded by dry, spiny bushes, ignoring the blind woman. Sara sat down next to him. Vaguely perceiving his sister-in-law's presence, Jacobo remained motionless and said nothing. He continued thinking of Chepén, trying to look through the thick fog. Nevertheless, all the muscles in his body tightened in response to the woman sitting next to him.

She began to talk mechanically about the day before when there had been a dinner in honor of Moisés. She described in detail the atmosphere of the Hebrew Union and gave the name of every guest. Carried on by the flow of her own words, she commented on the dresses worn by the women, admiring the taste of some, and sarcastically reproving that of others. Tenderly, she spoke of how proud and content Moisés had been, seeing the affection that was felt for him by the community.

With each passing second Jacobo went deeper into regions peopled by barely recognizable silhouettes. Indefinite streets and houses waved in his mind as he relived events from the past. Sometimes he saw himself with a cane in his hand, walking down the streets of Chepén. Other times he was praying in a room with shuttered windows, or preaching in the square in front of the church. He was publicly reproved by the priest. Guards took him from his house and dragged him through the streets. He was almost murdered by the people of Chepén. They dragged him to the square in the middle of the village. He had a cloak over his shoulders, and thin drops of blood were flowing down his forehead, clouding his eyes. Above the sea of ashen faces he saw the shape of a cross raised in the middle of the square. He broke away and began to run toward the outskirts of the village, followed by guards with whips and clubs.

On his first night in the hospital, Jacobo had had this same vision. Roused by his screams, two nuns had come into his room and found him crouching on the ground, his eyes tightly shut, shaking with fear. One of them had stayed by his side the rest of the night. The next morning, Jacobo asked her to remove the plaster crucifix from his room.

Jacobo's condition continued to deteriorate. He began to argue with the nuns about certain passages in the Bible. With vehement tone, he maintained that nowhere in the New Testament are the Jews blamed for the crucifixion of Christ. Each time he started on one of his speeches, the nuns listened to him with feigned attention, shaking their heads in compassionate agreement, not needing to contradict his words. But when Jacobo began to talk to them in Yiddish, the nuns stared at him, confused and frightened, because they believed they were in the presence of someone for whom there was no help.

After three months Jacobo had not improved, so Doctor Rabinowitz decided to release him. Convinced there was nothing more that medical science could do, he asked Rabbi Schneider to help his patient. Thus, on the 3rd of August, 1934, Jacobo left the hospital still believing the spirit of León Mitrani inhabited his body. Accompanied by Doctor Rabinowitz, he went to the house of Rabbi Schneider, who had promised to exorcise Mitrani's spirit and force him to find another dwelling place.

The rabbi, who lived about four blocks away from the synagogue, received Jacobo with great warmth and offered Jacobo lodging in his house until the exorcism began to take effect. It would be a difficult task. While the maid prepared a room, he told Jacobo with excitement that it had been a long time since he had had a chance to deal with a *dybbuk.* The last time had been in Poland in 1915, when he practiced an exorcism on a young girl who thought herself possessed by the spirit of a whore.

The room they prepared for Jacobo was on the second floor. The furniture was scant and modest: under the window there was an old wooden bed, and next to it, on the wall, a shelf with a copper candelabra whose candles gave out a weak but turbulent light and leaden smoke. Jacobo saw only the maid, who came up three times a day to bring him his meals, and the rabbi, who came up every night in his black cloak and bonnet. He would ask Jacobo to undress and stand in the middle of the room, then walk around him, reciting obscure cabalistic formulas.

On the third night, Jacobo began to feel a change. Mitrani's spirit suddenly became imperious. Jacobo's condition worsened: for seven days and seven nights his body was racked by tremors; he saw strange images in front of his eyes; he thought the maid was a blind woman who came to give him evil potions; he mistook the rabbi for the priest of Chepén. Jacobo began to pray to God to come to his rescue.

One night Jacobo Lerner saw himself surrounded by insects that came in under the door, and he became convinced that God would never again listen to him. To escape from his prison he opened the window, went out on the ledge, opened his arms wide, and flexed his knees in order to jump. But Rabbi Schneider, who had chanced to come in, grabbed him by his shirttails and stopped him from jumping. It was then that Jacobo realized God had in fact listened to his prayers, and had sent an angel to stop him from fleeing so that he might become completely exorcised.

Jacobo slowly began to regain his sense of reality. Recognizable faces and places once again filled his memory, and his imagination brought up images that were familiar and well defined. He saw his parents' house. He remembered a crossing on a ship. Bertila, the son he did not know, Juana Paredes and Sara Lerner, his brother Moisés, Daniel Abramowitz who had committed suicide, Marcos Geller, buried in the Cemetery of the Angels, his whorehouse, all came to mind.

But although he was regaining his sanity, he was sunk into a deeper depression than ever, because all these images were of a reality that he did not want to confront.

On the night of the 17th of August, Rabbi Schneider finally succeeded, and the spirit of León Mitrani abandoned Jacobo's body through the big toe of his right foot. With a restless flame in his eyes, the rabbi invoked Mitrani by his Hebrew name, and asked him to depart from Jacobo's body. There was a strangely familiar tone in the rabbi's invocation, as if he himself had known León Mitrani in the old days. Then Jacobo remembered what Mitrani had told him one afternoon in Chepén: a rabbi had come to the village on a donkey and stayed at his house for a few days. He had taught him some cabalistic formulas that enabled him to fly. What Jacobo had then thought to be the product of a diseased mind now had a meaning of its own, and reentered his mind as a real fact. When the exorcism was over, Jacobo noticed that blood was flowing from a small opening in his toe.

The next morning as Jacobo was getting ready to leave the rabbi's house, the rabbi told him, in an admonishing voice, that *dybbuks* pursued those who kept a secret sin, and that if he had been possessed by a wandering soul, it was to atone for his guilt.

Jewish Soul: No. 9—September, 1935

ON JEWS IN PERU

(Exclusive for *Jewish Soul*)

FRAY GREGORIO GARCIA AND HIS THESIS ABOUT THE JEWS AS POSSIBLE COLONIZERS OF AMERICA

In his work entitled *The Origins of the Indians,* Fray Gregorio García holds the theory that there might have been a Jewish migration to America. He discusses in some detail the possible routes by which the lost tribes of Israel could have arrived from Greenland, to Mexico, and then Central and South America.

INTERESTING COMPARISONS BETWEEN JEWS AND INDIANS THAT ARE ESTABLISHED IN THE BOOK:

(1) The lack of receptivity the Indians demonstrated toward the teachings of missionaries is seen as a result of atavisms of Jewish teachings.

(2) The great similarity in the footwear and clothes is remarked upon: sandals and tunics.

(3) The use of certain religious ornaments by the Indians is seen as identical to their use in Mosaic Law.

(4) Indian facial features are such that Gomara wrote, "When the conquistadores arrived with Pizarro they found Indians with Judaic faces."

(5) The custom among Indians of raising their arms to the heavens to give emphasis to what they are saying is seen to be much like a gesture of the prophets of Israel. The messenger who spoke with Huáscar witnessed that he raised his arms high to indicate his defeat. He finds this gesture similar to the one used by Abraham.

(6) Indians, like Jews, call each other "brother," even when they are not.

(7) Indian priests anoint themselves with *Ulli,* an oil substitute.

(8) There is a connection between the Jewish and Indian customs of taking the dead to their native land, where they are buried in mounds.

FRAY FERNANDO,
Lay Brother of the Convent
of La Merced

. . . .

XX

He raised himself on the bed as if he were a bundle, rubbed his eyes, and looked into the mirror. Jacobo Lerner had just passed his forty-second birthday when he was told he was going to die. After he had heard the news he spent a full week locked up in his house, opening his door to no one, not even to doña Juana Paredes who, unaware of what was happening, had come to see him three times.

When he finally decided to leave the house, he went to the post office, a couple of blocks away, to send a letter to Samuel Edelman. Since he did not know Edelman's whereabouts, he addressed the letter to the closed store of León Mitrani, trusting that some neighbor would give it to Edelman as he passed through the town.

As soon as he had posted the letter, Jacobo returned home where, from that moment on, he lived the life of a complete recluse. With the exception of the maid who took care of the house and of Doctor Rabinowitz who came to see him twice a week, Jacobo kept away from friends and relatives, holding onto the hope that through perfect rest he would soon be well.

Only now, after two months, lying like a fetus between the sheets, rising and looking at himself in the mirror, seeing his eyes bleary for lack of sleep, his skin turned to the color of dirty parchment, Jacobo began to believe the fact of his own imminent death.

He found it very difficult to recognize the image in the mirror. At first he thought that the being who looked at him almost mockingly from the silvery surface was his brother Moisés, who had come to take away the portrait of their parents. Then he imagined the thin figure with the dark circles under the eyes was old man Wilson who, after ten years, had sneaked into the room to bring him to account. Finally, as if a mysterious hand shuffled faded engravings in front of his eyes, he saw his father's face, that of Rabbi Finkelstein, that of the priest in Chepén, that of Bertila, and that of León Mitrani.

He looked at himself in the mirror for a few seconds, forced a smile, and let himself drop back down onto the pillow. As if through a veil, he saw the body of León Mitrani, the bloody face of Daniel Abramowitz on the night they took him to the hospital, the body of Marcos Geller in the Cemetery of the Angels, and the fragmented image of his son praying on his knees in the church of Chepén.

When this last vision came, Jacobo covered his face with his hands and, mechanically, remembered the time in 1932 when Bertila had come to his house to offer him his son. He had thrown her out into the street after insulting her and telling her that he wasn't even sure Efraín was his son; he thought he had done well to escape from Chepén in time. He imagined if he had stayed in that village he would have been, at that very minute, sitting behind a counter like León Mitrani, with dust in his eyebrows and his eyes lost in the distance like an old lame animal.

Exhausted by the tangle of memories, Jacobo Lerner sank his head in the pillow, and suddenly, as if a dream had become a reality, he saw himself a well man, healthy and happy, being visited by friends and family. He saw himself wealthy, living a long life in which he fathered numerous children, as if he were one of the patriarchs in Genesis.

When he opened his eyes he examined, astounded, the loneliness of his room. After a long while, his thoughts tried in vain to recapture some happy experience in the past. He held his breath to find out how it would feel to be dead, but his eyes continued to perceive what was around him: the slight waving of the curtains, dust shot through by a shaft of sunlight, a few gray clouds escaping from the frame of the window. He closed his eyes. He felt faint. He believed they were lowering him into the grave, and he saw it was to the right of León Mitrani. As if coming from a very distant place he heard the voice of Rabbi Schneider: "All, evil and good, go down to the *seol* where they lead a consciousless existence akin to sleep." Then he saw how they threw the first shovelful of earth on him, while Father Chirinos, standing by the side of the grave, made the sign of the cross.

When he opened his eyes again it seemed to him that the room was darker. He felt a slight chill running up and down his back. He knew it was going to rain all night and instinctively he put his arms under the blanket.

Trans. by Robert S. Picciotto

Isaac Goldemberg *was born in Lima, Peru in 1945 where he attended the Jewish school, León Pinelo. He left Peru in 1962, going first to Israel for a year, then to Barcelona, and finally to New York where he has been since. He received a Ph.D. degree in Latin American Literature from New York University in 1971, and has been teaching there since 1970. He co-authored a book of poetry with José Kozer,* De Chepén a La Habana *(1973). His book of poems,* Tiempo de silencia *was published in Spain (1970), and his novel,* The Fragmented Life of Don Jacobo Lerner *was published in both New York and Peru.*

Yaacov Hasson

Iquitos:* The Jewish Soul in the Amazon — Notes of a Voyager

In the Beginning Was the Struggle

It is difficult in a short article to give the history of Jewish labor in the Peruvian Amazon. I can't pretend to do justice to such an arduous task. The history of the Jewish pioneer in this region has been magnificently written about elsewhere. The subject, however, requires much greater development before everything about it will be known. For the time being, it seems to me that one can't speak of the present situation without tracing, however superficially, the principal lines of the past.

In the middle of the 19th century the exploration, by boat, of the Amazon began. These explorations upset the balance of the region, which now allowed commerce to extend on both sides of the river into places which had once been impenetrable. Peru and Brazil by now both understood the importance of this region, and encouraged commerce and incipient industries.

India-rubber trees grew along the banks of the Amazon like an uncontrollable flood. Many ventured into these practically unexplored regions in order to extract this richness. Adventurers from every nation arrived, in numbers equal to the times of the Spanish Conquistador who had imposed his law, mobilized the native population, and had expeditiously advanced into this region, dominated by the burning fever for wealth.

Between 1880 and 1890 the first Jews began to arrive, attracted also by the richness and this fabulous region full of mystery and danger. Principally from North Africa, Morocco and Tangiers, Sephardic Jews came and formed the basis of an organized and dynamic community. They settled along the banks of the Amazon and put their energies into the birth of restless cities. Until 1910, this movement continued unabated and energetic. In improvised boats, Jews navigated the waters of the Amazon and its tributaries in the incessant search for rubber and trade.

The Department of Loreto, with Iquitos as the commercial center, began to take shape. Rubber ran in torrents, as did money. But in order to consummate their plans, a great spirit was necessary for a labor that was full of danger and illness. Everything in this world had its price. Hence, the first tombstones were soon erected, the silent and

* Iquitos is about 1,000 miles from Lima, overland by plane. It is far inland, on the Amazon River, and has a population of 111,327.

imposing testimony to the Jewish contribution to this region. Nor was their contribution only that of wealth. The Jews contributed to the social life of the area. Some of them shouldered great burdens and identified their personal hopes with the prospect of a Jewish civilization here. Consequently, Jewish life, traditional and organized, began to manifest itself. A community arose which knew religious services, particularly those pertaining to the main festivals.

After the first decade of the present century the rubber fever declined quite suddenly. Great mineral deposits in the Indian Orient hindered the progress and retarded the initial advances. About 150 Jews had arrived in the Peruvian Amazon, ninety of whom returned disappointed, but not without leaving their fertile and prosperous descendants. Others were overcome by the various sicknesses of the region and the Israelite cemetery sadly became filled. And from that time until the present the bridge between those who remained and the outside world was destroyed. Sixty years passed; sufficient time to erase every Jewish vestige in this area. So it was thought. The established Jewish community in Lima closed its heart, believing that those who had settled in the Amazon and had had their children there, had learned to love the land of Loreto, had continued the struggle of their fathers, but were now forgotten kinsmen.

Rediscovery and Its Results

Eventually some Jews arrived in this region and learned about this community from others. Those who had remained had not lost pride in their Jewish past, though they sometimes had lost its meaning. I must say, in honor to the truth, in spite of what was known in Lima—even fragmentarily—of the existence of these Jews, nothing serious was undertaken to establish contact with them or to disinter their old sentiments. But there were those, precisely those children of those Jews who had been born in the land of Loreto, those who felt in their hearts, who could not sleep peacefully, these knew that this broken bridge between the Jewish community in the Amazon and its Jewish past must be rebuilt, that new roots had to be planted to reach that other ear in them, the ear of the Biblical people.

They started to make arrangements in Lima, to wait for the right occasion. The Israeli Embassy and the Society of Sephardic Benefactors came to their aid. Thus, after long delay, a plane carried us to Iquitos, and we felt a strange mixture of curiosity and uneasy pain. Only when the plane landed did we understand how much of this extraordinary history had been true.

The Peruvian-Israeli Cultural Institute is Founded

A small delegation received us with a surprising and emotional show of friendship. Ten Jews waited for us. They grasped our hands tightly. With smiles full of friendship and emotion they told us their names: Levy! Bendayan! Benzaquén! Edery! Samolsky! and they shouted: "Shalom ubrajá!"

We were taken to the Hotel for Tourists in Iquitos. Here we were again able to see the anxiety and love in their faces. The sun and natural forces had not diminished this forgotten Jewish race. They had remained in the land of Loreto and had sprung up again like a secret murmuring of intimacy and pride in their Jewish spirit.

Others soon came, young people and older people, men and women, they surrounded us. They wanted to hear everything, first about their kin in Lima, and then about Israel. But we let them speak first to us. And they spoke! They spoke with uncontrollable emotion of how their fathers had come there, of what they had done, of how a silence of more than sixty years had covered them. Many of them had been or were dignitaries in the city, loved and respected by everyone. That day, as we discovered later, all activity ceased: business, industry, even the schools. The people stayed with us and spoke of Israel as if it had been a tabooed subject for sixty years. More arrived and were introduced, and all of us looked at one another with amazement, with veneration. At this point, The Institute for Peruvian-Jewish Culture was born. The youth organized a small center for "exiles." We explained to them, and they understood, that time must pass before new roots could be born, roots that would be capable of rebuilding the bridge that had once tied them to their past. They were anxious to listen, to learn, to feel. A strange atmosphere surrounded all of us that afternoon. We were very tired and our bodies wanted to rest. But we were gripped by a compelling intensity, which we obeyed. We began to feel a great affection, respect, admiration for these newly found Jews. We were together with our kin. Nothing more could be said. All kinds of people were there, young people, professional people, businessmen, industrialists, shy people who hung back, and forward people who were ready to pack up everything and return to the land of Abraham.

At night, after so much talk all day, they came back again. In spite of the continuing heat, they returned with renewed vigor. They prepared a banquet for us. They spoke and they listened. We presented them with a gift: the first books to begin the library of their Institute. There was a silence and uneasiness at seeing these books which told them about the history of Israel, its geography, its traditions, its customs, its continuing struggle with nature. Later, I gave them another present, this one to be given to the Comté Directivo del Colegio "León Pinelo." It was *The Illustrated History of Israel.* The ambassador of Israel, through his representative, spoke to them about the creation of Israel, of its fight to overcome obstacles and to bring its message of peace and friendship to all people. There was great emotion in their faces. A heavy silence enveloped the room. We felt these emotions even more profoundly when later two movies about contemporary life in Israel were shown. This land of their ancestors brought tears to their eyes. Young children saw the Israeli worker and the Israeli soldier. They saw Israelis dancing and singing. When the films were finished, one man stood up and said, "I know that movies often give a false view of things. But I believe that no movie can capture the depth and power of our people."

Later, when the bell for midnight was sounded in the city we were joined again by more young people. We spoke together and made plans. They proposed an "Hebraica" which would state on paper their sympathy in the struggle for the rights of their Jewish brothers in Israel and the world. They chose a director who would have the right to receive an ambassador as well as to send back with us their message of one-ness and friendship.

The night was already full. Darkness complete. We could not see the streets of the city. Some of us broke the uniform silence of the city with a Creole dawn. Magnificent guitars appeared. And Peruvian music flowed from a singer. So, after having made this beginning to bind the torn knot, Peru gave back to us the present of her music and joy. Our first day ended.

The Beauty of the Amazon

The following day, after a visit to the Rector of la Universidad Nacional de la Amazonia Peruana, Dr. Emilio Gordillo Angulo, we went to the national radio station. They agreed to let us borrow air time in order to transmit the talk we had had in el Aula Magna de la Universidad.

Afterwards, we took a boat across the Amazon. Anyone who knows the beauty and peace of the Peruvian coast, who knows the Peruvian mountains and its people, also knows that its forests are beautiful. This conjunction of geographical factors has made Peru what it is. The Amazonian lands are majestic, enormous, tense. From time to time the monotony of the forests is broken by a village or a clearing of houses indenting the land like the teeth of a saw. People saluted us from their small boats that passed us by on the river. Their passengers smiled at us with peace and courtesy. We stopped in the village of Belen and went ashore. We wanted to explore the village, speak with the people there, to feel their anxieties and their hopes. There was poverty but no bitterness. And since there was work for everyone, there was no hunger. Small children bathed naked on the beaches and dived playfully into the water. Some greeted us; others, preoccupied with their own business, ignored us. The village moved us, but it did not inspire pity. In its inhabitants we saw the gleam of hope, the desire to improve their future, a determination to master the river and to gather its wealth. We returned to Iquitos. There, from a high balcony we overlooked the city and saluted it from our hearts.

In el Aula Magna de la Universidad

Saturday afternoon, Iquitos usually bustles with activity. But our Saturday was different. Many businesses were closed, and those which remained open kept their radios going. A great celebration was taking place in la Universidad Nacional de la Amazonia Peruana. The military band played national music. Many of the civic authorities were on hand as well as people of all kinds, including the students.

I cannot imagine a more emotional moment than this. We listened to the national anthem of Peru in silence. Then, for the first time in Iquitos, and certainly for the first time in the Amazonian forests of Peru, was heard "Hatikva," the national anthem of Israel. I can't say what passed through the hearts of the many Jews who were standing on the grounds of el Aula Magna de la Universidad, but I can imagine. Latin hearts, with their great spirit, wept openly. A speech from the president of the Peruvian-Israeli Institute of Culture, Dr. Werner Levy, opened the celebration, and Señor Emilio Gordillo, the rector of la Universidad, closed it. He spoke, among many things, about Israel, its geography, its inhabitants, and of their struggle against the desert, of the important function which this small state served for international cooperation among countries.

From the Jewish Cemetery and the Airport

In the morning, after visitng the surrounding forest and seeing the work that continues to be done by the University in the struggle against nature to put it in the service of mankind, we returned to Lima. More than fifty Jews accompanied us. We stopped at the Jewish cemetery along the way, this silent witness of spirit and conquest: white, clean, quiet. We said Kaddish in memory of these souls who had been delivered to the rain forest. We walked around the tombstones. All had inscriptions in Hebrew, the history of the Jewish soul written silently in the Peruvian Amazon.

Boarding the plane, we waved our hands. Our new friends looked back at us intensely, smiling, full of tenderness. "Shalom!" they called out, "Lehitraot!" Yes! Without doubt, we would return. There, in the land of Loreto, we left friends, human beings who in this rough and angry century, had been forgotten. We will return, my brothers!

Trans. by Roberta Kalechofsky

First published in Nuestro Mundo, *Peruvian-Jewish newspaper, July, 1969.*

Yaacov Hasson *is the Director of the Office of Human Relations of the Jewish Community of Peru, and a representative of the Anti-Defamation League for the southern region of Latin America. He is also a professor of Hebrew and the Bible.*

Ben Ami Fihman

My Name Is Rufo Galo

From the third floor the camera focuses on Nalewki Street. Since 1942, through time, today—tomorrow?—this badly treated piece of film hints at the presence of a man who will always remain unknown to us, the man who secretly operates the beaten up 16mm camera equipment, bought on the black market. Only hunger travels through the rotten ghetto air, between blackened walls, through the alleyways spread thick with bodies which convulse a while and then die. In the film marred with scratches and spots, in the faded black and white, one can see several wasted corpses on the opposite sidewalk. Two dark figures with a wheelbarrow come and gather up several bodies—they walk off camera. The camera moves a bit to the right and stops in front of a doorway. On one side there is a stone lion. A statue has disappeared from the other, but the pedestal remains, where a man we can identify as "Crazy Rubinstein," the poet, sits and contemplates the lion. Slow paw after slow paw the lion rips the bodies that hang in the patio filled with shit and rats. High in the parapets, their backbones full of cunning, the vultures are watching; from time to time they fly down to tear at a shrill, scraping rat that squeaks until it is nothing more than little torn up pieces of grey skin. All at once a paw curls, becomes entangled with livid flesh; the dead man's chest is ripped open, the ribs exposed to the air and full of blood. He strolls calmly among the hanged men, taking in the sweet air that comes in intervals and sways the guilty and the ambitious. I am the lion of this court, in which I have the job of watchdog. I look back nostalgically to times in other places where my great, great grandparents fought live men in arenas or in palace dungeons. However, I value this canine privilege, the same privilege enjoyed by the dogs in the Ahab legend. Here, instead of saying, "The dogs will lick your blood," they say, "The lions will annihilate your flesh." I've seen them hanging, I've quartered them with my claws; both the politicians and their assassins. Today is a day like any other, I can account for the remains of six once-powerful men. Below, the stupid lion tears them to pieces. Between the high, turreted walls that make him invisible there is a pasture full of manure and a swamp swarming with snakes. For one hundred years I was as stupid as he is; I enjoyed the sensual greed of my paws, and believed that my power over the powerful (over their remains), would last forever. Today I am no more than a bored bureaucrat, a poor government scribe in this damned reign of the 12th century, who longs to be able to sink down into the venomous swamp. I, who long before I was a lion, was a man named Rufo Galo, and was devoured by Queen Cleopatra's dogs; I, who after having been a man and a lion, am now the scribe who appears in these letters, locked up with the lion and the executed men behind these castle walls. Typhus has filled the ghetto streets with bodies. Crazy Rubinstein (Rufo Galo, lion, scribe and crazy man), composes these last satirical quartets leaning on my stone back and makes me think. I am Rubinstein who speaks from this ornamental lion, obscure stone lion from the ancient Jewish neighborhood of Warsaw, which the bombs will destroy within a few months, when almost all the ghetto inhabitants will have died in Treblinka. I am Rubinstein, I will not survive this typhus epidemic, as Ringleblum testifies in his archives. From the third floor the camera focuses on Nalewki Street.

Trans. by Marilyn Rae

Ben Ami Fihman

Revenge

In the middle of the heat which overwhelms the circus afternoon, the lion, favoring the straw loft of his cage, examines his past, plans his revenge. He recalls his routine fierceness face to face with his trainer on the track, together with the ritual silence of the public, restrained before the fling of the rose, the trainer's last gesture of hasty delirium. Uselessly, he counts the days in which gnawing hunger has martyred him. The nights in which, year after year, the drunken trainer has tortured him beneath the always tattered circus tent, behind the German wax museum made in Colombia. He holds fierce to the memory of cities forever unknown to him in his miserable circus animal life. Because, on so many impatient occasions when they changed to a new city (which for him, instead of the boulevard city, or paper streamer city, or foam city, or caramel city, was the amphibian city, ant city, scorpion city, or mosquito city), he had to resign himself to guessing the colors of the city just left behind. No one had thought about his anxiety, about his desire to leave his cage, the suffering stench of the dirty floor, the warm circus canvas that had never left the tropics, and which fit entirely into two trucks; no one had wanted to consider his longing to stroll through parks, to know the cities, the towns, the people.

He had never known a city (he had stayed in them, but only in shadow), not even through the tourist fervor of a parade, since it had been years since they had had one; circuses (now short on daredevil artists), were more like an incarnation of contempt and of everyone's lost imagination, the irreclaimable music that no one dares to whistle any longer.

For a moment his dog eyes were lit up with a vision of the imperious ocean which he had never seen, and the jungle which his ancestors had inhabited until falling into the prolific and intelligent Chinese traps of middle Africa. The Chinese had been the ruin of his species. The Germans, with their delights in zoos and exhibits, were the executors of their virtual castration. The Jews, although unknown in relation to circus business owing to their ability for camouflage, had been the only beneficiaries. Chinese, Germans, Jews: the irremediable history.

The lion, with the rib cage of an orchestra man, feels his throat burn with the consciousness of the incest they have forced him into, for years submitting him to cohabitation with his sister. He curses the men that he knows and those that he has seen through the bars. He regrets those whom he doesn't know, those whom he has never seen and never will, as one regrets an unread novel.

For a moment he scratches a visible rib with his back paw. He foresees a relapse into epidermic desperation, a plague worse than any illness, a plague of craziness that belongs to the reign of the invisible. He stops, he shakes himself, he gives a turn which is muffled in the murmuring of the floor, his glance crosses that of his sad sister, in whose non-existent mane are jumbled flies upon flies; he goes back to his straw corner, to his thoughts.

The heat continues spreading out over the afternoon; vengeance turns round in the head of the lean cat. His enormous yawn stops at imagining the trainer's head humbled in his humid teeth, but now he closes his mouth, realizing the futility of the idea. The daily reality, his arrows, his little claws, become known to him in the form of a general and permanent itch. The lion accepts this with the same resigned patience with which he has accepted his life, far from the only two virtues which could make the years tolerable for him: heroism and comfort. He scratches where his paws can reach, he turns over and over to bring his tormented body to rest. He feels that his eyes are two imperfect triangles and he is still what he is: a circus animal.

Once his paws have finished with the highs and lows of his rib cage, he tries again to examine his motives for risking himself in a plan of revenge. He thinks of the stupidity represented by the life of the trainer, his elaborate and false ceremony of power every night, every Saturday and Sunday afternoon. There is an unequal distribution of pomp and applause. Especially if you take into account the fact that he, with his performing-animal will, which has always prevailed, is the one who really dominates and directs the act. He despises the trainer as he would a mangy dog. He realizes, however, that the pomp and applause are not reasons for envy, since they are no more than component details of the same human conspiracy. He is no longer just a circus beast that has lived like a circus beast.

This is a much more personal matter. It has to do with the intimate irresponsibility of the trainer who, instead of showing himself appreciative off-stage, is cruel and dirty, having been taken in by the myth that they both create out on the track: from the first crack of the whip to the absolute fiction of the final fling of the rose. Wrapped up in the deceit, the trainer delights in tormenting him, adding day by day, strict and unfeeling punishments, reinforced by his alcoholism.

An irksome fly buzzes around his almost moth-eaten mane, enjoys gliding down to his tail, without the preoccupied lion noticing, surprising or pursuing him. He is thinking of a somewhat Japanese scheme. To let himself die, today or tomorrow, it doesn't matter, causing economic headaches for the circus which, like all circuses commanding attention and rank, has always had a thin purse. His death would ruin the futureless trainer, who would be helpless with only one wild animal, the lioness. His tail movement, which makes an enemy of the fly, coincides with his disapproval (it is a physical explanatory gesture), of this last response to his revengeful imagination; it would be a poor vengeance, crude, decadently iconoclastic.

Remembering the metaphysical nature of all his evils, including his body, which relentlessly demands to be scratched, the animal understands the futility of a stormy, irrational, whirlwind but ineffective revenge. He considers the subtlety of the survival of both parties. He spends the rest of the afternoon planning how to manage it; after a long winding search he finds an answer: the lion does not believe in fate.

The night, which has always had something of the lioness in her, arrives, and with greater skill than ever coincides majestically with all the poetic conventions of sunset. The lion feels content. He is full of detectivesque certainty. He waits only for the moment of reaching orgasm. He keeps track of the hours using his knowledge of sound. At 6:30, in the full chaos of the circus—clients, barkers, vendors, thieves—there is a melody which imitates Dostoievski and is distinguished as a path apart: the plan that waits.

Walking to the track between the guard rails, his figure is like that of his Bengali relative; there is an illusion of disguise. His step is slow; the distance, fragile beneath his feet. He stops a moment to let his sister, who is not surprised at the triviality of the fact, go by. Again he takes the straight path populated with damp sawdust. In the cage in the middle of the track stands the trainer, brandishing his whip with innocent arrogance. When the first animal enters, the band stops, paralyzing the open mouths of the audience stuffed with caramels halfway down. The cracks from the tip of the whip direct the circular path of the lion's sister; still he doesn't come in, everyone is waiting. The trainer's disconcerted face questions him. With an irresponsible posture, the lion doesn't move. The pyrotechnic persuasion of the whip doesn't work. His stubbornness grows, sea-like, before the trainer's impatience, the tension of the waiting public, which is less than the cross bar of a delta, barely a little piece of condemned ice. From her barrel, with the obedience of a nun, his sister observes him and wonders. Neither brandished cracks of the whip, nor prodding in the side, nor successive shouts are capable of moving the lion, who now waits like everyone else. Finally, facing the onomatopeia of total silence breathing beneath the circus tent, the lion takes a first step forward, then another, he enters the cage, examines the whole silence with wolf-eyes, situates himself in the center of the cage, next to the trainer who doesn't move, looks at him, moves his tail, and with pedagogical enormity, urinates long and drawn out.

Trans. by Marilyn Rae

Ben Ami Fihman

Counterfort

My love letters are not love letters but the entrails of solitude.
—Juan Sanchez Pelaez

New York April 26th

Cesar: I am not writing to you because I am drunk (in this letter you will notice that I'm not), or because dinner (ripe avocado, spaghetti with mushroom sauce, Brie cheese and New Zealand strawberries), has upset my chemical and emotional balance. I write you because it is logical that I write you—logical: though I am sure you don't like the term. This letter which opens like a metaphysical accordion, is the final point in a process. This letter doesn't mean that I naively, stupidly think that you are unaware of all that has happened, all that has happened to me, all that I was, all that I am, how it happened—Ah, bolero, bolero! Sentimental Caribbean!—no; I know that in spite of my wandering and random rumba, you have never abandoned me. Our communication has been more or less faithful, and we've never completely lost sight of each other—luck, luck and love, don't you think? But in this letter, which in itself is something notable, you will understand (we will understand?), that even when the habitual, the well-known and the common become letters, they become something else for me. I live a peculiar, double life in correspondence (as if this orthographic existence were more precise than that of a catalogue); writing is my way of breathing in the imagination and in my nothingness arena. Because of this, the step (I know, and I restrain my alarm, that you wear Bally shoes), that you, my accomplice and friend, give as a simple testimony (I almost wrote testicle), to the temptation of a postage stamp glued with nervous and blessed saliva, is the culmination, the tear kept in reserve for the funeral of a god or for the time when the apocalypse will remove the Asiatic veil. If I were Apollinaire or Lewis Carroll, with the few words that I write, the tear would be drawn on paper, damp and bloody. Discarding the graphic, you can see, feel, believe that the tear is coming out letter by letter, painfully. But it will remain suspended and won't touch the dark earth (and this appears to be the key) until your hand pulls it out of the mailbox, opens it and reads it—letters are read with the hands—then your head can celebrate the morning, your perplexity and your euphoria, like a soldier among willows.

Dr. Sanatorio, with whom I share an adoration for Gardel and Santos Discépolo, and with whom I've talked at length about Agustín Lara, Pedro Vargas and Leo Marini, Marlene Dietrich and Edith Piaf, once cited in Paris the phrase of a childhood friend: "The first duty of a man is to appear to be happy." I am sorry for both of them, but above all, for you, as I now dishonor the duty; I prepare myself to eat my memory.

Another place, another time, let's say another person. Hold on tight, I'm getting my chessmen ready. Do you remember? Let yourself go and listen to the great buzz; it's not a hurricane, but the footsteps of alligators and fish hooks and fish and Caribes, and deck chairs that don't come untied and rivers that run backward; and mineral deposits and diamond hunters and helpless poor people, powerless in the face of memory: I try to untie my knots and not eat my memories too hastily. What nostalgia I've suffered in that street full of yellowing, blind-eyed alchemists which is Prague, letting myself, in a certain straw-hatted plaza, possess retreats, cufflinks, a country gentleman's jacket, and colored houses and conversations in the backroom; the judgement on the vampire of Dusseldorf closely followed in the pages of the Universal, the little Caracas-La Guaira train, the adulteresses of Macuto, the Miramar hotel presided over by a general in a Panama hat; Sunday Mass and walks through Calvary; Los Caobos Park; the death of Gardel announced in a theatre, and the shouts and cries of women; the Petare scandal. If I had carefully placed my internal puzzle in an archive, like Miranda, who was in Prague and failed in political plans and in merciless loves at gun-point, it would be an archive of nostalgia! and how ugly nostalgia is; like egg whites, morphine and the soup of exiles.

It's horrible to remember; it makes me feel as if I'm exhibiting a flabby muscle at a freak show, and I'm the first to boo and hiss: First, because I hate muscular fraud and secondly, so that I can escape. Anyhow, do you remember? Ranches and drizzle; fruit baskets, *chicha* to drink, boat trips to Europe; I don't remember, I wouldn't want to remember; I ran away from all that, hating it, so that I wouldn't have to go back to that neighborhood house.

Do you remember school? You could say it was grey and without perfume; you could say it was a mountain fortified by clouds which showed how indestructible it was; but which changed, the mountain being destroyed by the heartfelt laughter of sober and gymnastic health; you could say it was corridors with colonnades and the school photograph, without surrendering to the corridors of the Benefactor, my Grandfather; you could say it was corridors lit up like refrigerators or morgues, don't you think? Remember? (Enough of these descriptions, I'm not writing a novel).

Can you recall all the vulgarity of childhood imprinted on the retrospective faces of our friends, whom I will not name for you, or describe for you, in order to keep from destroying myself with the very syllable that surrounds me with the robes of vulgarity, to keep from opening a weary hollow in the Black Virgin of the Crypt? Oscar Wilde was right: Vulgarity is the conduct of others, and how badly they do in school.

Do you remember? I had an obsession for fighting with Cabezon. It was always difficult to get away from him, he was always in front of me so that I couldn't forget him; his head was a four-faced die in search of my right fist, and my fist was a billiard cue putting a rebound shot in his eyes. Ending up on the floor became a ritual of expressing freedom from the instability and misery of mankind, the symbolic extermination of that which man still has in common with the monkey, as my dear Friedrich would prophetically show. His bone marrow contained a fixed clause which promoted his growth and which was in part, although only in part, the cause of Cabezon's failures in studies, women, and other things; for many years, the only thing that kept him from a truce was the thought that the Biblical day would come in which he would defeat me, escaping from my mold, the image and likeness of Sisyphus. He bought weights, did gymnastics, rode a bicycle, threw the shot-put and javelin, tried to learn judo, boxing and karate; the only thing he didn't touch was riflery; the desire to praise his purity is irresistible. He didn't gain anything over his daily oppressor, and if today he still walks the earth, I'm sure he has not forgotten. I wouldn't want to run into him, as my moral ruin would render me helpless in an encounter.

But his obsession was not the only cause of his earlier and later failures. I want to clear the air because it's possible that we have something in common and that the fatal sap in me may have underlined and produced this monstrous epistolary finger. I believe that such interaction unleashed bodily instincts that have resulted in aversion, in hands that could have strangled Cabezon and left him miserable on the floor every day. Without knowing it openly, I hadn't then reached the pearl of the matter; he was my mirror; something in me understood and wanted to break him, smash him, tear him apart, pulverize him and bury him.

Cabezon was myopic; his body odor professed the limitation of his olfactory sense; he was incapable of distinguishing Do from La; he used all the fingers of his hand to write owing to an acute oafishness; in all, he was one of the semi-useless that nature invents with infinite cruelty; not blind, not deaf, not mute, but having ineffective senses that only half-way respond. He half sees, he half hears, he half smells, he half feels, and he feels and suffers profoundly. Absolutely helpless (the torment of the semi-useless is unrelenting), he represents, with or without subtlety, purgatory. He does not even have recourse to the resignation of a blind man or to the compassion of others. He has been condemned to *waiting*, breathlessly and without rest; condemned to high tension in order to finally make a mistake and trip up. The refinement of the heart's torture: the semi-useless has a grieving soul, unperceived at bottom; and the only thing that crops out on the surface is a magnetic helmet for attracting blows and mockery. Life and semi-uselessness contradict each other and are mutually exclusive. As a consequence: weary infanticide in a park or sudden shooting with a telescopic rifle from a rooftop—and not without reason.

I am a semi-useless like Cabezon and because of this I hated him and because of this I wrote letters after a pathetic or prophetic morning, and because of this I know what suffering is and I know the meaning of the irremediable; I know what it is to be (filthy mediocrity!), barely intelligent enough to make myself understand that I am unsurpassably coarse. But the Black Virgin ordained all this before the wound glistened, that I should first meet with my other secret and, at the least, supernatural road, madeup of words leaping over white paper in a posthumous direction; the written word dies innocent and without anger on the road to communication.

It frightens me to risk novelesque fanfare with my metaphysical, secular accordion; I hate the art of the generous and the bored which is the novel, the salvation of editorials and of men who travel by train; I sin because it is inevitable for me to do so when I define myself and give flesh to our spiritual roasting. Radically I make a letter, or I don't make it at all; put on your swim suit: I have a feeling that this will not be your last submersion into my miasmas. Your susceptibility can go to the devil; I suffer more and I don't stop pounding little needles into myself like a Saint Sebastian miniature. I should write to you about the weather and the lions in the zoo; I should tell you what's new in horror films; I should dedicate a poem to you; my hand should drag you through a thousand spy adventures: I can't do it, that isn't why I'm writing. I write to you constructing my oxygen mask, without which I'd end up very badly. (In passing, there are two books you have to buy: *A Hundred Camels in the Courtyard* and *The History of Chimneys in Galicia*).

At that time of youth, homicidal teachers who taught stupid little boys and whorish little girls roman numerals, how to draw a map of Venezuela which is an anvil with these and those boundaries, and who confronted them with books that competed with each other in their tediousness, by tragedy, my happiness an unhappiness howled, unedited.

If at this unalterable point at which we are all alone, I should say something about Juanita, the verdict would be: insipid but tolerable. There was something about her face which bordered on the dream-like; but I had never talked to her: I preferred Joel's devilled sandwiches. One tearless night, it must have been around six o'clock, I found myself hypnotized by a blue, yellow, or black crack in the wall of the study, when they told me: "Someone on the phone for you." I had no feeling for this person on the phone, with whom I had broken before we had a chance to know each other. Body cold, heart pounding, I went into the kitchen and grabbed the phone; I heard a little mosquito voice running behind my ear inside the receiver. Too lame to identify, falling into an abyss which opened at the top of my stomach, like something glimpsed in half-sleep, I pronounced an indefinite goodbye and hung up. I felt as though everyone were looking at me and as though I were guilty; I knew that my life had been hopelessly obliterated. Mama looked at me, the cook looked at me, the dog looked at me, the roof made a church-face, the floor grimaced like a deceitful carpet, the furniture interfered; and when bathed in a polar sweat, I tried to return to my philosopher's stone refuge, to set myself at once before the blue, green, oily, romantic or parricidal crack, it winked at me, collapsing the ruins even further. Juanita. My eyes never spent another second on her. I prevented chance meetings. The beloved shadowy region of my soul became irritated; disbanded ravens, the inner coat in tatters, slavery, galleys, the ship thrown from one side to the other in the eye of the storm, the rigging made noise, the sails whined and whined, the waves rose up, up, lightning crashed through the foam, disappeared and reappeared in the foam, a flashing spike between the large, threatening clouds. Goodbye peacefulness of hidden cracks; drink water, lower the head, look up, the ocean's bitter saliva in my face, breast on the writing desk, graves, graves full of thistles; I tripped over the thistles and I fell, flying through a tapestry of anemones, to the ship, and to the sea I traveled, disturbed, my days growing dark, the teachers talking, the teachers snarling, the children whispering; I am disturbed; shit, I think, I loved Juanita and my life was a failure.

I repeat: forgive me for departing from my letter writing tone; but the fact is that I have arrived at that irreparable point at which one is completely alone; and setting the fuse that has saddened or enriched my life with these successive epistolary turbulences, impenetrable for others (and unchained), I let myself be overtaken by the violence of memory, the mercenary inventor of time. On the other hand, I can tell you from the edge of this abyss, the ravine of the years, that I loved Juanita, and that for the first time I was in love.

I drew away from her as much as I could, every day I ate more devilled sandwiches with satisfaction, with somersaults, hastily, taking many bold and unscrupulous mouthfuls.

Love! There were legs and pamphlets. I walked around loving, I ate more devilled sandwiches with Coca Cola and more Coca Cola, and with the most severe condemnation of dialogue.

One morning—in the early hour of dawn and with the sort of midnight sun on the horizon that my letters must resemble—my right hand wrote out a vile or happy note, whose contents I can't think of even today, but which embraced that magnificent, dirty face of that insipid but tolerable telephone caller. There I landed and took flight with Juanita who didn't find out (and find herself buried): I solved the labyrinth (very Peruvian) into which an inconsiderate phone call had placed me. First woman to put her sickly, opal finger into the groove of the brain which ruined the twelfth century troubadors. Dead love kept as good as new with pencil and paper. I enjoyed myself without realizing that what I was enjoying was my destiny and my ecstasy sealed, irreversible, following in the tracks of a bus that let Juanita off at the doors of school, where she bought peanuts before going to classes. Since Juanita, I don't talk to those whom I love, I write her letters; I don't kiss her, I write letters; I don't open her legs and caress her vulva, I write her letters; I don't exercise the archeological instrument, I write her letters; I don't visit the Rio de Janeiro of her body, I write letters; I don't listen to orgasmic shouts, the milky reward, I write letters; I don't eat flowers at her feet, I write letters; I don't sob falling to her side more alone than ever and like a tango; I write letters.

Cesar, Cesar, listen to me, Cesar forgive me for turning this letter into a bad novel; my unhappiness, my lateral fate, my definition is just that, and it began in a flood. Why was my declaration un-said (sad) and written, causing the perforation, foundations of my unhappy (un-spoken) future, of my life on the edge of life, never saying what should be said and not written, and writing it without saying it aloud so that the words could die en route to communication, with a flood of tears from within and shouts from the depths. Was it a masochistic, or perhaps amorous but not matrimonial, mortal pleasure? I don't know: unruly destiny. My love builds its own breakwaters; that is, it has prospered in messages sometimes sent, sometimes not, always dead. Distance and love or distance that is love.

Distance is no joke; even less of a joke in the aftermath with pile upon upon pile of loved women like so many dolls in the attic. Juanita was the first filly on my erotic carousel. From little year to little year, my skin felt precise sensations and frisked about with the linguistic game of fantasy and memory. I still maintain with perfect lucidity, that love's opportunity is to be found in distance, and that masochism and self-love, in addition to the loved object reduced to stimulation and little more, are of prime importance.

I imagine that you glimpse something of this development in me, uncertain and in darkness, but no one can touch the future until it happens—remember the captains who don't shipwreck until they shipwreck, the men who don't die until they die—lacking a strict theory, I went from enlightenment to enlightenment with the vertigo and power of a highway at night, lights high above, with traffic going in the wrong direction. Look Cesar, I've been around and have seen a number of things and events; catastrophes, erupting volcanoes, unbelievable weddings, earthquakes, moons gathered in Arab books, coral beaches, civil wars, final exams, black markets, lovers who have nothing in common, and in spite of having witnessed with complete tranquility, nature, God and man untied simultaneously, and having earned a certain delivery to glory, the esoteric distinction of the dachshund, that I share with others in our long history which moves crablike; and in spite of my having impenetrable armor since that day in which my father called me to his side, pulled out a yellowing eye tooth with his fingers and ordered me to pound it into the nape of his neck, so that he would remain paralytic, and could renounce the velocity of the world that made him dizzy: I am not strong enough to look at the immovable, tragic carousel which Juanita, together with my father's death, pushed into movement, without becoming weak and crying like a wounded vulture in front of the family mausoleum. Oh! my Indian cows! She was a literature teacher, English immigrant, one two three, a waltz rhythm, bon bon boxes full of clouds, rainbow, cornucopias, horses with horse laughs, up and down, centurions, hippogriffs, and one two three, violins, the carousel goes round to the point of nausea, sun on icecream, Helen, Marisela, veils, grey fuzz, one two three violins and scarabs, bass and contrabass, the carousel goes round, mixing Fragonard colors, and holding on to the wild animals—one two three four five six, little breasts, hips, gray, red, black, blonde fuzz, one two three four five, stirrups inverted between the legs so that I can mount the horse of indifference, of sweet meat waters, one two three, waltz rhythm, cotton candy, the center with little rings, unchained, escaping into forgetfulness, one two three, waltz rhythm, piano chords, the violins come in; my eyes resting on his back as though he were a lantern, crying inconsolably; Ah! my Indian cows!

April 27th

I interrupted this letter and I'm picking it up again after revising it. Last night I was up writing until 4 A.M. After that I couldn't do anymore; the temperature wear and tear is tremendous. However, I've started and there's no turning back. But I have to correct my style, my novelesque deviations; it is very difficult to unmask myself, especially if I use disguises: specifically your disguise. I use convention because solitude makes it inevitable, quivering banners of madness. My progressive ostracism is not fatal and unconscious; rather, it comes from the exercise of will and the diaphanous syllogisms that wink at me in the limbo of the semi-useless.

I was talking about my love carousel. (I left out the star with the golden feet, EVA; I include her now because she was pretty and blue-eyed). All through adolescence, I wrote anonymous letters, avoiding impossible confrontations with the women I dreamed of at my desk, on the bus, or in the sacred confines of the bathroom. The literature professor, Helen, Marisela, EVA, all showed me the way to the precious instrument that in the long run, made things bearable for me: masturbation. One could say: anonymous love at one extreme and solitary masturbation at the other.

I left Caracas and my adolescence, going away on the pretext of buying merchandise for my widowed mother's toy shop. I began to navigate through third rate hotels, always further away from the valley, from Avila, from the outlying farms—Sanatorio has told me they no longer exist.

The world was a huge river we traveled on by bicycle; I would not deny that the futurists and their followers were hypnotized by speed, but there was still room for carriages; and seated in them, we saw the obscene trails of cars and little propeller planes go by. How many travellers "listened" to the sunset; how many people were thrilled with Gallito de Oro; passing over the strident music of Schoenberg and Stravinsky; Warsaw was still Warsaw and on the Vistula, a town called Prague was budding; explorers didn't run out of virgin land, and archeologists had enough ruins to last forever; Germany preserved things in zoos; people danced the tango and bolero and the blacks played jazz; there was talk of the Far East; in fact, that was the moment in which I passed from being a not-so-calm gentleman, to being a knight errant.

It happened that I went from masturbation to accompanied masturbation: whores. In their habits, the whores harmonized with a world of romantic frisking. They weren't whores just for business reasons; they chose their work, and with the callousness of their social marginality, they took hold of the silent thread that ran through the centuries, rivalling the prestige of Jezebel and Cleopatra.

I gave free rein to my weaknesses and my mounts dragged me by the head to perversions which couldn't be reconciled with the light—and I understood then that, like truck drivers, whores and vampires, I belonged to the night, I went on to excesses that I have paid dearly for. My heart was violated by indifference to domestic scruples. I was visited by women who were old; by thin women who nail you to their pelvises, hunchbacks, bad smelling women; women who were blonde, pretty, fat bottomed, flat-chested, masculine, one-eyed, lame, hard, soft, black, crystalline, made of china; religious women and women who had become pregnant and who had miscarried.

We will see! said the blind man. The libertine of letters, the monarch of dissipation died guiltlessly. My calendar wasn't disturbed; and one third-rate-hotel-night, there erupted in the middle of my equilibrium, which blushed because of its fragility, EVA, nude and white, with wounded chewed tits and the shadowy treasure hidden between her legs, climbing the balance beam of half-sleep: EVA; EVA without a top; little creature of my light; and depositing her little pieces, her little golden pieces over the rug, she led me into an empty room, where I was exposed, without a springboard, without my swimming pool.

I wrote at dawn, before and after masturbating; I wrote during my fabulous and always more gigantic meals; I wrote on trains; in King of Denmark Park; in cities and on ships; I wrote, leaving my undigested past (distant, so distant), passing through a corridor of oily walls that took me away from the passions that impassioned the city. All the cities were one city; my journeys, one journey; my labor and the demands I made on myself were one. I wrote letters that almost parodied themselves although I lived in them, a wild boar coming from the palm groves. I salvaged this manuscript territory *from the rock of the rock* of tenderness; and shipwrecked against caresses, and being salvaged from caresses I shipwrecked against passion; and being salvaged from passion I shipwrecked against violence; and being salvaged from violence I had to shipwreck against necrophilism by correspondence; and without being a tautological bruiser, I stopped there. My sails billowing in the storm toward a deep, far away sea, a monstrous lake.

From backwater town to backwater town, from capital to capital, eating like a hungry bear, and accompanied by great catastrophes which gave me a reception without fail; I ate; I was silent, and I wrote. An airplane crashed; Käeseschnitten; twenty-one thousand died in an earthquake; tacos, enchiladas; thirty terrorists were shot: fillet of meat with Chevreuil sauce; a madhouse burned down and the patients were carbonized during their sleep cure; Alexandrian camels have something wrong with their humps: Paratha, Falafel; destruction of the Doblegado bridge: cat soup and cuttle-fish ink; invasion of doves in Katmandu: rice with Cobra; battle of the Kidneys: Campurriano chicken; shipwrecks, tigers, accidents, amputated babies, cyclones, floods, bombs, grape-shot, court judgments, ruins, poverty: apple Dauphine, chestnut puree, fillet of tongue, chicken in almonds, partridges with chocolate, Tin Suey Kai, Shangai spiced meat, lamb Curry, Goulash—and letters, letters, letters.

Letters on napkins, in notebooks, on toilet paper, by typewriter, by pen, by pencil...

April 28th

Last night I went on with the letter I began to write to you the day before yesterday. I didn't keep at it for too long because I didn't have the patience. What a night last night such a nightly night; if it hadn't taken place, I could not see your clear face in this letter, which has as its point of departure a vague, helpless intuition of great urgency, of the last round. If I had gone on last night I would have said something like this: that my landscape was formed by masturbation and letters, whores, and coarse gastronomy. That I have lost myself in the letters, and that you have disappeared too. That I have committed suicide in every greedy letter; that I have killed you beyond mercy.

What happened when I went out into the street is a black reflection of the stage at which I've arrived, my irreparable point. I've spent three days writing a letter; unusual for these times when the telephone governs the uneasiness of distance. The epistolary tradition of long beards remains today in perhaps only two or three vestibules of Prague, although not in Warsaw which was destroyed at the instant of its greatest disgrace and grief; what truth is there to the rumor concerning a certain Morel of German origin, a specialist in venereal disease, and supposedly the greatest epistolary writer of the last twenty-five years? I lack reliable information. We know that what is being accomplished here will stop your breath; you first and particularly next the specialists of this genre, within a century. It has to do with an unheard of juggling, of an intermingling of functions, with the final question of feeling.

For the first and last time I am writing you. I'm not writing about one more stage of my life, I'm writing about *the* stage. With these pages I construct my beast, I station myself in its entrails and I devour myself; there can no longer be any outside recreation; with this beast and with you I will die. Last night I found out that there are no rails or roads at the irreparable point; the worlds, the carousels, the wax museums, the circuses have all been reduced to disgust, and I feel this humiliation with the very soles of my feet.

I left the letter for the alcoholic rats of temptation. First, I went to Chinatown; a nest of spies that coil innocently among the tourists. I was bathed in hot mustard seed, almonds parading over mild chicken tacos, greens curled up in the claws of parrot chili sauce, multitidinous handfuls of rice cohabiting with herbs, peas and mushrooms, fried vermicelli (immemorial inhabitants of the Great Wall), that come together to prevent the intermingling of races, sweet sauces, and soy sauce dressed up like an ancient executioner of Slow Death. Caresses of tea, and the final kiss of almond cookies.

From Chinatown, with a card from a Buddhist temple (*The solitary walk in silence beneath the starry heavens*), I went in the direction of Broadway, and with my food in my head and not in my stomach—carnival, *danse macabre,* a festive assault on reason—I went up the stairs of Tango Palace.

I paid the dollar cover charge; behind the door, black lights emitted confusing forms of bottoms, howls of exaltation, bosoms offering battle for the daring capture, a line like an avalanche contained only by the veranda, the boundary between moral and monetary ruin, between a puppet show of sex and the plain beer at the end of the bar. Darling, come here. Darling. Daarling. Let's talk. Darling. You were a boy in Caracas, you loved Juanita, you were in Tango Palace, my darling, Juanita was not in your school, co-ed schools didn't exist, neither did Coca-Cola, you can't walk on water; slips and stumbles toward the bar or toward the fat cats, the terrible human waste to the right; daarling, let's talk; surprise attacks and the tragedy of impulse; breakwaters without sails, hopeless wrecks, darling. The somnambulists overpower the footman, taking him by the feet, and in the back of the mind the literature professor and thousands of letters murmur; we are going from the gesture of pretending to hold on to the glasses of beer, to certain hugs and certain proposals, files of teeth on parade, endless piano that finishes in the right hand which searches in the right hand pocket for the $6.50 to pay for half an hour of dancing.

Bolero: well you know how it goes; no, I don't know; if you give me a tip we'll come closer; no, I don't know, get out of here professor, woman, get out of here Juanita, get out of here EVA, leave me alone, I don't want to hear anything of Caracas, I live on a different planet, in different places, I live punishing those who devour love letters, yes, yes, today you can travel to Caracas in four hours, I don't want to go, kiss me, kiss me a lot, as if it were the last time, twenty dollars more and we'll really have fun, get away tears or I'll flood the Guaire river, take twenty dollars so I can cry on your shoulder before tearing it to pieces, until your skin is like what the literature professor's skin must be like now, or EVA's, EVA who was born in Coro, a face of sand; but you know darling if you make me another gift I'll go topless, my life air-mail paper, my libertine life like an air-mail envelope; my life take your twenty dollars and make your tits into two pillows so I can sleep, die without fetus; those were the days, my friend we thought they'd never end; bah! change the record, boleros, boleros, nothing but boleros; love do you really want to enjoy it? give me twenty more and I'll show you, twenty more, you didn't go where she goes, Juanita, you didn't crave me with that professorial right hand, you didn't open my fly and you wouldn't do it for twenty dollars, Marisela, you wouldn't put a rubber on me like diapers EVA, you wouldn't caress me with the lullaby of your hand to the point of delirium Helen, I'm crying, I'm crying, I'm crying like a bolero, I'm crying with my whole body, she moves me and I cry without compassion in her hand, in the rubber, I change the record, clock don't mark the hour because my life is being snuffed out. The half hour is over and I hastily go downstairs and I'm gone.

That wasn't all—I ask you for the eighth time to forgive these defective novelesque deteriorations; could I say it any other way? I can't find any. I'm the same age as my father was when he died, and Cesar, I'm so far away! What a pathetic act I'm living out, what a precipice, what clarity! I see the serpent shimmering, I will drag myself down with the poison of a single attack, I will become an acrobat. Forgive me, forgive me.

Bar, alcohol, forgive me, alcohol. I succumbed to a whore ignoring the fact that New York whores are the worst; they've always been the worst, since before the flood. I gave her my lean dollars (I don't have any more and bankruptcy won't help me) and we went over to Tenth Avenue to a building that was being wrecked. Uselessly, we fought in the dark, on a mattress on the floor. We stopped, went down to the street.

Two men stopped in front of us and, waving an arrest ticket, they jolted me with obscene questions. In the station, the police continued the investigation and took down my name. Short step to the paddy wagon and a cell on the East Side.

Next to the latrine (I couldn't think in that slat board bed), accompanied by the deathly complaints smeared on the walls, I finished my business and the letter which I finally completed in my hotel room.

Prostitution; period. That's it; forgive me; I spoke without changing to my next place of refuge; I chose it at the end of an exceptionally long theatre evening: excuse me; I looked for my father in the back of the stage. forgive me, there was a perpetual movement ordering me to nail the tooth into the nape of his neck: forgive me.

I closed my eyes for two hours (and what if God went mad?), and I got up with the vertigo of the fall of the world after a frenetic turn of the moon in bottomless space. At center stage my father shouted to his son: nail the tooth into me! I can't bear anymore! and his son awoke from a cosmic nightmare in which no one could help him. The son approached an understanding with his father; his son was in a Manhattan jail for paying a whore.

Cesar: the step is the step of the world in the abyss.

My strange journey unraveled across the night, going out of the reach of years, flying over the abyss. The earth was round and floated alone. I was alone on the lonely earth with my origin, and my father who had pounded a tooth into his neck so that he wouldn't have to go on alone on a lonely earth. The jailer opened the door. He wasn't interested in my weariness. They handcuffed me to a black man; the guard: cruel joke, of course.

They moved me from one place to another, from cells to cells, from unhappy faces to sickness, to the crime, to the miserable ones: forgive me. They interrogated me over and over again in a building which had hidden doorways and high, uneven passages; they emptied my pockets and they confessed my crime: forgive me. An engine of masturbation, letters, whores, father: forgive me. Above, the judge worked his lips without stopping. It was my turn and I had the audacity to not know the answer; and the judge repeated the allegation in the drunkenness of his anger. I didn't answer and they held back his lordship, who was climbing over his desk to smash me. At the third try, someone prompted from me the "yes" that I shouted. My pockets couldn't help me with the fine and they sent me away with a citation to pay the fine. Forgive me.

For blocks and blocks I walked, analyzing: forgive me. I realized that the carousel, circus, and the wax museum hadn't done anything since the past but revolve around the center: a great self-love. Concessionless self-love which nothing or no one can reduce. In loving, I had wanted others to love me; in eating I had adored myself, in writing I had written to myself.

The lesson of the father was learned by the son after a cosmic dream; the letters were a treason allowed as an error of youth; the alliance with prostitution was ended in order to sow disorder in families; the figure of my father brought to the front of the stage said that the tooth was inevitable.

We have touched on the real meaning of this three-day letter, Cesar. It's the gurgling of a drowned man; the inward and transcendental exhortation of self-love; I strain my neck writing to you; if I've misled you through gluttony and letters, I rescue you without going back because I am nothing more than your reflection; and tomorrow when you walk through the halls of the hotel to get your mail, I'll go with you; and being bound to you in these lines which you already know as well as I do, we'll never again separate; the whole tooth will be buried in the nape of your neck.

Cesar

Trans. by Marilyn Rae

Ben Ami Fihman *is an attaché in the Venezuelan Embassy, serving in Bógota, Columbia. Like Elisa Lerner, he is familiar with the New York scene, particularly the sections of lower class hotel life which he draws upon for much of his writing.*

Isaac Chocrón

Break in Case of Fire

1. Dear Chocrón:

Today I thought of you. I was seated alone at a table in the Gijon Café, watching the clamoring of the Spaniards, without any desire to find out what they were talking about, when a newspaper man who sometimes sits with me and tells me horrors of Caracas, came up to me. For a few miserable years, he lived at Candelaria Plaza, waiting for the stroke of good luck which he, together with thousands of his compatriots, had come to look for in our country. In order to survive, he took whatever work he could find, including a job as a waiter in the "Alvarez" restaurant, where you and I had lunch together many times. The first and second times that he shared my table in the Gijon, he insisted that he had seen me back in Caracas, and I played along saying, "probably," until he suddenly mentioned you and remembered us both seated at one of the tables he served. Since then, you have been our bridge. Every time he sees me he asks after you as if the three of us were close friends. I know that you and I are in spite of our different interests, or perhaps I should say in spite of the fact that you have always known exactly what you wanted to do, while I have always done exactly what's been least difficult for me. Always, until the earthquake, that is, and I suddenly found myself with nothing to do. We never talked about that in Caracas and I prefer not to now because I think it's more pleasant to tell you that, thanks to the waiter, I call him that because I still don't know his name (he's told me several times and as many times I've forgotten; I don't remember the names of people who don't interest me), thanks to him I met your friend, Catena.

The two of them arrived and, after shaking my hand, they sat down across from me. I invited them to have something to drink and the "waiter" asked for a shot of whiskey, while Catena ordered white sherry. The waiter went on and on in this charming tone so common among Spaniards, and spoke of all the banalities that fill their mouths. You know what I mean: conscious of their fossilized mediocrity, they like to form opinions and pass judgments on everything that can be changed in the world. Because their surroundings don't change, they like to theorize about other changes that occur on the planet. They don't talk, they gush. But Catena didn't say a word, or rather, he said only two things. When he sat down he asked, "And how is Chocrón?" and a few seconds later, taking advantage of the fact that the waiter was getting some fresh air so that he could go on ranting and raving, he added: "He wrote me that you were coming."

When I got up to say goodbye, so did Catena and the two of us went out into the dying afternoon of this Madrid summer. It must have been eight-thirty, and still night hadn't set in. Along the Gijon sidewalk going toward Cibeles and all along the wide walk-ways that form La Castellana Avenue, people were walking as if drinking the air. Here the people don't walk fast and they don't run in front of one another as they do in Caracas' narrow streets. These people slide along, they stroll, the pairs arm in arm, walking deliberately as if in a slow motion movie. Since time doesn't exist, it doesn't matter that time passes.

Catena and I walked as far as Sol, without saying much, he choosing his words in order to avoid touching on tender subjects. "It's not quite so hot now." "Next month everyone will come back to Madrid." "They're still celebrating La Paloma Saint's Day," and I realized that you had written him a good deal about me. This isn't a reproach. I'm grateful to you for your goodness as I'm grateful to Catena for not having submitted me to an interrogation. When we crossed the wide Sol Plaza and we came to the newspaper kiosk, I bought "Time" and "Le Monde" and Catena asked me if I was thinking about going to Paris. "Probably," I answered him, just as I had done before with the waiter. Lately, I answer many things, saying: "Probably." We crossed the street to a taxi stand and there I said goodbye. Almost without looking at me, and very casually, Catena said: "You have my number, don't you? Whenever you like. . ." I thanked him, shook his hand, and got into a taxi. Now I'm in the hotel. Tomorrow or the next day I'll call him and invite him to lunch. We get along well. I like his discretion and his generosity. Thanks for having given me his telephone number.

What else? I haven't said what I was going to say. What I wanted to tell you—and this is the reason for this letter—was that on my outing with Catena I felt you at my side. It was as if I were walking with you on our Urdaneta Avenue, at two in the afternoon after eating, when there's no one in the streets and the heat is terrible. We would walk slowly, with our stomachs full, while it drew closer to the time for me to go back to the Chancellory and for you to go home, most likely to have your siesta. Once you told me that your friend Cabrujas had said that for him, Urdaneta Avenue was the center of the world. I laughed, looking at that street full of dirty ads and insignificant little shops that sold pots and pans, where the few people on the street walked very quickly. Annoyed, you asked where I thought the center of the world was, adding as if to hurt me: "The Chancellory?" I remember that I answered you: "My home," and you called me bourgeois because I chose the most comfortable spot where I had Rebecca and 'Little Face' to protect me from the world. You always called him 'Little Face,' and I was glad you called him that and not Jacob. I still like it.

One of the things I have to do now is go back and choose my center of the world. But in order to choose it I have to have some possibilities. I hope they may appear. I know that it's not La Castellana or the Puerta de Sol, in spite of the fact that I felt you with me while I walked there with Catena. I promise to call him.

I hope you are well. I send you a big hug.

Daniel.

2. Dear Cousin:

The trip was neither as long nor as bad as you had predicted. Thanks to the sedatives, which I'm still taking daily, nothing seems to affect me, especially not a plane full of people who ignore you if you stare fixedly out the window. In planes, privacy is respected more than one would think. It's true that the Briceño couple bent over in their seats from time to time in order to arch over and look and smile at me (they practically touched me in the side). And the old man, after an insipid lunch, leaned over to ask me how I was. Receiving no more than a half-smile from me, or more likely, a grimace, he said something like, "time cures everything."

Time. It goes. It's true. Yesterday was Wednesday, tomorrow will be Friday and each day has its own morning, afternoon and night. I go along with the daily rituals of any civilized being: I wake up at nine (here in Madrid nothing happens), I shower, I shave and then I brush my teeth, I comb my hair, I dress and the breakfast I ordered the night before arrives: tea with milk, toast with butter. Then I go out, I buy the A. B.C. and sometimes go to the Retiro park to read it sitting on a bench. In the mornings the park is almost empty, except for the gardeners watering plants or raking the paths. I sit down in the shade of a tree and go through the pages of the magazine which is the most important daily periodical in Madrid and which eternally reviews the doings of the decrepit Spanish aristocracy.

I swear to you I'm not feeling badly. After breakfast I swallow a couple of pills that good Oscar prescribed for me, and that give me a terrifying serenity. I see myself as if I were another person who goes along beside me. I observe myself. I walk along slowly, peacefully, as if someone had asked me to go for a stroll, and when I sit down and open the A.B.C., I go through the pages at a good rate. From the Retiro, I usually go to the Prado, and I'm getting to know almost all the rooms. I parade in front of the pictures, almost all of them portraits facing front. Curious, how such a large part of the history of art is portraiture. People and more people, all looking to the front as if they were passengers, not on a plane but on walls. Or as if they were people looking into a mirror. I suppose that the mirror would be the spectator. Don't laugh; I'm becoming philosophical. I express opinions.

I'm writing you these opinions because I don't have anyone else to tell them to. I still haven't called the friends of the friends who recommended them to me. I'll do it, but first I've preferred to spend a few days alone. I haven't even called Melilla. Every morning I tell myself that I should do it, knowing that they expect my arrival and must be worried. I don't think it would occur to them to call Caracas. Who would they call?

What I want to do, what I am doing, is preparing myself. Don't think that I lack courage or decision to face new friendships here in Madrid, or to face the family in Melilla, now that I have all this serenity from Oscar's little pills. Neither is it aversion or apathy, because if I wanted to I could leave today for Caracas or Paris or London or China. I can come and go as I please. I can drop this inconclusive letter or finish it. I can send it to you or let it lie around for a few days or tear it into four pieces and throw it into the basket at my side. It's a willow basket, the glory of Spanish artistry. Very pretty. It adds a homey touch to this hotel, whose manager welcomed me saying: "This is your house. I'm at your service." The "at your service" took me back for a moment to my childhood in Maracay. Now I sometimes think about my childhood: all that training, all that education while I was growing up, to convert me into what? Into a man dressed in a black suit, white shirt and black tie, with two briefcases and a portfolio, also black, who must have looked like an accountant or a lower court judge when asking for his reservation at the desk in a hotel entrance. I don't think that either the manager or the workers have any idea of my real situation. I doubt that in the Madrid press they've dedicated much space to what happened, because then they'd have to omit the news about charity bazaars and teas and banquets for the future monarchs. Since they looked at me so cautiously and treated me too carefully, the next day I dressed in grey, keeping the black tie in case I should run into some Venezuelan on the Gran Via. I like walking down this avenue because the steep hill tires me. I arrive at the hotel tired for the night and I almost feel as though I don't need the sleeping pills in order to sleep. I should tell myself to (little by little) get rid of the three bottles I put on my dresser. It irritates me to know that they control my temperament. I'll throw them out after my trip to Melilla. I suppose it will be a quick trip: coming, selling, going.

Thanks for your letter and for your decision to write instead of calling on the telephone. Reading and writing are less painful than hearing. At this time, either of our voices would be disturbing. We can say more to each other with more control with the written word. I never wrote letters much before, but I like doing it. It's enjoyable to fill up one page and then another, with a certain dominion of thought. Thanks also for your visits to the cemetery. Thanks so much. The business of the gravestones can wait. We will wait. Kisses for the children and a brotherly hug for you and for Oscar.

Daniel.

3. Dear Graciela:

Thanks for your affectionate letter which I just received this morning. Affectionate and long, giving me so much news about so many acquaintances. I spent almost all lunch time reading it. I go to a different restaurant for each meal and I try to arrive as early as possible so that they won't wrinkle up their faces at me when they see that I alone will take up a whole table. They always seat me in some corner or right next to the wall, and as soon as I sit down I open a magazine or, like today, the envelope with your letter and I try to read. I say "try" because I inevitably start to hear the conversations around me. I live, listening to the conversations of others and I've begun to talk to myself. Even worse, I like the conversations I have with myself. Fortunately they are silent and don't attract attention, but who knows if one of these days my voice won't burst out? I suppose that the waiters would serve me very rapidly and they would arrange to remember my face and not let me in again. Because of this, I sometimes think that solitary people like myself should be allowed to approach others, especially in restaurants, and say to them: "Could I listen please? I promise not to interfere or interrupt. Only listen. I will be as quiet as a chair or this vase with daisies, or the salt and pepper shakers, or the sugar bowl. I promise to be just one more element on the table where you have sat down to talk so richly." I, who have so much free time (so much? I have all the time in the world!) should go to a printer and have some cards made up to say: "I would like to thank you for not mentioning the word earthquake in my presence and for not asking about my family. The two things are the same for me." I should carry a number of these cards in my pocket and hand them out to everyone I know, like the deaf-mutes and the blind people do. I should do it. I probably will do it one of these days. One of these days. . .

But why am I telling you these depressing things? Not because I'm depressed—on the contrary, I'm calm and the days go by without anything important happening. I told you all this because I remembered when the waiter, hearing my accent, asked if I were American. Here, everyone who doesn't pronounce their c's as th's is an American, while those who speak English are North Americans. They also call us "hispanoamericans," perhaps to revive the umbilical cord, but they never call us "Latin Americans" because that is a term of contempt. As I shook my head affirmatively and before I could open my mouth to tell him what I wanted to eat (always the same: "beefsteak platter, green salad, no dressing, bring the vinegar and I'll put it on"), the waiter asked me: "Where are you from?" Everything was so quick that I automatically answered: "From Venezuela." "Ah!" exclaimed the skinny man with the big eagle nose, "then you were saved from the terrible earthquake. What a tragedy, sir! We knew about it here because the brother of the owner was saved by some miracle. He lived in Altamira where everything was demolished, but he and his family were lucky enough to have gone to the beach. When they got back, nothing! They didn't find anything, no apartment, no anything. But they have money and people with money. . ." I took advantage of this conversational lag to ask for beef steak and salad, and as soon as he started to leave he turned around to ask me, "You didn't lose anyone?" and seeing my impassive face, added: "Not so bad. You are calm. I'll bring your lunch right away. You shouldn't be on a diet. You're in Spain and here we have tripe you wouldn't believe!" With an impassive face I returned to your letter and the waiter disappeared through the swinging kitchen doors.

My impassive face. What would that cadaverous family man, with yellow coloring never exposed to the sun (And how is our red hot sun, dear Graciela? Do you remember our days on the beach? Jacob and your Perlita running as if to chase the waves that broke one after another, and we sitting under the umbrella talking and dozing off. . .), what would he have done hearing me say: "No, in my family there were no miracles. I was the only miracle and that was because, tired of so much siesta, it occurred to me to go to the American Book Store (North American, of course), in order to buy the latest issue of "Time." Rebecca sometimes joked with me saying: "You read the whole thing every week and you don't realize that every week you have your brain washed" and if papa heard her (poor papa, his was a really circumstantial death: we think that his only intention of visiting us that afternoon was, as he would say, "to make a fuss over Jacobo"), if papa heard Rebecca going on about "Time," he defended me saying: "Why shouldn't he read it? It is an international magazine. Besides, this is what he was educated for at Columbia University." For this, papa? In order to read "Time" so religiously that, it being already Saturday afternoon, I felt it necessary to buy it before they closed the bookstore? I got there in time, I bought it and then everything happened and I think until midnight I must have had the magazine with me in the pocket of my old corduroy jacket, my favorite because of its little pockets, or maybe I dropped it somewhere. I don't remember. But I know I didn't read "Time" that week.

Does the length of this letter surprise you? How could it have been any shorter after you sat down to send me eleven pages? But I'm not writing a long letter to pay you back. Suddenly, I like writing letters. It's a good way to communicate: a letter is a perfect monologue. You don't interrupt me. There aren't any conversational changes. I talk and I talk and when I get tired, I sign my name. Then it is many days before the person who received my monologue answers with his monologue. It is a very civilized way to communicate, very respectful, very controlled. What happens is that sometimes my hand gets tired from so much scribbling, but tomorrow or the day after I'm going to buy a portable typewriter that I chose after exhaustively comparing the different models and makes that they sell here in Madrid. I've visited various shops asking (a good way to pass some time) and I think I've found what I like best. I should have been more impulsive and bought the first one that I liked but then I would have had one less task to do and I try to find stupid tasks to occupy the hours of my day. It's easier at night. I go to the theater and watch the predictable plot of the play go by, and the actors who pretend to be who they are not. Or I sit in an open-air café and watch the tourists and watch the people of Madrid watching the tourists, and watch the prostitutes and the pimps who make a career out of watching the people of Madrid and the tourists. Almost no one looks at me. I must look like a Protestant pastor or a secondary school teacher, not because of my gray suit (am I gray, Graciela?), but because of my general appearance or more exactly, because of my countenance. I see myself as being too serene, as if isolated. I know because I see myself in the store windows. It must be the tranquilizers. Three a day plus a different one before sleeping. I think I should begin to ease up on the dosage. One of these days. . .

What did you want to tell me about the Synagogue? Why didn't you tell me? Tell me. Now it's your turn. Letter writing is like playing chess long distance.

A big hug.

Daniel.

4. Dearest Sara:

I've barely been in Madrid ten days and I've already received three letters from you. How can I thank you for everything you've always done for me? You came running as soon as you found out what happened and you didn't leave my side. You are in the middle of all those moments that I remember now, in my Madrid days, as if they were photographs bouncing me here and there. I see you bringing coffee in a red thermos and consommé in a blue one, on the chance that I might want something to drink while waiting on the corner, surrounded by friends, waiting for the firemen to clean up the rubble and pull out the bodies. . .

I don't know when I'm coming back. I thought that I could do everything I had to in only a month, but I've already been here two weeks and haven't done anything yet. Yesterday I finally called Uncle Abraham in Melilla. It was very difficult. When he heard my voice and when I said who I was, he started to cry. Aunt Luna talked to me and told me how much she wanted to meet me. They asked me to please try to arrive on a Thursday so that we could go to the cemetery early Friday morning. I told them I'd come this Thursday, that I'd come on the afternoon boat. As soon as I hung up, I was sorry for having committed myself so suddenly. But it's better that I did. Sooner or later I have to go, so it's better to go now. The day after tomorrow, Tuesday afternoon I'll take the plane to Malaga. I'll stay over, and Wednesday I'll make arrangements for the boat, which I understand leaves early Thursday morning. I hope to return Monday or Tuesday. I hope I'll find another letter from you.

If all goes quickly and well, as I would suppose, I hope to return to Caracas, let's say, within a month. Sometimes I think I'd like to go to Paris and London, and probably Rome too, for a few days. I haven't been in those cities since my honeymoon trip, and then Rebecca and I were the perfect tourists, always tired of seeing ruins and museums. I don't know if I have the courage to retrace my past. In any case, I'll never go back to retrace the past in those cities. If I were to go, it would be to sit in cafés, to walk about, to go to book stores or to the theater. First let me go to Melilla and arrange everything there. Then, we will see.

I tell you again that if you need anything for the house or for you, you can ask Dr. Benchetrit, another one who is a lawyer, not a medical man. I will write him saying not to forget to give you everything that you ask for.

I'm happy to know that the plants on the balcony are growing. How could they do anything but grow, with your green thumb? Each plant has its mystery and you know each mystery. Tell anyone who asks about me that I'm doing very well. Seriously, dear Sara, I am fine and everything I've written you has been to make me feel better. Although you don't understand, keep this letter and don't tell anyone anything. What would be the point?

My affectionate greetings to your children and grandchildren and don't hate me too much for having put you back to work. Many kisses and hugs for you, from the one who loves you so much.

Daniel.

. . . .

7. Dear Francisco:

The Chancellor's letter came yesterday and yours today. His generosity strikes me as excessive. I only asked for a three-month leave without pay, more than enough time to finish what I came to do and to try to recuperate and get accustomed to. . .well, you know to what. Even writing it is hard. It's hard because I'm terrified I might inspire pity or, worse still, my own self-pity. But to have granted me unpaid leave for an indefinite period is either pity or else a recognition that what I do in the office is not indispensable. It's like telling me, "Never mind. Take all the time you want. And besides. . .as far as your work is concerned. . ."

The truth is I really didn't do that much. Mine was not an earth-shaking task. In fact, neither was anybody else's around there. Let's be frank: does anything really concrete, really and truly beneficial, ever get done in that big beautiful Yellow House, which they should either give to some rich family with lots of kids or else open up to the public, out of historical nostalgia, complete with the furniture and curios of its era. As I remember our work days used to go like this: you got there sometime around nine o'clock and for the first half hour we'd all say good morning, pass along the latest gossip (appointments, transfers, scandals) and read the morning papers. Though we would have already read "El Nacional" at home or "El

Universal," we would leaf through whichever ones we hadn't seen simply because they were there on top of our desks, the "full assortment" Pacheco the messenger would have handed around two hours before we ever got in. We didn't get this stack of papers because the higher-ups thought it might be good for us to absorb their contents, but rather because this massive subscription, not only in our Ministry but in all the other government offices too, represented a juicy contract for the publishers of all those papers. Cutting subscription quotas would have meant to run the risk of being censured and criticized for whatever measures the Office might be carrying out.

And what did we do after turning newspaper pages and gossiping? By then it was ten o'clock and we'd sit down to work answering the correspondence they had assigned us. Letters from Embassies and Consulates asking information which we would patiently gather, no hurry, and letters from other Offices asking information of our Embassies and Consulates which we would transcribe practically word for word for our secretaries to type out, and then the entire stack of letters stuffed into a maroon pouch would constitute the "Account" which we presented to the Director for his signature. "I am pleased to have this opportunity..." to inform you, notify you, request that you...or "This is to advise you of the receipt of your memorandum number such-and-such, dated such-and-such, in which you were kind enough to..." send me, notify me, request that I, and always the same closing: "On behalf of the Minister, the Director." By now it would be twelve or twelve-thirty, and we would already have drunk at least two coffees in those little plastic cups Pacheco would go around filling from a silver thermos. Many of you would already have smoked your first pack of cigarettes of the day. Remember how the smoke bothered me and how sometimes, to bother you back, I'd say I couldn't stand any more of it and go out to the lobby to get some air, but also to listen to all the grumbling from everyone waiting to see the Chancellor so that he would give them a post abroad or speed up their transfer to some other embassy? I'll bet some of them are still out there waiting to see him. You'll be amused to hear that as of a couple of days ago I too am a smoker. "You, a smoker?" *Sí señor,* me a smoker. "Whatever for?" I'm not sure, someone offered me a cigarette and I took it. I didn't inhale but I blew the smoke all around. Then I smoked another and another and yesterday I bought my first pack of *negros.* They're called "Ducados." But I also want you to know that besides smoking I now drink wine. "But you were the only diplomat who never touched alcohol," Augusto told me. Well, I touch it now, twice a day: dinner and supper. You probably think I'm sliding into the gutter, like they say in tangos, but I like the taste of wine with a meal and lighting a cigarette over a cup of coffee. I had to come to Spain to acquire these passions, which proves I'm as slow as ever in everything I do with my life.

I don't mean to sound bitter about our work, but seen from over here, at this distance, it seems a bit pointless. The greater the distance, the closer you see things. Every so often the truth of this dawns on me with blinding force. It seems all one has to do is to go away and suddenly you see in great detail what was right on top of you, or right in front of you, or all around you. And at a distance, my job in the Ministry keeps looking more futile and less important to me every day. Whatever was I doing there, sitting at my desk next to yours, both of us facing our secretaries, two pairs of twins at four little desks, answering letters and phone calls all day long? I know you'll say that sometimes we carried out tasks "of broader scope," to use our Chancillorese, and that we did them competently, but in reality what good are those instructions to delegations or international conferences or all those memorandums (I know, I know—the plural's memoranda) to interministerial meetings, or those confidential reports on positions and alternatives, if none of it ever gets translated into action that might better the lives of our people? I think my disillusionment began when I came out of the Second Commission of the United Nations Assembly, so late that night, after spending days, and hours and hours of those days, discussing a Draft Resolution on raw materials in which the seventy-some developing nations won a clear victory over the industrial powers in relation to minimum prices and conditions. I walked out at one in the morning from the silent United Nations building, my briefcase hanging from my hand and tears stinging my eyes (I know I've already told you this several times, but never in writing and I'm writing it now perhaps more for myself than for you), I walked out excited thinking, at last we had won something tangible, and I drove to Middletown where I found Rebecca sleeping as peacefully as if she already knew the Resolution had been approved without a single no vote, only two abstentions: The United States and the Soviet Union. The rest of the story you know as well as I do: not only was the Resolution never implemented, but while, of course, the information was reported in *The New York Times*, the Caracas papers ignored it just as everyone ignored it in the Chancellory when they got our cable announcing it. Another paper was written. Still another. And that is the sum of our labors in the Chancellory: papers written, papers written to be filed, papers written to be numbered, papers written to be received and answered, papers and papers written to make a gigantic pile of words crowning forever, for centuries and centuries, our abuse of the language.

A simple letter like this does more good, I believe, because it tells you something concrete and asks something from you, while the papers written on our job tell you everything and ask everything of you, but, when you add it up, that everything means nothing, it's something vague, fluffy, that you can't get hold of, pin down, make it yield results.

So I guess I've ruined your day with this letter that no doubt Pacheco brought around to you, telling everyone he meets, "Martinez got a letter from Benabel." He's probably come strolling by two or three times while you've been reading it to see what he can see.

Tell him I'm fine. That's what everyone always says. And really, I am. Instead of bothering you with my same old complaints about work, which you already know inside out, I should have been telling you about myself since that's what you ask about in your letter and I know you're concerned about me. I'm fine. The slow pace of Madrid, worthy of a good private hospital, is having its effect on me, as you've probably noticed by the outburst I just got through with. I'll stay on here longer than planned, since the paperwork on the houses is complicated (more papers written) and since in Melilla, that least little crumb of Spain, they do everything at a camel's pace. What's funny is that when you convert the price of the sale into bolívares it doesn't come to much, but it had to be done that way since I'm papa's only heir. Probably including the money that's supposed to go to the uncles. Or if they don't offer a tempting sum, I'll arrange the papers in my name and won't sell anything, letting the uncles keep the rents. I can't tell you anything either about them or Melilla since I still haven't been there. I'm waiting for the lawyer down there to put everything in order, and to let me know when it's all ready, before I go. I think I can take care of everything in two or three days and then return to Madrid to leave for Caracas. Your idea of a "swing" through Europe had occurred to me too, but your reminder about knowing someone in our Embassy in almost any capital doesn't appeal much to me because I know that as soon as I would give them a call they would come running to the hotel for a sympathy visit. That's what happened here in Madrid, and not only did Gutiérrez come by but also his wife and daughter, a skinny kid with eyes bulging out of her head, probably at the thought of seeing the victim (me), and one of the secretaries came along too, I think his name is Alvarez Luengo, very pompous with his double surname. (Do you remember what Jiménez used to say: "These double names will have to go—they're underdeveloped. Everyone should have one given name and one surname. Not a single more." He started talking like that after he ditched his second name because when he went to whatever conference that was in Washington, nobody called him Jiménez but. . .now I can't remember what his second name was.) The four of them were here, the two women in black, all sitting across from me in the hotel lobby. I asked them if they wanted something to drink and they all ordered coffee, probably thinking that was the proper beverage to begin asking me in the strictest protocol how I'd liked the trip, how I liked the hotel, how I liked Madrid, how I liked the weather, then a long silence which I finally broke with some silly story or other, just so they wouldn't have the opportunity to sit there gawking at me as if I were the loneliest orphan on the face of the earth.

The same thing would happen wherever I went, and if I ever feel friendly towards an ambassador it will be because I'm sure he would leave all protocol aside and ask me point-blank, "How'd it happen?" And what could I tell him, Francisco, or you either? Who could ever tell, or better yet understand, how it all happened? So if I do happen to travel, I'd prefer to do it anonymously. Naturally I'll keep you informed. But it will be a quick trip: two or three days in two or three cities. And then back to Caracas. What bothers me is knowing I'm coming back to the Ministry. It bothers me because that job bores me now. I like being around you every day. With you and with Maria Esperanza and with Amparo, our devoted servants, and with Diana, who sent me a very amusing "memorandum" which I've already answered, and with almost everyone we work with. Even with Valdez, who's always so impressed to think we're polyglots, and of course with Pacheco, our blessing from the Holy Spirit. The people all attract me and I would gladly be around them again, but the work, Francisco, the petrified routine. . .for how long? Sure, I know that at our age it's nearly impossible to make an about face and that the best thing is to keep accumulating years until we get our pension, but I've been in the Chancellory for eighteen years, I entered when I was twenty-two and now I'm forty. And for that sweet pension, which they can give me after twenty-five years of service, I still need seven years. Seven years, Francisco! The seven fat cows and the seven lean cows! I might use up my seven lives (like a cat) outside the Chancellory but inside, what ever happens? And in seven years I still won't be old enough to get my pension unless I can find someone to pull strings for me. And what would I gain by my pension? A monthly stipend which I certainly won't need, now that everything my family had is mine. In short, it's not worth it to get myself worked up like this, and even less to worry about the future. First let me do what I came to do, and along the way I have a feeling that whatever's in store for me will get clearer, or what I might like to do with myself.

Thanks for calling Sara. Go have lunch with her whenever you want to. You know how she loves to show off her culinary talent when Doctor Martinez comes to visit. And between the next notice of receipt and memorandum, slip a sheet of paper into your typewriter and write me a long letter. (What do you think of the typing job in this letter? When I don't have Maria Esperanza to rely on, I take pride in how well I can do.) A kiss for her and one for Amparo. And a very special one for our friend, Diana.

A brotherly hug.

Daniel.

Trans. by Marilyn Rae
and David Pritchard

Isaac Chocrón *is considered one of the three most important playwrights in Venezuela today and is a member of the influential group, el Nuevo Grupo. He has also written three novels, and the excerpts here constitute the first twenty-five pages of his epistolary novel about a wealthy Sephardic Jew who attempts to go back to his roots in Madrid, Melilla and Tangier.*

Dr. Josef Goldstein

Agarismo: A Biblical Method Against Sterility

It is not a matter of adding to or of subtracting from the devotion we already have for the Bible, or of believing or not believing in its writings, and even less a matter affecting the Commentaries. The fact is that the Bible is the oldest literary work and the only book that has become the universal treasure of a civilization whose prominence continues to the present moment. It is also obvious that the people who lived in the Biblical age confronted similar problems and difficulties to those we find in our own time, the Age of the Atom. The problem of human sterility is at least as old as the Bible and perhaps older because by that time it was already considered to be a grave problem. Torah, in no small way, deals with this problem and in such a manner as to suggest that the natural law of human procreation, with all its problems, was initiated with Adam and Eve and continues until now. Among the many and serious problems of that time, the problem of sterility occupies an important place and we Jews, in our condition of peoplehood, would not now exist, if our ancestors had not discovered the appropriate solution to this problem in their own time.

I don't know if it was a coincidence or the will of the Divine Creator, the fact that the first Hebrew and his wife lived until old age deprived of children. The circumstance tormented them so that God had to console and encourage them so that they would not lose the hope of progeny.

The first man who spoke frankly of his grief to God was Abram (he was not called Abraham at that time), and his feelings were expressed in this way: "Oh, Adonoi, God, you who have recognized me, consider that I am alone." And the tragic figure of Sarai appeared, wife of Abram, the first woman to suffer from sterility, who had to experience humiliation before she could be blessed with the fruit of her womb.

At that time, Sarai was one of the richest and most beautiful women. Her beauty was so famous and celebrated that Abram, in his migrations, was obliged to keep his marriage to her a secret. Precisely she, this famous beauty, admired by princes and kings, the woman who was perfect in physical condition, was not blessed with children and the best years of her life passed in tears, prayers and supplications, as it is written: "And Sarai, wife of Abram, had no children. The years passed and Abram was eighty-five years old."

In desperation, Sarah agreed to adopt a method that would be quite disagreeable to anyone, let alone to a woman like Sarah. She suggested to Abram that he cohabit with his servant, as it is written: "And Sarai, the wife of Abram, having no children of her own, had an Egyptian servant called Hagar. Sarai said to Abram: God has asked me to be delivered of a child; therefore, cohabit with my servant; perhaps you will have children through her." Abram heard the voice of Sarai and Sarai, Abram's wife, took the Egyptian Hagar, her servant, ten years after Abram had dwelt in the land of Canaan, and gave her as a spouse to her husband. He then approached Hagar and knew her. And, as the Bible continues: "And Sarai conceived and bore Abram a son in his old age." Abram was eighty-six years old when Hagar bore him Ishmael, and a few years later Sarai bore him Isaac.

It's obvious that Sarah had adopted a very original method. With the idea of obtaining a son from her legitimate husband, she urged him to take her servant, Hagar. It's clear that the request was hers and not his, from her expression: "Bo na" as it is written. And he obeyed, as the text says: "And Abram heard." Torah emphasizes Sarah's part in this deed by stating: "And Sarai, the wife of Abram, took Hagar, her Egyptian maid, and gave her to Abram for a wife," an idea that Sarah not only agreed to, but in fact had originated. Who knows what would have happened had Abram done the same thing without Sarah's knowledge, whether she would have remained childless.

Let us sort out the religious issue from the emotional one, the emotional confusion and the internal struggle which must have taken place in Sarah's soul. Because it is obvious that a step such as this was not a simple or easy one, particularly for a highborn woman—to submit to this humiliation. Certainly, she could not have been happy when she pleaded, "Take, please, my servant." No woman would want to find herself in this situation, nor can there be a more profound humiliation to the feminine pride than this.

Thus, her decision was not undertaken lightly. Without doubt, her decision was the result of a prolonged and painful internal struggle, perhaps taken after previous medical consultation, if such medical help existed for such a purpose at this time. But having exhausted other recourses, and having tried the possible and the impossible without results, Sarah valiantly decided to take the one step that promised hope of obtaining success, and it was then that she commanded and pleaded: "Take, please, my servant; perhaps she will bear children." Truthfully, it was the only method available at the time, failing other medical explanations. So, in spite of everything, she resolved to take this risk for the sake of her own health.

"And Abram heard the voice of Sarah." Abram restrained himself, for it seems that he did not immediately carry out Sarah's suggestion, but merely listened without responding, to his credit, hesitating. Torah does not tell us why Abram did not hurry to carry out Sarah's request. Some believe that Hagar was not as pretty as Sarah. Others maintain that he found Hagar very much to his liking—she was younger than his wife—but that he pretended not to want her, even though Sarah had obligated him. It is then written that after the deed was consummated, Sarah said to him: "I gave my servant into your bosom." Another opinion has it that Abram agreed immediately, but that it was Hagar who refused, for Abraham was much older than she was, and, as proof of this, it is written in the text: "And Sarai, the wife of Abram, took Hagar, her Egyptian servant."

There are still others who expound that Abraham couldn't believe what his ears heard and he was not able to act on Sarah's words, that he remained astonished before these words, without knowing what to say or how to act.

Therefore, Torah says: "Abraham heard the voice of Sarah—" It says that he heard her voice, but not whether he believed her words. Sarah, observing his lack of enthusiasm "brought her servant Hagar to him" and bid her lie down on Abraham's bosom, as the text expresses it: "And Sarah, the wife of Abraham, took Hagar, her Egyptian servant and gave her to her husband, Abraham." Only then did he hear her voice: "And he entered into Hagar who conceived."

Abraham and Sarah continued married, the problem of children being present constantly as a daily theme and we can be certain that during the first years of their marriage without children that all kinds of experiments were tried.

The usual idea about childless marriages that people have even today is that the woman is to blame for this, in spite of the fact that it has been amply demonstrated that it is the man who is usually sterile. This would be true even for Biblical times when gynecology did not exist, nor laboratories, nor any equipment to test for sperm count. Sarah was therefore equally certain that she was at fault and consequently said to Abraham: "Look! God has made me sterile; therefore, enter my servant to see if you can have children." In other words, Sarah said: "I am suffering from a gynecological illness and cannot bear children but you, Abraham, lie with Hagar; perhaps I will bring forth in this way." She believed she suffered from an illness which could be cured by Abraham's lying with Hagar.

Sarah was the first known woman who suffered from sterility, but she was also the first woman who knew how to cure it, and she chose a method which brought success; and it is necessary that we undertand that she did use this method very successfully. Since Hagar was the first woman who served as the instrument of this method, I have called the method Agarismo.

Sarai, Hagar and Abram: two women and one man, three eternal figures in the world of medicine who were able to cure serious sterility by a natural method, without medicines, treatment, or surgical intervention, while our own scientific age still does not grasp or understand the method used by these people thousands of years ago. One feels even greater admiration for this method because it was applied so successfully to patients who were already advanced in age: "Abraham and Sarah were old, very advanced in years, and Sarah's menstrual periods had ceased." It is very rare when a woman whose menstrual periods have ceased bears children. Under normal conditions, women who have ceased menstruating, cannot conceive, but a miracle happened here: Abram and Sarah, in spite of old age and impotency caused by senescence, achieved success thanks to Hagar. And I emphasize these words: "thanks to Hagar." It is here that we Jews, in our condition of peoplehood, must understand that we owe our gratitude for our existence to this young Egyptian girl, of whom we only know that she became the instrument which allowed Sarah to give birth to Isaac. It is certain that but for the intervention of Hagar, Abram and Sarah would have remained childless.

Torah follows this narration with that of Isaac, their only child, who was forty years old when he took Rebecca for a wife. I don't know if it is merely coincidence that our three matriarchs were sterile. With respect to Rebecca, the Bible says: "Isaac prayed to God because his wife was childless, and God heard and Rebecca conceived."

It seems that Rebecca did not use the same method which Sarah used, known as Agarismo. Moreover, Torah doesn't even mention the name of Rebecca's servant.

After this follows the episode of Jacob and his two wives and their respective servants, Zelfa and Bala. Jacob, who truly loved only Rachel, the younger daughter of Laban, was burdened with four ladies: Leah, Rachel's older sister, Rachel herself, and the two servants.

According to the Biblical text, we read: "Jacob loved Rachel and said to Laban: I will serve seven years for your younger daughter, Rachel." This, in spite of the fact that he knew that Leah wished to marry him. He wanted to marry Rachel because while Leah's eyes were tender, Rachel's eyes were elegant and beautiful. This feeling in a young man is natural. It is surprising how much Torah tells us about the erotic sentiments, describing the sexual passion of a young man in the same way we would describe it today. Jacob loved Rachel because she was pretty and had a beautiful figure, motives which move any young man of flesh and blood with natural instincts and sexual desires who quite simply prefers a young lady, perfect in beauty and bodily proportions, as the text says: "Laban had two daughters; the elder, Leah, the younger, Rachel. Leah had tender eyes, but Rachel was slim and beautiful. Jacob loved Rachel."But this love was not to be so quickly consummated. Jacob had to suffer and to sacrifice a great deal to win Rachel. His love for her was so great that he made Laban the following proposition: "I will serve seven years for Rachel, your younger daughter." Laban had not wanted this and perhaps would never have demanded it, but Jacob feared that he would not get his consent if he did not offer to serve him for the seven years. For his own part, Jacob asked for a very small dowry: that Laban give him the two servants, Zelfa and Bala, as it is written: "Laban give him the two servants, Zelfa and Bala, as it is written: "Laban gave Leah, his daughter her servant Zelfa to serve her." And the text continues: "Laban gave Rachel his daughter to wife and with her Bala her servant to serve her."

We are accustomed to thinking that servants had little value in those times, but Torah suggests otherwise, because later it became impossible to free ourselves from our debts to these servants, even difficult to imagine what the course of the history of the Hebrew people would have been but for the worthy intervention of these servants whose names have been immortalized in this history.

We return again to the love of Jacob and Rachel.

I extend my subject matter a little further now, because in spite of the strong passion which united them, nature punished Rachel with sterility. This contradicts the opinion held by some scientists who believe that the strength of sexual passion is a means of combatting sterility. Could a love greater than Jacob's for Rachel be possible?

There is a verse in the Bible which has stirred up many problems in the medical world: "God, seeing that Leah was not loved, opened her womb, while Rachel's remained closed."

According to this text, the woman who is not loved by her husband bears the children, while the beloved does not. We don't find a single reference otherwise, throughout these passages, which describes Rachel's and Leah's activities with Jacob; the writings are limited to informing us only of Jacob's love for Rachel, in spite of which he married Leah though he loved Rachel more: "But he loved Rachel more than Leah." And in spite of which, even without mentioning anything of Jacob's feelings for Leah, Leah was blessed with many children, and Rachel, the beloved, was infertile. How explain this? Is it a matter of mere coincidence? Or should we see something else in it? Is a medical explanation at all possible?

Medical investigations in this area do not agree. Partly, many doctors do not agree that there is a relationship between sterility on one hand, and love or hate on the other. Certainly, in daily life, we find couples who profess great love for each other and who have no children while, on the other hand, there are couples who marry for the sake of convenience and who have many children.

Others who have thought about this problem relate sterility to the psychological relationship of the couples. But if this were so, those marriages based on love should have a better chance of children. However, there are those who believe that the very passion of a couple can be the cause of lack of procreation. Among all these various theories, there is one more theory which presently is rebutted by many doctors.

This theory, in agreement with the Biblical text, explains why "...God opened her womb..." because "Leah was not loved." The theory is not accepted by the scientific community. Furthermore, their theory encourages us to believe that the bonds of passion do have a greater possibility of fertility than the kind of relationship which existed between Jacob and Leah. Only one thing is clear at present: there is no certainty in the medical world about the problem of sterility.

"Rachel, seeing that she had no children, was jealous of her sister and said to Jacob: Take my servant, Bala; enter her, that she may bear on my knees, and I will bring forth through her."—"She gave her servant to Jacob to wife, and he entered her." The text then says: "Leah, seeing that she was permitted to bear children, took Zelfa, her servant, and gave her to Jacob. Zelfa bore Jacob a son." The text continues: "And God heard Leah, and she conceived and bore Jacob his fifth child." And Leah said, "God has rewarded me for giving my servant to Jacob; and she called him Issachar (Yesh Sajar—I have been compensated)." I cite the verses from the Pentateuch, word for word, to demonstrate the important role undertaken by these servants. No writing tells us what they looked like, if they were pretty or ugly, because this fact is not important. The only important point is to allow the deed of the three wives of the patriarchs: Sarah, Rachel and Leah, to stand out: they chose to give women to their husbands, and that this is one of the important conditions for combatting sterility, to which we later ascribe scientific explanations.

In some way these three ladies who suffered from sterility already knew, thousands of years ago, how to employ the method called Agarismo, and they did it with great success. We must acknowledge that this method served them as a means of curing sterility in the select circles of the society of that time. And we should be able to acknowledge this without further considerations or hesitation. It is obvious that from the sentimental point of view, we can say nothing about the relations between Jacob and his servants, whether these relations had an emotional basis, or were merely instinctual. But putting that aside, the result was still that the servants came to be the wives and mothers of Jacob and his children. Concerning Jacob's feelings about them, the Bible remains absolutely silent.

Trans. by Roberta Kalechofsky

Dr. Josef Goldstein *was born in Rumania, finished his medical studies there in 1933, and has been living in Caracas, Venezuela since 1948, but is a frequent visitor to Massachusetts where he has a married daughter. He is a specialist in Biblical medicine, and has written many articles on this subject in Yiddish, which have appeared in periodicals in Israel, Venezuela, Mexico, South Africa, New York, and elsewhere. He has also written books on cancer.* The Fourth Sign, *on that subject, was translated into English in 1968.*

Alicia Segal

An Interview with Dr. Elena Blumenfeld: Someone Who Has Put Her Finger On the Wound

It is forty-six years since Elena and Jerónimo Blumenfeld arrived in Venezuela. Jews, originally from Poland, they graduated medical school in Prague in 1924, and immediately emigrated to Argentina where he worked in the Cancer Institute with Professor Angel Roffo, and she in the Children's Hospital of Buenos Aires with Professor Bassigalupo.

In 1925, Mr. and Mrs. Blumenfeld went to the interior of Argentina, in Tierra del Fuego, to practice their medical apprenticeship for five years.

Norma, their only child, is also a doctor, head of the Department of Investigations of the Blood Bank in Caracas. Her professional career, as a hematologist and a university professor, together with that of her husband, Dr. Virgil Bosh, who is an endocrinologist and also a university professor, forms a valuable chapter, meriting its own attention.

Our subject, however, for this interview, is Elena Blumenfeld, a leprologist. In a few days she will have completed thirty-seven years as the head of the leper colony of Cabo Blanco. Our conversation revolved around her long and consecutive experience in this field.

More Than Nationalisms

—Why did you and your husband choose to come to the malarial part of Venezuela in 1930?

—My husband had a brother here, Maximiliano, who was also a doctor, working in Altagracia de Orituco. When we arrived here we also went to practice in the interior, in the rural districts of Cúa Charallave, San Casimiro and San Sebastian. We were there from 1930-1938, the year my husband died.

—Doctor, since illness in general is a situation which produces in one a mixture of recoil and pity, why did you choose to specialize in such a sickness as leprosy, which carries with it the tradition of fear and aversion to such a degree, more than any other sickness.

—It was the suffering which the death of my husband brought me, so intense that I sought some activity which would allow me to be with others who were suffering more than I was, in order to give them some hope. The very month in which my husband died, I entered Cabo Blanco where I have been for thirty-seven years without interruption.

First, I was the head of the laboratory until 1945. At the end of that year, Edmundo Fernández, who was then the Minister of Sanitation, gave me the official title of Resident Leprologist, a position I held until five years ago. The first twenty years as Resident Leprologist, I left Cabo Blanco every fifteen days to see my daughter, who studied in the College of San Pablo and was living with the family of Roberto and Conchita Martínez, who were her guardians.

—What is your work like in Cabo Blanco?

—After my daughter had been married for seventeen years, I was able to divide the work of the lepersarium with the help of my three grandchildren. In Cabo Blanco itself, I work seven hours a day. Also, as a specialist in leprosy, I have been giving classes on the subject for twenty years, to students who are in their sixth year of medical school, who want to study here as part of their course in dermatology.

—If this is not too indiscreet, what is your salary?

—Including the recent increase, I now receive two thousand, five hundred bolivars a month. *

Neither Monstrous Nor Bloody

—How do you explain the unconscionable terror which leprosy has always produced in all times and places where it has been observed?

—Look, when I arrived at Cabo Blanco, thirty-seven years ago, ideas about leprosy were the same then, as they had been for centuries. Identical. It was believed to be the most contagious of the infectious diseases. One for which there was no cure. One which brought terrible injuries to the stricken in a horrible way. One which caused such a psychological state in the stricken that it turned them into irritable and difficult people. Today we know that these ideas are entirely or partly false. Because leprosy is the least contagious of all the infectious-contagious diseases. To such an extent, that a person who has leprosy, and I want to make this clear, has two weaknesses. One is the Hansen Bacillus and the other is the genetic factor, which allows this bacillus to develop in the organism. Very well! By luck, the majority of people, almost all of us, have defenses that impede the development of this bacillus. Only a small number of people do not have this immunological system. Then, when they come in contact with the bacillus, yes, they can become very sick. This explains why one does not become sick if you marry a leper, or after five children, for instance, none, or all, or three or two, become sick.

—What exactly is this immunological failure?

—There is a certain type of white globate which forms very specific antibodies against this bacillus. These macrophagi can synthesize a

---

* a bolivar is worth approximately 24 cents of American money.

lisogenic substance that destroys these bacilli. After four decades I now work with these sick people without gloves and I don't catch the disease because, as with most people, my lisogenic system is conditioned for defense.

—What are the early symptoms of this disease?

—There are various kinds of leprosy. Lepromatosa, tuberculin, and mixed. But these details are too long to explain. In general, the majority of the first visible symptoms are hypochromic spots, or a small discoloration, whitish, that with time acquires coloration. Or leprosy can sometimes begin with a disturbance of the tactile sensitivity, because leprosy is a disease of the skin and the peripheral nervous system.

—What treatment is required?

—When I first arrived in Venezuela, leprosy was treated with derivatives of oil from chaulmogra. Today, treatment is basically with sulfur derivatives and other experimental drugs, sometimes combined very effectively.

—The leper—what makes him an invalid? I ask this because one notices that the sickness produces dull, slow movements, or even none, in the extremities.

—This happens because the normal reflexes toward heat, cold, pain, or whatever, are partly or totally lost. For this reason, they can scald themselves, wound themselves, injure themselves, without realizing it. Then, secondary infection appears, which is very rapid and injures the same leper again. Put yourself in their place. In order to educate them about the first phase of the disease, they must learn to use sight as a substitute for feeling. Another phase is when this sickness begins to exert pressure on the peripheral nerves, one has to learn how to free oneself from this threatening condition, to see oneself differently, in order to lessen the danger of wounds, in a word, to practice preventative medicine.

—You said earlier that lepers are known for being intractable and disagreeable.

—That's a lie! A lie! I have been with them for so long that I can prove that's a false notion. At first, obviously, they behave like anyone who is confronted with misfortune. They are human, you understand, and they have suddenly lost their jobs and they see that everyone around them shies away from them. If you help them, they know how to be agreeable. I have many personal examples of this.

—Are there many who in time recover and go back to their families?

—Leprosy is a sickness like any other. Actually, there are about 11,000 lepers in Venezuela, who are treated as outpatients. In Cabo Blanco there are only 250 and a few more on the island of Zuliana de Providencia.

Why Are There Leper Colonies?

–This being so, how do you justify the existence of special hospitals for lepers. Why then the new leper colony of Cocollar which will soon be in use, according to newspaper reports.

–Today, with the electron microscope we know that the treatment of the Hansen Bacillus can be modified so that it loses its infective potency by being disintegrated. But that is not the significant thing. What is significant is that our ideas about leprosy should be transformed. Since we have changed the concept of this sickness, it is only suitable that we also change the means and reasons for a lepersarium. The most important thing is to end long hospitalization, and this is now being accomplished. Formerly, when a sick man entered a leper colony, he was sure he would never leave it alive. Modernized hospitals should exist for those lepers who have not yet been treated, to teach them how to protect their bodies against lesions that can hurt them, to practice preventative medicine, to experiment with treatments that will facilitate even shorter cures, and clearly, also for those who are completely invalided.

–Would you include a laboratory?

–Not primarily. The hospital's purpose should be to prepare the individual to be re-integrated with society, mentally and physically. Why do I feel that this should be the main function of the new leper hospitals? Because long hospitalization is very damaging to the individual and to the state, economically, socially, intellectually.

–Is it possible to detect a family contagion?

–This is a very important question which the greatest authority on this matter, Dr. Jacinto Convit, Head of the Department of Dermatolological Health of the Ministry of Sanitation and Social Assistance, can answer with more knowledge and details than I can. From this one great center of study, there are twenty-nine lesser centers in the interior, all co-ordinated, and they keep track of those treated on an outpatient basis, and the surrounding families as well. There is, for example, an introdermic injection, the antigenic Mitsuda-Wade. When this preparation is injected, and the person responds to it with evidence of a nodule, it means that he has defenses against leprosy. Someone who does not respond in this way is apt to contract leprosy. The children of a leper undergo this test so that we can determine how to treat them. Look! This past year in las Jornadas, when representatives from the whole world came, it was shown that Venezuela, with Dr. Convit at the head, was in the vanguard in the treatment of leprosy, and I believe it is because of what he has done, honestly and tenaciously and because, fortunately, until now, politics has not invaded Venezuelan leprology. Moreover, experience is not written in just one book of the world.

Education Combats Myth

—How can we substitute these new, useful, clear ideas to take the place of fear and disgust?

—By changing the old concept that is taught in the schools.

—Would you advise those who plan education that the doctors revise their ideas according to yours, to implement these changes?

—Obviously, yes. But it is difficult to achieve these modifications, because repulsion is too firmly rooted in all of us.

—Have you noticed changes after forty years, even minimally, in the prejudice which views the leper as a sacred punishment imposed by God?

—Not much. Because it seems as if people want to cling to this idea that has formed a part of their culture.

Work With Love

—What kinds of pleasures and rewards have you gotten from your work with the leper?

—I don't believe that leprologists merit special prizes. Still, in 1966, I received la Orden Francisco de Miranda en su Segunda Clase. Above all, I remember when in 1968 the lepers of Cabo Blanco named me their Spiritual Mother and when in 1972, the students nominated me to be their godmother at their graduation, because these were the first times in my life that I was given something for nothing. The homage came from the young people, and this is exceptionally valuable because it is free and spontaneous. In 1973, I had no wish to accept another honor, because it was too much, but they presented me with a diploma which you can read for yourself: "Doctora: Thank you for teaching us to work with love." What more could I want?

—Do you ever feel tired or feel a need to change your activity?

—I will be seventy-six next April. These circumstances which I have lived with for thirty-eight years are adequate for me. I have many friends in Cabo Blanco, the most loyal friends. When you listen to them, they give you much love.

Published in the review, Resumen, *March 21, 1976*

Trans. by Roberta Kalechofsky

Alicia Segal

el Hembrismo (Feminism)

Different social commentators have come to the conclusion that machismo is inextricably woven into the economic and psychotechnical processes of Latin America's mixed ethnicity and colonialism. In the interpretative text of a previous article (The Supermachos 15-5) I sought to encourage the uneasy reader to reflect upon this defect of underdevelopment which is so strongly connected to the essence of the Latin American persona.

But there's more. One of the most regrettable defensive reactions to machismo, can be labeled "hembrismo" (for lack of a better term), which has been predominately connected with women's liberation movements. I use the word, regrettable, because if good, profound, irreproachable analyses like Kate Millet's *Sexual Politics* could create a true social revolution beginning with a conscious change in the irrational treatment of today's women, it is no less certain that the majority of women in the modern world don't know how to advantageously use reformed postulates and instead proceed towards "feminist" extremes which at times reach ridiculous proportions. The North American writer Norman Mailer satirizes these excesses in his amusing polemic, *The Prisoner of Sex.*

Nothing could be more detrimental to the possibility of women achieving complete integration with men in both public and private stratas than those associations, political groups, etc. which consist only of women; because they devalue the biological essence of womanhood and an essential masculinity that can fully actualize the existential communion of the couple. Therefore, discussing problems of reform among men and women separately is to grotesquely continue and reaffirm the highly criticized "machista" tendency and the tradition of female segregation in our inherited neomedieval culture.

One of the present results of this attitude is certainly a depressing contradiction. The women's sectors of various elected parties offer equal rights to the public. But they are incapable of making even one mature judgment of their own. Like catechisms they repeat already familiar offers as representatives of the "supreme candidate." Where does that leave us? Do the legal problems which affect women and children demand this politicized female isolation in a country that seeks to guarantee "paternal responsibility." Why not discuss these serious matters between men and women, both of whom are equally involved and responsible? Is it then a question of promising laws (which are commonly known to be in writing but not in practice) or gaining a change of behavior and attitude on the part of the Macho? Consider women like Anne Parker, Madame Nguyen, Golda Meir and Indira Ghandi. They never belonged to women's groups, yet precisely by associating person to person with men in their political work, they obtained respect and achieved concrete gains for their causes.

It's no secret that the mother-child situation and male-female behavior regress, stagnate or evolve in accordance with the economic and mental processes of those who are encompassed by them. Thus, it is necessary to uncover the collective Latin American as well as the local unconscious in order to demystify idolatries and prejudice. It is imperative to start at the beginning in order to achieve this difficult task of creatively uniting male and female in a just, logically organized society; woman and man together, in agreement. Because from the direct communication of "macho" and "hembra" can arise the integration of man and woman.

Otherwise, it is only a matter of words, words, words.

Trans. by Susan Riva Greenberg

Alicia Segal

Una Visita Sin Antesala: An Interview with Elisa Lerner

After having obtained the title of lawyer in la Universidad Central de Venezuela, Elisa Lerner wrote her first theatrical piece, the monologue, "A Press Interview or The Women of Intelligence," published in the review, Sardio *(nos. 6 and 7, 1959) and first performed in 1960, when she was in the United States to take postgraduate courses in law. On her return, she wrote the poetical play, "In The Vast Silence of Manhattan," which received the prize, "Ana Julia Rojas," from the Artists' Guild of Caracas, in 1964.*

Her work, "El País Odontológico," is the result of her experience with the audiovisual medium which she used for a series of television interviews called "The Other Generation." "El País Odontológico" was first published in the review, Zona Franca Magazine *(no. 39, 1966). She also did the sketch, "La Envidia," for her part of the spectacle, "Los Siete Pecados Capitales," performed by el Nuevo Grupo, in 1974.*

"Vida con Mamá" was first performed in May, 1975 in la Sala Juana Sujo de Caracas. It was directed by Antonio Costante, with Laura Zerra in the role of la Hija and Herminia Valdés in the role of Madre, for which this actress received the prize of Círculo de Críticos de Teatro, as the best actress of the year. "Vida con Mamá" brought el Nuevo Grupo the award, el Premio Anual 75, for the best theatrical production to be given by el Concejo Municipal del Distrito Federal. Awarded the prize, Juana Sujo, Elisa Lerner was chosen as the outstanding playwright of 1975.

A selection of her essays and newspaper articles have been brought together in the anthology, Una sonrisa detrás de la metáfora, * *published by Editorial Monte Avila in 1969. They also published "Vida con Mamá" with a prologue by Isaac Chocrón, in a volume which includes some of Elisa Lerner's most distinguished pieces, as well as her new monologue, "The Lady of the Afternoon Newspaper."*

The plays of Elisa Lerner, together with that of Isaac Chocrón, José Ignacio, Cabrujas, Chalbraud and Rodolfo Santana, among others, constitute what is known as Nuevo Teatro Venezolano.

An Authentic Grief

–There are many who say that the "Allende Affair," the gigantic photograph of him, and the lines which some of the actresses say in

---

* The Smile Behind the Metaphor

"Vida con Mamá," was a demagogic act, your concession to the Left.

—Look, the only one who says this is the journalist, Pablo Antillano. In reality, I have suffered a great deal of loneliness, precisely because I have never struck a demagogic attitude. I have been branded on several occasions a cosmopolitan, by Adica* and, I imagine as well, a Jewess, and now when many Leftists have quieted down and are busily employed in the cultural bureaucracy, how do they dare accuse me of being a demagogue?

—But what motivated you to include in a play of this kind, of such penetration, this slap in the face to the spectator because, with this Allende matter you interrupted the dramatic flow of the play.

—I agree the play is strong. I didn't do what I did for the purpose you suggest, but because theatrically it hit the mark.

—Elisa, this is a country—and I am able to say so in this interview with you—where politicians make demagogic use of intellectuals. Isn't it reasonable to assume that sometimes the reverse could happen, in artistic form?

—I have not produced demagoguery. His dignified death pained me. It has been said that my entire play is the political history of the country for the last fifty years. Though it is written in a discontinuous form, there is a secret coherence between the two protagonists. Allende's death pained me enormously.

—Why?

—At bottom, it was like a mask of the fall of President Romulo Gallegos in 1948. Ever since then, I have felt that this subject would make a profound drama for this country, an event that was felt only by a few at the time because our democracy was only three years old, and not only had it been brief but it was immature, I would even say ungovernable. Because before that, after Gómez, Venezuela had lived through ten tepid years.

—Do you think that Venezuela is now accustomed to democracy?

—The problem now is different. When Allende fell, Chile had had half a century of democracy. It was a rude blow for the whole of Latin America.

—Do you think you projected this in "Vida con Mamá"?

—I think so. Because if I had written only about Gallego, it would have remained a local question and the play would not have achieved the continental, historical worth it has, and which the loss of Chilean democracy signifies.

---

* Acción Democratica (Right Wing political party)

The Country—A Mother

—Why did you choose such a domestic title instead of something like, "Life with the Nation"?

—Well, it means that, but for me, the nation is like a mother, because Venezuelans think of it as a mother. Other Venezuelans didn't always have their own families. I have a father and a mother, I am a first generation Venezuelan, of European descent. In this "family" way, one guards fidelity, confronted by discontinuity and the historical drama of the European centuries. At least, there is a familial coherence. A great many Venezuelans, of many generation, have lived as if the nation were their only hope. Moreover, "Life with the Nation" would have been very pretentious, don't you think?

—When one reads your plays, for example, "In The Vast Silence of Manhattan," it seems to be very dense theater to read.

—That depends. Because at bottom any play must be for reading, until a director takes it over and makes it over, like a seamstress, making the proper cuts—

—Since you are an incisive critic of the Latin American Creole personality, why do you use the theater instead of the direct essay?

—I have written essays and journalistic pieces about the country. Remember my article, "Country and Memory," among others? Generally speaking, literary genres are not important to me. In this age, there are no divisions between poetry and prose, and the same thing is happening in the theater, to the essay. It all depends upon my mood. If I feel somewhat divorced, I write plays.

—You have certainly achieved fame as being a somewhat distinct and singular person, sarcastic, caustic in work and in conversation—on those rare occasions when you go to a cocktail party.

—I don't like it, when in a particular interview, one is described as a "caustic intellectual." Particularly, if the subject happens to be a woman, because women are stereotyped as sarcastic, while it is accepted that a man in this country can use a gun to express his hostilities. True? This expression seems dangerous to me. But sarcasm can be creative—and hopefully, I have used the theater so that the sarcasm there is mature, distancing, so that it does not express a personal perspective—well, now, that's different. What disturbs me are people who are sarcastic in the anecdotal, in tale-bearing, who have no ideas, and when they write, suddenly write about matters seemingly profound but which are rhetorical and boring.

—Then, yours is an "abstract" sarcasm?

—Yes. I apply it to the country.

Loss of Memory

—In your play, "El País Odontológico," you developed the theme of deceit and cultural blackmail in Venezuela with a rather bitter humor, no?

—Yes. Because anyone who says that democracy is all good, that all the vices in Venezuela can be attributed to the early dictatorship, is telling a fairy tale. I used to believe this myself. I expected too much from democracy, as I said before. Then I began to understand that these Venezuelans had no memory. So we mourned those youths who had no party connections and who simply, by reason of the generosity of the era—because there are generous ages—and because of the impetuous nature of the Venezuelan, we did not inherit hatreds. I too felt that a new Venezuela was beginning, because I had no memory of the past. Afterwards, I was disillusioned.

—Why?

—I'm not sure. I have the impression that hardly had I begun to write when I didn't know what I was, because to write is a very serious thing, perhaps the most serious thing except for dying—and then it is a daily death—I think that we who believed so strongly in democracy, those who were our friends during exile and secrecy...

—I don't understand.

—Look, I want to say that perhaps we asked too much from them and they weren't able to give it because they had to make too many compromises. Suddenly, they became weak.

—Weak or inconsequential?

—Both, I believe. Weakened by the people who served the dictatorship, for example. It seemed awful to me.

—One hears rumors that now you suffer persecution, that the Seguridad Nacional taps your telephone and that you were questioned by the head of this repulsive organization...

—That was the least of it.

—And that as a result you were not able to publish.

—Well, besides, I don't want to publish.

—Perhaps you realize that even in a democracy you can't say everything you want to.

—Now I have said all I wish to say and it has cost me. "El País Odontológico" brought me many problems. But I don't want to speak about that anymore.

The Theater of Text

—How did the Third International Theater Festival given in Caracas a

few days ago strike you?

—It was a big effort on the part of Ateneo, of María Teresa Otero, and Carlos Giménez. There were many important things. Right now, there prevails, perhaps, the criteria of spectacle rather than of text in the theater, because the theater of text is not in vogue here. But I think that ultimately intelligence will prevail, in spite of the appeal which spectacle now has, because spectacle is fleeting. On other occasions, I also think that the selection of companies and countries should be made at the widest possible level, with the participation of directors and dramatists, but in such a way that it fulfills criteria and does not leave the theater of text unprovided for. Here nothing of the new English dramatists is presented.

—Like Harold Pinter. . .

—Not only Pinter. For example, Stoppard. Or even a play by a traditional or living North American. But, on the whole, it was a great gesture of vitality on the part of all the organizations and the public. It's not significant that it missed being a total triumph of creation of the best theater. Within certain Venezuelan intellectual groups, for instance, there is a depreciation of theater because they don't realize the great mobility theater has.

—How can you say this? "Vida con Mamá" attracted masses of spectators in the first three months of presentation, and equally so a second time and now, in the Festival one hears that the European and Latin American critics are very enthusiastic about it. Furthermore, I remember what positive reactions were stirred up among the intellectuals and local creative talent of all political and esthetic tendencies.

—Yes, but the exception proves the rule. In general, they don't realize that a theatrical play is capable of better language and greater introspection than a novel. But since there is this tradition that we are a profoundly visual country, if we had good theater with good language, we would be able to help those who read novels. Furthermore, I am a woman of strict literary forms. I have been formed, literarily, by the reviews, *Sardio, Zona Franco, Imagen.*

—This is very obvious, particularly in "Vida con Mamá," where there is little action and a great deal of nostalgic memory.

—I don't believe that action must be a battle or violence of some kind. That is a very Latin American view of action. One can achieve the same effect of action with a song, or the way in which an actress stands up and says something.

—Is that why you put old and new songs in your plays?

—Yes, it's because the popular song, in Latin America, has been a way of identifying ourselves and even a way of relating and defining ourselves. Since we are a country of little dialogue, the song has kept the silence from becoming complete. The radio was one of the earliest inventions to take us out of our lethargy. For the generation of our parents, the radio was a miracle.

–But why are you so fond of that particular mode of inquiry? The viewer of "Vida con Mamá" feels as if he is a secret viewer, spying, poking about in distant lives.

—These modes of inquiries—yes, they are a spontaneous form of dialogue that rescues us from the disconsolateness in which the country lives. Now, the Venezuelan has rejuvenated the old dictatorial guard for his mercantile interests and ambition. Every Venezuelan has become a new Juan Vicente Gómez of the condominiums. This new kind of dictator does not punish or remove the public liberties, but maintains caution in order to enrich himself and to remain in power, whether or not he has democratic convictions.

–Why do you have this obsession with the "earlier" Venezuelans?

—Because it is like the ambiguous visit of the "friend of the chief." One sees it for what it is in the official dispatches. This bureaucratic "visit" has not lost its tradition here. The other kind of friendly visit is gone. Right now, the Andean intellectuals, who are in the majority, are completely cheap. They still pay visits, but they never invite back. They only go, particularly if someone offers them a meal. . .In a like way, these kinds of meetings persist, because the politician in a democracy doesn't offer solutions, only cheap consolation.

A Certain Distance

–How do you account for the habit you have of disappearing every so often, as if you went into quarantine?

—That's a personal matter.One day I may think, how sad it is for me to write today! Then I have to subject myself, in this country, to a kind of quarantine, that's for sure. Because if I permit myself to go to all those parties and suppers—because, as you know, instead of a simple visit we now have elaborate suppers—I would not be able to write. You hardly write half a dozen articles in Venezuela and suddenly you have graduated as a writer, and everyone invites you to supper. And I never lacked food in my own house, because of my European Jewish origins.

–Well, that's true, we eat a good deal at home.

—Right. As if in case anything should happen, before one is taken off to a concentration camp, we should be well provided for and armed —Very good, the first stages in writing for me are like a preparation for a tournament or a competition. I know that there would be more sympathy for me if I accepted everyone's invitation, cigarettes, whisky. It is possible that in my isolation I write very little, because my raptures are intense but brief, and if I can accomplish three hours of work that's already like a marathon for me. Yes, I have to keep myself distant from society in order to maintain an effective discipline.

—But, can you then get to the real Venezuelan if you keep your distance?

—Everything that I write doesn't work out in every detail or very punctiliously.

—You read a great deal, don't you?

—You should know that I possess all the egotism of the intellectual. Caracas offers so much sedentary stress and boredom, that I don't feel that I am giving up external adventures, and I am quite able to write. I believe that literature is the product of a great boredom.

—That sounds like a pose. Your own writing is too full of lively intellectual resonances.

—Thank you. About your earlier question, I would say that we now have more professional writers.

—Has the scene changed from—the harpies you describe in "El País Odontológico"?

—The Venezuelan politician who is in charge of culture can deal better with these harpies who acted deceitfully during the dictatorship of General Marcos Pérez Jiménez while others, because of wanting to keep their dignity or because of ideological conviction, did not act at all. But this is already known. Fortunately, it was a fleeting moment. Because cunning, like desire, is of short duration. And true work, like love, is of long or eternal existence. Anyway, I believe that now there are more potential readers.

—And also potential spectators.

—No. The genuine spectator already exists, above all, in the upper middle classes. As I said before, we have the means to fight the harpies, because there are people who write seriously.

—Does this have anything to do with democracy?

—I believe so. There is one thing that one cannot deny the government of Acción Democrática, and that is the founding of Monte Avila. With all the mistakes this publishing house has made, with the realization that at times it too easily publishes Venezuelan writers who are very mediocre, I still believe it has been a major stimulus because since there is no true criticism here, it offers the only opportunity for the Venezuelan writers to produce and to get to know other writers. Because of Monte Avila, I know Djuna Barnes and Clarice Lispector.

—You are sufficiently intractable, and you know how to flee from cultural manipulation. When you were bound up with "Vida con Mamá," everyone was your friend again. People who hadn't remembered you or didn't want to remember you, suddenly discovered you—.

—During the years in which I wrote essays and newspaper articles, I found people who praised me, among them yourself, and Adriano González León, Isaac Chocrón, Orlando Araujo, but really when I was named among these writers, I was regarded as secondary. The critic, Néstor Leal once told me that the great writers of this country always dealt with the fragments of life, and that all my work, the newspaper articles, the essays, is significant. After the success of "Vida con Mamá," I still think that perhaps many of these articles are more prfound and more valuable than the play. Because either by occupation or vocation, I am a prose writer.

—How do you explain this neglect? Is it because the Venezuelan writer is regarded as something of a chronicler?

—In countries like England and the United States, Norman Mailer and Susan Sontag, for example, are well known by all their numerous works. Yes. Many of the ideas in "Vida con Mamá" really first matured in these earlier articles.

—Certainly those articles in Una sonrisa detrás de la metáphora *and later articles, even the most recent, give evidence of your devotion to good cinema and of your very original understanding for the universal film phenomenon. Perhaps you are one of the most qualified people to judge Venezuelan cinema today.*

—Perhaps one should clarify what is called "the national cinema" with a new name. The Age of the Four Letter Word. Because it is filled with crude and gross language. But one can't have good cinema in a country that is not provided with cinematography, in spite of the passionate will of a Margot Benacerraf and of a Rodolfo Inzaguirre. Our impressarios are not daring, they think more of box-office. The movie-goer then is not prepared for good cinema. And the movie-maker here is a self taught person, a wandering photographer. Certainly, at times television has brought some important pictures here from the 40s and the 50s, but one would have to become a detective to hunt down those instances. On the other hand, our film makers think that reflections about violence should be deliberately harsh, while I believe it should be a mental process, fear should be digested in the fantasy, in a living interior terror.

—One forbidden question. What are you now writing?

—That question does bother me. Because in Venezuela over the years there have been a series of books announced, whose titles have become famous by now. And they have never been written.

Partially published in el Suplemento Cultural de Ultimas Noticias 6-6-76 and in Nuevo Mundo Israelita, 6-18-76.

Trans. by Roberta Kalechofsky

Alicia Segal *is a Professor of Literature at la Universidad Central de Venezuela and a well known journalist in her country, writing for the newspapers, El Nacional and El Universal. Her books,* Entrevistados En Carne Y Hueso *and* La Venedemocracia *contain interviews with major political and intellectual figures of Venezuela; and her two books,* Trialogo: Notas De Critica Urgente *and* Cuarta Dimensión *contain her comments on such contemporary issues as feminism, ghettoes, blacks, Harlem, and Bangladesh. Her father, Máximo Freilich, who is the subject of an interview in this volume, is a well known Yiddish periodist. She considers her husband, Dr. Jaime Segal, to have been a great stimulus in her intellectual life. They have two teenage boys, Ernesto and Ariel. She is also executive secretary of la Confederación de Asociaciones Israelitas de Venezuela.*

Elisa Lerner

from

In the Vast Silence of Manhattan

A Poetic Drama
(12 Scenes)

CHARACTERS
(In order of appearance)

Rosie Davis	
Her Mother	
Miss Mary	Office workers
Mr. Jones	
Jean Harlow	
Mr. Robert	A boss
A New York Man	
Joe	An office boy

Group of men and women on Lexington Avenue, in which there are three voices, one of them a woman's

Julie	A madwoman
Nurse	
Psychiatrist	

Group of women in the Depression

Murphie	A secretary
Jim	A former suitor of Rosie's
Man in the Episcopal Church	
Mary	A friend of Rosie Davis
George	A Madison Avenue type

1st Man 2nd Man 3rd Man 4th Man 5th Man 6th Man	6 bosses from Rosie's office

Woman dressed as a chorus girl

Tom	A handsome young man
Vanessa Merton	An actress

1st Old Lady
2nd Old Lady

Leni	A young woman renting a room from Rosie
Mr. Lubko	
Priest	

SCENE I

(A room in early evening shadows. It is the room of a New York suburban working girl.)

TIME: (The early Thirties. A bell strikes eight times, probably from the bell tower of a nearby church. Rosie is onstage, seated in front of a dressing table with a mirror. She holds a powder box and a powder puff in her hands. Hearing her mother's voice, she drops the box and puff on the table, a little startled, as if she were just coming out of a long dream. From the rear of the stage comes the Mother's voice.)

MOTHER'S VOICE: Did you hear, Rosie? (Without waiting for Rosie's answer the Mother enters. She wears a cheap black dress of coarse cloth. Her hair is pulled into an austere knot. Her face is hard, her eyes glitter, her voice has a slight tremor. She is carrying two beautiful silver candelabra. She goes towards where Rosie is sitting, but stops in the middle of the stage.)

MOTHER: (Repeating) Did you hear, Rosie? The clock on the First Church of New Rochelle has struck eight. I hope you're ready. I hope your cheeks, your lips, your eyes are all shining, are all neat and tidy like those linen closets in the best houses in town. That's how they'll need to be.

ROSIE: I know. Soon cousin Emily will come in her car and we'll be off to the dance.

MOTHER: This dance is important, Rosie Davis, my daughter Rosie Davis. Very important that you should go to it. Are you listening, Rosie?

ROSIE: You know I am, Mother. You even know how. I'm listening to you as for years I've always listened to the water we boil for tea with our supper, thinking I could hear the whistle of trains bound for streets I'd never seen. I'm listening to you...

MOTHER: I don't know, Rosie. I still have the feeling you're hiding in your sewing box, like satin.

ROSIE: Mother, you're exaggerating.

MOTHER: Maybe so, my daughter Rosie, Rosie Davis. The truth is I would like something savage like desire, something savage like a man to drag you away from those satins, from that shyness. Something savage like desire to shatter that belly into smithereens. Then you'd have to start seeking your belly from the beginning, your vulnerability, in every fragment of the world, in all the blood.

ROSIE: Mother! The flames of your candelabra look so terrible—they dazzle me like those white birds on October mornings that make the sun so vast, so empty. And your words seem to spin more light than your candles. Mother, you frighten me with those candelabras, those words.

MOTHER: Rosie, all I want is your advantage. An advantage is simple. Every advantage is simple. Every advantage is a wedding, a season... Yours will be going to this dance. Out-of-town men have been coming to them of late, with breaths as cozy as meat and potatoes. (She goes up to Rosie. She strokes her cheek with a certain tenderness.) What I want is to see you married, Rosie. What I want is to see a wedding ring blossom on this finger.

ROSIE: Mother, what you want isn't easy. And besides, these aren't easy times. The men all left town in the Depression. First the bread shortage got so notorious that the Governor shut down all the restaurants. "For Reasons of Public Order" the authorities wrote on all the tables, chairs, glasses and plates in every restaurant in New Rochelle. If you wanted to eat it would have to be in private, as if keeping the secret in your stomach. Then more than ever, Mother, I thought the tableware looked like silver-plated minnows you could never fish from the tablecloth. And now, finally, nobody in town has ventured as far as New York this winter. Hunger and poverty have made the city trains too cold. Nobody goes on them now. They've been thrown out like the king's dirty dishes.

MOTHER: That is why, Rosie, Rosie Davis, it's so important that you go to this dance. Where there's no bread on the tablecloths, you won't find men on the sheets of love. Still, cousin Emily drives her car all around town and in her car, like in a shameless basket, she collects all the rumors. Those rumors...

ROSIE: Those rumors...

MOTHER: Rosie, those rumors say that men are still coming from the city to this town, men with shining blonde whiskers and mugs of sparkling beer. They will get rich. At night their money will glow like mirrors, like lamps. The bread we lack today they will be seeking at the bottom of mines, of ruins. They will build vast factories, theaters, banks, huge stores...

ROSIE: Mother, you're delirious. Sometimes you seem to be seeing mad flashing lights.

MOTHER: What I want is something concrete. There are no kings' crowns anymore. Hardly any dreams. What I want is to see a ring bloom on your finger, the youthful vigor of your marriage. (Silence.) Yes, you have only to get married, climb out of that oppressive sewing box, and after a time you will forget all about that clumsy first ring, maybe even forget your hands as well. All that will exist for you will be those long black gloves from the best stores in Manhattan.

ROSIE: Mother, I don't understand you. Now you seem to be chasing metaphors in the sky. It's an audacity to go chasing around these cold weather skies. These skies darkened by the lack of winds and birds.

MOTHER: You must listen to me, Rosie. If I have to I'll smash your sewing box. I'll make it blaze like burning castles and I'll trample your satins on the sidewalk. It's time you learned about desire, about a lover's tongue.

ROSIE: I'm afraid I can't climb out of my sewing box any more. The palest of all my satins is my face.

MOTHER: Rosie, I don't mean to upset you. These last few years we've lost that sense of something metaphysical that exists between one being and another. That was all I wanted to say to you. Cousin Emily should be coming any minute. I've talked too much and the flames on these candles are starting to go out, but even so I can still see you. You look very lovely tonight, Rosie Davis. Leave your fears in your sewing box, in your mirrors that clarify nothing. I'm going to my room now. Bless you. Be happy! (Mother exits. Rosie is alone on stage.)

ROSIE: Cousin Emily won't be much longer. But I still feel full of my fears. Soon I won't be able to look myself in the mirror, I won't believe in them anymore. I will think they're waters, waters my face alone can join. Then I'll have nothing to believe in. Other faces, the flesh, have never been mine to hold. Mirrors, though. . .are vast, are oceans that have never known other land than what my face paints on their lonely cheeks. Because mirrors are vast, they grow without end when the multiple flesh of life or love has kept distant, like a sky we are not allowed to touch because it is white and birdless.

Is that cousin Emily? No. Cousin Emily is about to arrive, but not yet, I know, because when she comes her black car swishes down the street like a big black patent leather slipper. I am full of fears. I didn't want to go to this party. The truth is, I think my belly will be smooth forever. It will stay like the face of an adolescent. Besides, I know how those New Rochelle boys dance the Charleston. They dance so fast! It must be the times we live in. But while they're dancing, their bodies sometimes seem to rise like actions on the stock exchange, over the highest skyscrapers on Wall Street.

Then again, I'm so clumsy I might slip and fall down. My heels might even break, like champagne glasses. And then how will the couples go on dancing if my heels are lying scattered in the middle of the floor like fragments of wineglasses? By that time we must suppose that these couples have drunk too much and would have a hard time telling if what was strewn all over the floor were my broken heels or the shattered champagne glasses. Thanks to my awkwardness, the party would be paralyzed and maybe no one would know why. Most people might think that the dance was stopped because of hungry and desperate people outside throwing sharp glass, and bombs, since it isn't right to dance the Charleston when for many months the banks have been silent like undiscovered planets. But I would know the truth: it was my clumsiness that ended the party. Then I could never forgive myself. I'd end up in a madhouse. I would sit, overwhelmed by remorse and guilt, where I could see only grass, smell only salt. Besides, I must begin to face the fact that I will always be Miss Rosie Davis and that if wholesome men still do come to these parties in New Rochelle, they'd never pick me. They'd want a strong, solid woman to bear the wedding ring they offer, and they'd see right away that my fears and my dreams could never bear anything, could never bear a wedding ring. It would tire me too soon. What's more, the strong, solid wedding ring might just crumble like mysterious sands as soon as my dream shoots the first flickers of entrancement. I am definitely not suited to those men.

The man I love now is writing a book or fishing all night and naturally can't see the fish very clearly because he is fishing in the dark. Or the man I love seeks a forest but will undoubtedly get lost without ever finding it. There aren't any forests any more. The wood, nearly all of it, has been used by the government (a growing scandal) to make the chairs in their waiting rooms, since with the Depression we're living in, it's getting very difficult to solve the problems of the people. But in the government waiting rooms, the wooden chairs are increasing and the forest is a dream forever in ruins. Which means the book, fish or forest man can't come to the party tonight in New Rochelle. The ring they would offer would weigh nothing. It would blaze like footlights in Broadway theaters. My belly will stay smooth. I don't want, I wouldn't ever want to go to this dance. The Charleston confuses me. But my mother is a vigorous woman whose eyes glitter like the flames on her two silver candelabras. That's cousin Emily, she's here. Cousin Emily, her coach and her horses gleaming like some fantastic patent leather pump.

. . . .

SCENE IV

(The set is from the same time as the previous. A street in downtown New York. From above hangs a series of red and yellow traffic lights which should be arranged a little after the manner of a Calder mobile. When Rosie Davis mentions traffic signals or red lights, the red signals should light up. When she mentions the apple pie or the flowers, the yellow signals will light. At the tensest moments of the monologue, all the traffic lights should flash on and off at once and almost continuously.)

(Rosie Davis's monologue on Lexington Avenue)

ROSIE: I still have. . .exactly one hour before I have to be back at the office. That means I could still buy Mama her apple pie at the Lexington Bakery. Really, I do like this Lexington Avenue, with all its stalls of yellow flowers. Not to mention Bloomingdale's. But in another hour I should be on my way back to the office. Some other day I'll go to Bloomingdale's: I'll wait for spring and all the sales to do that. Now I have to hurry and get the pie. Though I really could come more often to get Mama her apple pies. As of today, I'm getting a five dollar raise. Today is payday. Now I can afford to go a little easier on the overtime. Five dollars' raise isn't bad. No, I can't quite see the traffic lights on Lexington Avenue. No, I haven't gotten married.

At the office everyone says back and forth between the desks, "To think Miss Rosie Davis hasn't gotten married. As ready as she is!" And the typewriter keys pick it up, "As ready as she is!" And I certainly am ready: now I'm getting an extra five dollars. . .I'm thirty-six years old and there's nobody left in town except Nilson in that frail-as-an-eggshell house of his. Nilson, Nilson, who never answers the cards I send him every year on his birthday. . .I think the light has changed. Now it's red. Am I losing my mind? If I don't hurry up and cross the street I'm afraid the light will start telling me, "Hurry,Rosie. Take a taxi if you have to. You can do it. Come on, hurry. Take my splendid red city light for a lover's face." Well, I made it across the avenue. That's hard to do at this time of day. I couldn't seem to see the red light. Suddenly I thought I saw it on top of a hill. Like out in the suburbs, like in New Rochelle. But that's absurd. They don't have red traffic lights on top of hills, over New Rochelle. Now I'm making my way through lines of cars and café tables. I'm not hurt and I can stop and think how my favorite was always Jim. Jim is in California selling insurance. At first he sent snapshots. Poor Jim. Mama and I hear them saying around town that he isn't happy, that his wife is cheating on him. Jim got married when he got to California. That usually happens in the insurance business: you end up taking a lot of risks. But meanwhile it's nice to think that from now on I'm getting five dollars more, that I'm going to buy Mama an apple pie, and that Jim is still my favorite. In short: I think what I like most are these flower stalls in the middle of Lexington Avenue. These yellow roses. Maybe what I would like would be to eat a pie of yellow roses. . .I could have been Nilson's wife or rather Jim's. My belly is a neglected gift, a planet. But why am I talking about my belly? Why talk about something as unknown as the ocean the fishermen never catch? Though I can't remember what kind of pies Nilson and Jim liked to eat. Does that have anything to do with my belly? If your own belly is lost in the fog, doesn't the world miss it? The pies Jim and Nilson liked must have been. . .apple? And . . .my belly? Maybe Nilson and Jim didn't like eating pies, but I can't see their faces either. They're lost in a fog like my belly. Personally . . .I would prefer a pie of yellow flowers. (One of the yellow lights goes out at this point and an invisible stage hand lowers it slowly into Rosie Davis's hands.)

Although. . .now I've got the apple pie. But I do have to admit I'm a little tired. . .so many people buying apple pies. Could all those people be. . .hopeless? I'll have to be careful trying to cross the street, that light was telling me to take a taxi toward life. . .saying over and over, "The taxi, Rosie. Take the taxi and not the pie. The taxi." That red light, isn't it Nilson's face, isn't it Jim's? I can't make it out very well, the light is blinding, Nilson doesn't answer the birthday cards I send him and Jim hasn't sent any snapshots for a long time now. I can't see very well. Nilson's face, Jim's. Besides, that light won't stop talking. It keeps saying something about a taxi and life. It's saying something about life. I have to listen closer. I'll hurry. But there are other taxis, other lives. I can't hear very well. I think I should leave the pie. I need to get free, to find the talking red light. I should go up to that red light, but before I get there, I lose. It's as if that light is on the highest point of the hill in New Rochelle. There's a taxi I should be taking too. I can't see well. But I'm beginning to believe that if I ever get in the taxi, life, and the taxi too, will soar higher than the red lights along the avenue. Higher than the hill in the suburb of New Rochelle. But the taxi and I might end up destroyed. Because, isn't it maybe too daring to try to devour the red light like a lover's face? There's no reason I should risk so much for a red traffic light, for a yellow taxi ride through life. I shouldn't risk so much: I still have my five dollars and an apple pie. Besides, I don't know which taxi to take. . . (Rosie starts to rush out into the street. The red and yellow traffic signals light up suddenly and voices seem to be coming from them. There is also a bewildering blare of automobile horns.)

1st VOICE: Hey lady, look out!

2nd VOICE: Don't jump out in the street. Don't jump out!

3rd VOICE: The taxi could be your death! Your red death light!

(A scream is heard and Rosie falls in the middle of the stage like the victim of a hit-and-run. Immediately several people sprint out, most of them men in winter overcoats. Some take their coats off and throw them over Rosie's legs, then stand around the body.)

(Voices of the crowd.)

1st VOICE: Someone call the police. The woman is hurt, though her face looks happy.

2nd VOICE: She's got an apple pie.

3rd VOICE: (A woman's) Then naturally she must have been very happy. An apple pie is one of the few things to make some people in this city happy.

1st VOICE: It's a very strange pie. It has a red light shining on it.

2nd VOICE: Probably a cherry. Maybe the pie isn't all apple.

3rd VOICE: Maybe it's an effect from the red traffic light.

(The stage grows dark.)

1st VOICE: But look. How strange! Now the red light in the pie is going out.

(The two men and the woman pick Rosie Davis up from the ground and say in unison:)

THE THREE VOICES: Only the yellow lights on the taxis shine down the avenue.

3rd VOICE: (Coming alone to the front of the stage) And only the taxis shine down the avenue, flooding the traffic signal and the apple pie with its yellow city light, its yellow city roses. . .

. . . .

SCENE IX

(Rosie is standing off to one side of the stage, in her accustomed corner, where she speaks in the voice of a radio announcer. Usually this spot, when Rosie speaks from it, is lit by yellow light, but on this occasion the light might be violet. Center stage is in shadow.)

ROSIE: Really, everyone in the office has been so kind to me. Even that nasty little Italian in the Collections Department. That sexy Italian! They say. . .they say he spent last summer in bed with three servant girls. I am quite overcome. Profoundly grateful. Everyone in the office has been so very considerate. "Take as much time as you need," they told me. "We're sorry, we're so very sorry, Miss Davis." Suddenly it seemed I was getting a raise, another check for five dollars. In short, from now on I'll never forget the kindness in this office. "Miss Rosie has lost her mother," said the secretaries, salesmen and elevator girls. The typewriters, all of the typewriters stopped for a few seconds, making the day and all those words more enigmatic. . .And what a wreath they sent! My God, it must have weighed more than the Sunday New York Times! Then all the office bosses filed in grave and silent, as if they were attending one of those planning and coordinating meetings so popular today. . .Mr. John came too, the top executive, whose smile my mother always found so benign. I guess it reminded her of other smiles of power. (The corner grows dark. Onstage, Rosie Davis: pale and in a high-buttoned black suit, standing by a dark, somber tree. Suddenly six men appear in single file. They are all in black, with black bowler hats. They approach Rosie. The first, Mr. John, removes his hat and puts his hand out to Rosie, while the others also take off their hats and say in unison, gaily:) "What a great loss, Miss Rosie! How very sorry we are!"

ROSIE: (Radiant now) Oh Mr. John! Mr. Phillips! This really truly is a great day! The highest executives in the office taking time off from figuring dividends and giving orders, though there can be no question how dearly you love the clauses of your Commercial Code. You are standing, with such delicacy, right here, next to Rosie Davis's only possession (pointing to the tree): her mother's coffin, wood from a tree that in springtime, maybe, used to blow like a sailboat. (Changing) I'm so delighted! I was always a sociable girl! I always wanted to offer my summer sandals to a man! (The men, like actors in a musical comedy, almost festively, raise their bowler hats while saying:)

1st MAN: Now we'll say goodbye. Some of us have to go to one of those business meetings they now call "top-level."

2nd MAN: Devotion, you understand.

ROSIE: I always tried to accept the human condition and its heartfelt dialogue!

(A brief pause. Then:)

3rd MAN: (As if accusing her, very rapidly) You lost your mother.

4th MAN: (Same) You've been in a mental hospital.

5th MAN: (Same) You never married.

6th MAN: You who are a fragile rose, whom the New York City traffic lights have hammered like faces.

1st MAN: (Quickly) Like memories.

ROSIE: (A sudden cry) Jim, Nilson.

2nd MAN: (Quickly) You and your apple pie.

3rd MAN: (Quickly) Your yellow rose pie.

ROSIE: (A dramatic cry) Enough! Let the asphalt silence swallow our voices...

(Tense silence. Then:)

4th MAN: (As if speaking from a remote distance) Summer's coming.

THE MEN: (Repeating soberly) Summer's coming.

5th MAN: (Turning to Rosie) Take some vacation time, Miss Rosie. We'll speak to the personnel manager so he won't cut your pay while you're gone.

6th MAN: (Also turning to Rosie) And if you go to Barbados, for example, Miss Rosie, we'll get you in on our employee travel plan. 40 percent off.

ROSIE: (With great poetic dignity) There are men and woman who for days on end turn to bathers, engulfed by towels and ocean, seeking happiness in the water, a fullness they no longer find in people's faces. (Transition. Leaning with a certain coyness towards the men, who have gathered around her) I've heard tell, from one of our church goers, that in Barbados the grass grows nice and smooth.

1st MAN: And there are bathers who almost believe they're eating it on those little salad plates they get at dinner.

ROSIE: (Timidly) I. . .once wanted to stretch myself out on the grass, to know the splendor of the world.

2nd MAN: Yes, Rosie. You should go, now, somewhere where you can touch the sand, not this asphalt acre of death all around you.

ROSIE: (Returning to her earlier poetic dignity) When we have touched sand a long time, for many days, we can go on to touch skin and faces. But I couldn't say whether that is enough: sand soon crumbles, leaving our cracks and hollows unfilled.

3rd MAN: But even so, Rosie, the earth goes on lifting the island and its people.

ROSIE: Then it's a lovely island. I. . .always wanted to see that precious basket that holds the world. (Changing. An apprehensive tone) But now, death has also made my flowered chair vulnerable, the wallpaper roses in our rooms. . .

CHORUS OF MEN: Forget, Rosie Davis, the flower-covered chairs that that come between you and the blood of men.

(Here a woman dressed as a Radio City chorus girl appears, showing her legs and pulling a typewriter, or stage prop to look like a typewriter, by a string. In a very sweet tone she says:)

GIRL: But gentlemen, don't you have a meeting of the Anticrime Commission to attend?

CHORUS OF MEN: (While filing out after the girl) Yes, we do. But it's been nice seeing you, Miss Rosie. And we're sorry. We're so very sorry. But really, more important are our riches and our offices, our personnel manager, our anticrime commissions, and the lovable breasts of these cute little chorus girls. A pleasure, Miss Rosie, to see you. A real pleasure.

ROSIE: (Remaining alone by the tree, in a mournful voice) Oh Jim, oh Nilson! This winter the city winds have been fierce and New York has blown like a huge trumpet. (A final flourish) What immense blank spaces we are!

. . . .

SCENE XI

(Some years later. The scene takes place in one of those automats so common in New York City. At one of the tables, on the left, are sitting two old ladies, pale, thin, brittle, resembling as closely as possible the wooden statues—pop art sculptures—of Marisol Escobar. One of the old ladies is wearing, as a hat, a small brown pot with the leaves of a green bush sticking out of it. The other lady's hat should be a kind of miniature bright red window-box. The two old ladies might well be real-life images—harsh and ordinary—of the present Rosie Davis. At a table to the right sits a Rosie Davis who has now definitely aged, but who still seems to gaze off into a dream, though the dream is turning more and more melancholy.)

(The two Old Ladies talk:)

1st OLD LADY: Do you have your own house?

2nd OLD LADY: No.

1st OLD LADY: Your own car?

2nd OLD LADY: No, no...

1st OLD LADY: Then obviously when you were young you went into...social work?

2nd OLD LADY: Recently I've been involved in selling real estate. Could you take a peek at the newspaper and see what it's been up to this last month?

1st OLD LADY: Maybe sometimes, you worried about where you might live?

2nd OLD LADY: No. Still, I think that before long, city apartments will disappear and we'll all have to live in garages of dreadful asphalt.

1st OLD LADY: (Sighing happily) Not us. What a relief! We won't have to hear about any more wars or...teenage unemployment. We'll have died and our eyes will be like wedding rings that have lost all earthly brilliance.

2nd OLD LADY: In any case, days we'll never see again, we are like horses they turn out to pasture.

(The two Old Ladies sigh and sit a moment in silence.)

(Rosie's monologue:)
ROSIE: I believe I've ordered my life rather well. In a year I'll be 65. I can retire from the office, I'll have gotten my pension. Then, no doubt, I'll take a trip, a trip around the world. I'll see rivers and cities. In the blue places in the rivers are the boats and summer. In the gray places, the city and next autumn.

(Old Ladies' dialogue:)
2nd OLD LADY: How did you say to make chicken again?

1st OLD LADY: Nothing to it, dearie. Just stick it half an hour in a slow oven.

(Rosie's monologue:)
ROSIE: Now that I really am starting to get tired of working in the office and pounding the typewriter, like pounding my own insides.

(Old Ladies' dialogue:)
1st OLD LADY: (Leafing through a newspaper) There's a meeting next Tuesday at our church. We could go.

2nd OLD LADY: I don't think I'll go to any more of those meetings. Do you know what the topic was at our minister's last talk? Homosexuality. To go to church to hear people talk about. . .homosexuality.

1st OLD LADY: I didn't know that at your age you could care about sex. Especially not having had either a car or an apartment when you were young.

(Rosie's monologue:)
ROSIE: Because I need a river for love.

(Old Ladies' dialogue:)
1st OLD LADY: Yesterday after dinner I was listening to the news on the radio. I think this country's in big trouble.

2nd OLD LADY: Too many millionaires in government.

1st OLD LADY: They don't know what it is to earn their bread with the sweat of their brow. They don't know that before there's bread there's the brows of men.

(Rosie's monologue:)
ROSIE: Tom never came back. In his beauty he seemed to hold all the semen of the world. We could have been like fish of love. Sure, I was much older than he. But maybe that wouldn't have mattered so much. Woman carries man in her belly and then later, again, in love.

(Old Ladies' dialogue:)
2nd OLD LADY: For over a week, and after working more than twenty years in the office, they've stuck me without a desk. Do you know what that means? One day my desk is on one floor. Another day, on another. So that after a while I've worked every desk, every department, every floor.

(Rosie's monologue:)
ROSIE: That's when I decided to rent a room to Leni, that young Swedish girl. In my memory, in its boundless personnel, of course, Jim and Nilson stayed on with me. Leni was a strange girl. She wore her slip all day and threw her underthings all over the apartment. "I like going around in a slip, Miss Rosie. So I can be closer to the hopelessness of the world," she said.

(Old Ladies' dialogue:)
1st OLD LADY: I don't think it's proper for ladies like us to rent rooms under any circumstances to young girls.

2nd OLD LADY: Of course not.

1st OLD LADY: The last time I did it, the girl brought men to the house when I stayed late at the office. She even told me about it. "I like sharing my bed as if it were bread or daily life." But at my age it was disastrous to get a reputation as an old lady with men in her apartment.

(Rosie's monologue:)
ROSIE: But Leni in nothing but a slip, with her other underthings tossed all over the apartment, began to get to me. It kept reminding me that once I had wanted to stay close to a man's lips. I had wanted to kiss a man's face like kissing the world.

(Old Ladies' dialogue:)
1st OLD LADY: This morning Mr. Miller came to see me, he used to work in my office. He's been drawing his social security pension for over two years now and at present lives in Vermont. He brought me a present, a bottle of floor wax.

2nd OLD LADY: Yes, I remember him. He spent more than twenty years among our desks and typewriters. He seemed to loathe us all.

1st OLD LADY: He's changed a little now. He has nothing to do except at Christmas. So now he sends Christmas cards to all the office mates he used to hate.

2nd OLD LADY: And the business about the wax?

1st OLD LADY: He can't get along without his wax. In his retirement home up in Vermont he makes and bottles floor wax and then gives it to people because, up to now, he hasn't gotten the authorities to grant him a license to patent it as an industry. The wax keeps him active. At the same time it performs a great service: most of the people he gives it to are rheumatics, but when they walk on waxed floors, thanks to the bottles Mr. Miller gives them, for a few moments they feel spry.

2nd OLD LADY: They feel a radiance spreading from their thighs out into the world?

1st OLD LADY: Not quite. We know we're old and that even when we were young we didn't have pretty legs. Sometimes the wax makes us fall and have accidents.

2nd OLD LADY: Accidents?

1st OLD LADY: Sure. The last accident I had my leg swelled all up. Of course they gave me permission at the office to spend a week at home.

2nd OLD LADY: You mean a week with pay?

1st OLD LADY: No. But anyway I had a wonderful time writing letters to the insurance company and answering the phone. (The first Old Lady strikes a pose as if answering the telephone.) Everyone was so kind, asking after my leg. I'd say: Yes, Miss Wilson, I woke up a little less swollen today. No, Miss Porter, the insurance company hasn't answered me yet. And besides. . .those were peaceful days. Christmas was coming and I could sit down and pen all my Christmas cards at leisure.

(Rosie's monologue:)
ROSIE: Sundays in June or July, the man would have spread a tablecloth with me and on the cloth we would have served dinner, like someone setting roses in the grass. But really, it would have been like spreading the wings of an enormous butterfly living in us, because we would have been happy and smiling.

(Old Ladies' dialogue:)
2nd OLD LADY: I think the best thing for me right now would be a planters punch. It seems like only when I drink can I sing songs that bring me old faces.

1st OLD LADY: And if someone buys you a drink?

2nd OLD LADY: Even better. Then I feel like a courtesan. A prostitute of great renown.

(As soon as the 2nd Old Lady says this, the invisible stage hand should drop a big sign just over her head, with heavy block letters saying, EXPENSIVE PROSTITUTE. After a few seconds, when the 1st Old Lady starts speaking, the sign should disappear.)

1st OLD LADY: I'd rather they bought me ice cream. Ice cream brings back my childhood and my father. I see red sailboats.

2nd OLD LADY: Didn't you soon find your father in other men's faces?

1st OLD LADY: I guess not. Because, until now, I've always done better with the private sector than with the public.

(Rosie's monologue:)
ROSIE: (Gets up. She comes forward, not very enthusiastically, to the proscenium) Black winds have been covering my skies and my blue and more favorable suns. (Rosie exits slowly.)

(Old Ladies' dialogue:)
1st OLD LADY: I see you're taking your hat off.

2nd OLD LADY: You should too. We musn't count on spring and summer gardens. We still have a year before they give us our social security pensions.

1st OLD LADY: (Takes off her hat) We are women who never gave birth.

2nd OLD LADY: Our only spring and summer roses are here in our hats.

1st OLD LADY: Should I look for water and a watering can?

2nd OLD LADY: You'll have to.

1st OLD LADY: Take my hat. I'll be right back.

(The 1st Old Lady exits. The 2nd puts both hats on the floor. Soon the 1st appears with a tiny garden watering can.)

2nd OLD LADY: You were gone a long time. I'm afraid it's winter again.

1st OLD LADY: Where I went they were having a run on watering cans. A legion of old maids all telling the clerk, "Please, one of those watering cans so we can grow spring and summer in our hats."

2nd OLD LADY: Did you see an old lady with a pink hat on her head?

1st OLD LADY: (Brightening with memory) One who was also carrying an apple pie in her hand? (Silence. Sudden doubt) No, I don't remember.

2nd OLD LADY: Then let's water the hats.

1st OLD LADY: And sing a song.

2nd OLD LADY: A song to bring us old faces.

(The 2nd Old Lady starts singing a song popular every summer in America, while the 1st Old Lady sprinkles water over the hats as if they were a shrub or a garden.)

SCENE XII

(At the far right stands Rosie in a white nightgown, a garland of natural roses in her hair and a long black velvet glove in one hand.)

(To the rear, toward the middle, could be standing a few chairs, the kind usually set out at funerals.)

(After several minutes Leni comes onstage. [This is the girl who in Rosie's later years, for a while, sublet a room in her Long Island City apartment.])

Dialogue I

LENI: (A slight tremor in her voice) Rosie. Rosie. Miss Rosie...

ROSIE: (Rather abruptly, in a suspicious tone, and still at far right) You should be on the job at the café.

LENI: I left work for a few minutes. Mr. Lubko, the landlord, came by this morning for a cup of coffee and he told me...

ROSIE: (Coming out rather listlessly to the center of the stage to greet Leni) He told you I was dead?

LENI: That's right. That's what he said.

ROSIE: Don't worry about seeing me still around. I'm only here to receive some of the people who will undoubtedly be coming to pay me their respects. Though the funeral homes do a fine job of it. A lot better, maybe, than most public administration offices. The experience my own death has given me leads me to believe that in the future they should choose the highest officials in the land from among the funeral directors. If their urns shine like tea kettles, think how the rest of the country might shine...

LENI: I understand that nevertheless you don't want to leave all the work to the funeral parlor and that even in the midst of the sober occupations of death you are ready to receive your friends. You always took pains with your education, Rosie, and with your manners, like you took pains with those white curtains in the autumn windows...

ROSIE: Education, Leni, also living alone, compel me to this final effort. Why, only last Christmas I received 150 greeting cards from 150 different friends...

LENI: Maybe lots of them will turn up to admire your tea kettle urn. Your transcendental tea kettle. But (affectionately) you mustn't tire yourself too much, you don't have much strength left, you're getting quite old now and besides, you're dead. (Change. Drily) There's no life left to lean on.

ROSIE: In this country we develop a great agility that death can't snatch from us right away: the agility of having existed 65 years, paying the supermarket bills and the rent...

LENI: That's true. At your age, you still dance on city subways and escalators, and you ascend tirelessly in elevators, looking for something. (Suddenly critical) I think it's only your nose that made you look so awfully old.

ROSIE: (Tensing) I have to stay here. Naturally, since I live alone, there is no one to receive condolences for me. You have to get back to the café. But I also stay on here because, maybe I have something to confess. (Serious, firm) I have something to tell you, Leni.

LENI: (Wary) Tell me what?

ROSIE: You came here. But you're not sorry, really, that I died.

LENI: Rosie.

ROSIE: It's the truth. I didn't love you. I think I. . .envied you, because you were always in your underwear around the apartment, maybe, because love turned your tongue splendid and a magnificent masculine saliva brought the vastest oceans to your fingers, all the waters. . .

LENI: You don't know what you're saying. You're dead and you still talk like the living. But I forgive you because you are dead. You have suffered much, Rosie: you have died.

ROSIE: I deserve this death, this black urn. The truth is, I didn't really care that the rug in your room was covered with the darkness of winter. What hurt me was that you were young and that the bright juices of men kept you happy.

LENI: Quiet, Rosie. Obey your death. You're talking nonsense. Black streams of death have deprived you utterly of life's clear-sightedness. (Changing) Now I have to get back to work. It's time to put out those cups of coffee that lonely people like to drink. I just work there. (Leni exits.)

Dialogue II

(Rosie stays alone on stage, but soon a fat character appears, with white hair, rather coarse and solid-looking. He is dressed in a dark overcoat and carries a ring of keys which, for scenic purposes, should be large and visible. It is Mr. Lubko, the landlord of Rosie's Long Island City apartment. When Rosie sees him, she rushes to meet him with an effusive uncertainty.)

ROSIE: Come in, Mr. Lubko. You were truly a landlord deserving of admiration. I always paid my rent in full. But not only that. I trembled with friendliness and fear: you were the owner, you had the money. Towards the end, money that came my way made me shudder with pleasure and respect. But you know, this accident happened to me: I died. I died, Mr. Lubko. Now I can't pay any more rent. I won't be paying any more. I'm very sorry. I beg your pardon.

MR. LUBKO: (A little embarrassed) You musn't take things so seriously. I knew life's needles wanted to sew more splendid fabric than your spinster's skin, that the needles of life were slowing down for you. We landlords are prudent folk: I've already found somebody else for your apartment. What's more. . .I didn't give it to any Black or Puerto Rican family. You can rest in peace. (Coming up to Rosie) This is a very pretty urn.

ROSIE: (Coquettish, stretching her long black velvet glove) Think so?

MR. LUBKO: (Very solemn, very sure of what he is saying) Without a doubt, one of the most sumptuous urns I've seen in recent times.

ROSIE: (Very pleased) I thought so too. I had to be sure it was a good urn because I knew that the highest men in the office would be coming, people from the church. . .you. (Assuming a certain intimacy) The rents brought us together in recent years.

MR. LUBKO: (Very sensibly) Of course, of course. The rent linked us rather solidly.

ROSIE: (Sighing, and as if to herself) The rent and not love. (Louder and more rapidly) The rent, not love. . .

MR. LUBKO: (Interrupting) I don't understand, Miss Rosie. You talking of love, now that you're dead. The dead are practical folk. They've pushed love utterly to one side. Love is something for the living, for the credulous and inexperienced, Miss Rosie: they haven't experimented with death.

ROSIE: True: I'm dead. I have no right to talk of love. I never held that hard splendor in my legs. From the beginning I was very practical. Eventually I acquired the lucidity of the dead. (As if talking to herself) I mustn't talk of summers or men: I am dead. (Turning to Mr. Lubko) Excuse me. I don't want to bother you with my personal affairs, with my death.

MR. LUBKO: Death is one of the few personal affairs that do concern us in others. Poverty or loneliness, naturally not. Death, yes. We are human, Miss Rosie, and the death of others concerns us. I trust this is not a socialist sentiment: I'm a landlord. . .

ROSIE: (Still coquettish and playing with the long black glove) Then, my death worries you?

MR. LUBKO: Of course it does, Miss Rosie. To feel moved by another's death is a human sentiment, almost a law, though it's understood this has nothing to do with popular demonstrations or revolution. But now I must go.

ROSIE: So soon?

MR. LUBKO: Today is the day I collect rents in this building. Miss Rosie, you were always so punctual that your death fell on the exact day your rent was due.

ROSIE: (Remembering) You came in winter to see if I had enough heat in the apartment. You climbed four flights...

MR. LUBKO: You paid your rent. Now you're dead. I'm sure more people will show up...

ROSIE: I hope these people who show up will take my death and my presence as an invitation to drink tea. That would be most proper: I was so old. Besides, I always loved the little tea cakes. . .Mr. Lubko, do you see any cakes on the urn?

MR. LUBKO: No cakes. Only the urn.

ROSIE: Then I must have eaten them. (Rapidly) Before you go around to the tenants, could you go buy some tea cakes for me? Don't forget to put them on the urn.

MR. LUBKO: I'll get you some cakes right this minute... (Mr. Lubko exits.)

Dialogue III

(Rosie remains on stage, but this time her presence is not so noticeable: she looks almost to be waiting in a very odd train station. A middle-aged priest enters, pink cheeks and soothing manners. He has a small paper in his hand. He doesn't see Rosie at first. He walks about the stage as if looking for directions, and asks in a soft voice, rather timidly:)

PRIEST: Miss Rosie? Rosie? Any Miss Rosie here? The Miss Rosie who died...?

ROSIE: That's me: Miss Rosie. I see I surprise you. Of course. I'm very tired. Understand: I'm dead. But someone had to take charge of my funeral. The very day of my death, and still I can't rest. First I have to attend to those who are coming to my death reception: Are you one of them? (Stroking the long black glove) Can I tempt you with some cakes? If you ever played canasta here you'd know which ones I mean. They're on the urn. (Changing) Your suit looks familiar. But it's so hard for me to recognize things now: between your skin and my own, blind waters of death are rising this very moment...

PRIEST: (Rather moved) You have no reason to know me. I'm new in your church. You came on Sundays: the Episcopal Church, off Wall Street.

ROSIE: (Distant) The church, of course. That man was certainly right: "Miss Rosie, you should join our church this year. Don't wait too long." I myself never saw him in church, but later I found out that the next year he had died. It was as though, not being able to offer me anything, marriage, for example, he proposed that I join the church. His intentions, no doubt, were good, were refined. A man like him couldn't offer me brushes, though... I believe he sold them.

PRIEST: We will pray for your soul.

ROSIE: (Still distant) Oh yes! My soul! These last years, I've only thought about my social security pension, about how much the Workers Union would pay me. Now, suddenly, I'm dead and my soul is like an ocean full of ghostly fishes.

PRIEST: Now you are suffering: You are dead. But let us pray for your soul, Rosie. For its sake do we discard our skin. But now, I must be getting back to the church.

ROSIE: (From very far away) Father: The fish are very ghostly, I can't make them out. The water in this ocean is very cold and gray. Now I understand nothing. Nothing.

PRIEST: (Turning toward the rear) We have discarded our skin. And the soul is just a tiny gray stone that only on certain days becomes warm and blue.

(Priest exits. The stage grows a little darker.)

ROSIE: (Sobbing) But, these ghostly fish...

(A little light returns.)

(Voices off stage:)

1st VOICE: Rosie Davis can be happy: It was a bona fide funeral. A very sober affair. She managed to bring together a landlord, a top executive and a priest.

2nd VOICE: It didn't seem such a sober reunion to me. I didn't see a single politician.

ROSIE: (As from a great solitude) But I begin to feel, again, as if I'm alone with the ghostly fishes. My long black glove that I never stopped stroking, triumphantly, all the time I was talking to the landlord and the priest, is falling down. (Rosie lets the long glove drop. Then she walks slowly, to the front, towards an imaginary coffin and with a loud exclamation says:) Finally, I go to my coffin, grave as a ship that never knew birds. . .

Trans. by David Pritchard

Elisa Lerner's *life and work is represented in her interview by Alicia Segal, printed in this volume. Other relevant facts are that her family came to Venezuela from Rumania at the beginning of the 1930's and that the author was born in Valencia in 1932. She graduated with a law degree from la Universidad Central de Venezuela in 1959, and her first play was published in 1960. She has been to the United States to study and work under the Children's Bureau in Washington and has spent a good deal of time in New York, becoming familiar with Broadway and Off Broadway. Her play,* Vida con Mamá, *was recently produced in Los Angeles, as well as in Mexico. She has won several awards, and her play,* In The Vast Silence of Manhattan, *written soon after her return from New York, won el Premio Ana Julia Rojas, del Ateneo de Caracas, in 1964.*

Alicia Segal

El Musiú:*
Interview with Máximo Freilich, her father

–Tell me, Señor, why did you come to America?

—Over there, in Poland, they began to treat us as the Germans did afterwards—they didn't like Jews—then, although I had what to eat and it did not occur to me that I would ever lack food, still I wanted to leave, although no one in my family was happy. I left secretly, by foot, for Germany.

–Where did you come from?

—Me? From a small town outside Warsaw, called Blenden.

–How many kilometers did you walk?

—Many, as many as a three hour train. I entered Germany without a passport and they seized me.

–How old were you?

—In 1924, I was twenty.

–And after?

—They let me stay a month in Germany, and after I went by train from Berlin to France. There, also without a passport, and they let me stay five weeks and then I left in a boat for Havana, Cuba. When I arrived there they arrested me for something or other, but said that if I paid thirty dollars they would let me go free. I managed to get the money on credit and I stayed in Havana until 1929.

–What did you do then?

—I learned how to be a shoemaker, to make the top part of shoes. I did not know how, but I learned. I lost a lot of blood from my fingers. I earned fifty dollars a month and with this I helped my parents in Europe a little.

–And why did you also leave Cuba?

—I was a socialist, but some of the communists from the factory where I worked began to disgust me, to threaten me because they wanted me to become a member of their party. Moreover, the dictator, de Machado, was truly terrible—no one was able to say a word. The communists had to work secretly in La Casa de la Cultura.

–Then?

---

* slang word for "foreigner," like "gringo," or "greenhorn."

—Again, I exposed myself to danger, in a small boat, a launch as they now call it, for the United States. The pilots got lost and instead of the one hour in which we were told we would arrive, we spent five days on the open sea, without food, without water. Of the eight people who had left, one died and others went mad. When we arrived in Miami, half dead, luckily, they took us in and put us in a hospital for eleven days. Afterwards, they sentenced us for entering without visas. They put us in prison for a year, and told us that if Cuba would take us back we would have to go back there, if not, we would have to go back where we were born. —And as Cuba said no, afterwards, a journalist from New York by the name of Vladek who knew me because I had written for his paper, and Governor Lehman, they got us out of prison after a few days, with the permission of the governor of Florida. Then I went to Venezuela.

—How did that happen?

—On the beach, where I used to walk with a man there, who was well known in Venezuela, we would talk and I told him my story. He said to me: "You should go to my country and you will be able to work in peace there." He didn't tell me about Gómez—Even so I went and this man and his family took me into their home for eight days until I found work. I started as a door-to-door salesman, but it made me irritable because it exhausted me. I tried a thousand things in order to make a living. I tried making frames, I sold glasses, many, many things. Until I went to Valencia.

—How come?

—Because a friend of mine by the name of Winer said to me, "Why are you here? In Valencia one can be a collector if one can't be a vendor." So I went and I stayed until 1937, the time of the World's Fair in Paris, when I decided to return to Poland because I knew that war was coming.

—How many members of your family were still in Poland?

—I think about fifty.

—And?

—In France, I obtained, with some difficulty, a visa for Poland. I stayed there until 1938. Here I met a young lady, by the name of Rebecca, and she married me there, and I persuaded everyone that I could, to come back with me.

—Why didn't you stay?

—In Poland! I would have been crazy!

—Why didn't you take your whole family, then?

—I begged them to leave, I told them there was going to be a war, but they laughed at me. Moreover, they didn't know the language, they didn't want to leave. They didn't know what was going to happen, if they would have a chance, if they could be saved.

—What was the antisemitism like then?

—The Jew couldn't work, nor could he go to school or the university, and other things.

—And you, where did you study?

—I only went to Yeshiva, that is the Jewish school where one learns to read Torah and the Sacred Books.

—And when did you begin to write for the newspapers?

—In Poland, as a young boy, when I was eighteen. I wrote poetry and stories. In Cuba, I began to send my articles to the Jewish newspapers in New York, and in Havana we had a Jewish weekly newspaper.

—Do you still write?

—For newspapers in the United States, Mexico, Colombia, Israel, but in the last few years not so much, I am getting old—

—Why do you maintain that the first Venezuelan Jewish community after the war was in Valencia?

—Because. Here in Caracas they asked two thousand bolivars for a permit to sell from door to door and for a warranty from a businessman. In Valencia we paid only thirty bolivars and we were free to sell in every house. But when I returned in 1938, I stayed in Caracas.

—What was the city like then?

—I don't remember a single big building then, not even one that had two floors. One could find work by walking from here to Petare, without a bus, even all the way to La Vega. Today, I recognize nothing. It seems like another city. Proportionally speaking, Caracas has grown more in these forty-seven years than New York.

—And you? In addition to business and Yiddish journalism, what else have you done?

—Many things. Together with some others, I founded the school, "Moral y Luces." I founded Herzel Bialik, and also the Bikur Holim, which help the sick and the aged. Between us, we help others. I help direct a Cultural Club that is called "Sholom Aleichem," named for the great writer.

—And what is it for you to be Jewish?

—Since I was born Jewish, why should I change? I don't see that others are better. I see everyone as equal.

—Are you religious?

—No. I am Jewish because I was born Jewish, without further discussion.

—And if someone asks you to convert?

—Never. Never in this life.

—Now, after your little rest, tell me, what do you think of Venezuela today?

—It is the best country in Latin America. There is not now the dictatorship that used to be before you were born.

—Were there more workers among the earlier Venezuelans?

—To tell you the truth, there was no trade, there was nothing. What they call, "los musiús," us, the foreigners who came from Europe, we began industry here. That's the truth. Even cloth was very rare.

—And how did the people treat those who came to their doors?

—Very well. Magnificently. These people are very noble. Many times they didn't need the cloth, but they would buy it if they saw a man walking with a suitcase, for pity's sake, they would buy something from him to give him a weekly bolivar, and at times, truly, they didn't even have it for themselves—they gave us coffee, they spoke with us, they are a refined people.

—What do you call those who came?

—Ja, ja. Los musiús. Each country has its own words, gringo, musiu. And they treated us very well, no antisemitism. I have never seen it here.

—Do you believe there is antisemitism again, in some other places in the world?

—There are many ways to tell the truth, but for the sick, for those who wish everyone to be what they want them to be, antisemitism seems to be a remedy. Some declare themselves outright to be Hitlerites. Even today there are many such in Germany who would permit Hitler back. There are many who are secret Hitlerites, as well as many who are open, who openly declare themselves to be Hitlerites. And since the government is today, as they say, more democratic, they can't complain that they are not permitted to speak out. But even today they have the same idea. And in Russia, it is the same too. If you are not as they want you to be, you are not. For me, the government of Russia is as antisemitic as Poland and Hitler's Germany. In Russia, the father cannot speak with the child, as we do here, and there is much to fear. There are many Jewish writers who saved themselves from Stalin, and they wrote the truth. We should translate their books into Spanish. If I were to say in Russia that the government does not please me, the following day they would take me from my bed at dawn and no one would know where I am. This I know. There are thousands and thousands of arrests. I love Venezuela very much, everone here can speak and write as he wishes, it is a democratic country. It pleases me to be able to be openly critical, it does not please me to be made a prisoner for it.

—Wasn't there some antisemitism in the past on the government's part?

—A long time ago a Jewish delegate who was also a writer, came and asked me to go with him to speak to President Rómulo Gallegos. He spoke in Yiddish, Gallegos in Castillian Spanish, and I translated for the two. The delegate asked him why in the Venezuelan consuls in Europe there was a sign which read, "There are no visas for Negroes, Chinese, or Jews." The president answered him, as I remember it today, that his government had not made this law, but that everyone was free to come to Venezuela, regardless of color or religion. And this was the truth! Absolutely!

—How did Gallegos strike you?

—Very well. You would have to look far and wide for one like him.

—Where did he receive you?

—In the Palacio Miraflores.

—Have you met other politicians?

—No, because the fear of Gómez is not cured in a day. Although one spoke of freedom, one remained afraid of speaking because of earlier memories. Something happened to me when I first arrived in this country. I was in a café near San Juan with a friend, and we left to take a walk. Walking in the street with us, were men who wore earrings and had their faces painted. I asked my friend in Yiddish, if Gómez permits such dress. Behind us walked the police. They wore sandals, a deep, brown color, and a fur cap such as worn now by our firemen. These, the police, began to beat us and took us to the chief. I was imprisoned for two days and the civil chief, Señor Ochoa, asked us what we were doing there. I answered him in my Cuban Spanish, and he called the police again. He said that we should be imprisoned because we had been speaking about Gómez. So this was the thing. I never again used the word "Gómez." This was a dictatorship that I had thought existed only in Russia.

—You are famous for having a terrible tongue, for always speaking what you think.

—And also I think about what I say.

—Why are you so direct, even to the point of being one of the most argumentative people in the community.

—I was born like this. My father was a rabbi and he was also a bit of an anarchist. Once he said to my mother, he put his hand in his pocket and said to her: money is a false god. And this is very true. If it were not for money, people would be better.

—Doesn't your outspokenness annoy your friends?

—Oh, very much, very much indeed!

—Which Venezuelan writer do you admire?

—I would like to write like Uslar Pietri. Also, I should say newspaper writers rate very well here in comparison with others in the world.

—After forty-seven years in Venezuela, what do you think is the major fault in Venezuelans?

—They drink too much. It has always been this way. Alcohol is good, but in Europe, for example, we take wine with our meals, and that was good. Too much alcohol, without food, is very bad for the health.

—What would you like to see improved in Venezuela?

—To lend money to the poor, this is moral and beautiful. But the rule is always first me, then you. There is good land here, and with a little money they would be able to have clean houses with baths, with water, with light, with medicine, with schools in the interior, so that the people could work the land and could take from it their rice, tomatoes, potatoes. The people here are good. I remember when we used to sell, no one ever said "no" to us. Sometimes they said "another day," or "come tomorrow." One day a friend who was also a pedlar, who had just arrived in Venezuela and didn't know a single Spanish word, some of us bought him a suitcase filled with merchandise, but he always returned without selling anything. One night we asked him: "How come you don't sell anything? What's the matter?" He told us, bravely, "I don't sell anything because, as with you, they always say to me 'another day,' that's what they say in every doorway. I would sell very much but you never give me another day. What do you want me to do?" I remember also another friend who didn't know any Spanish and he went through the streets selling stockings, and he would shout: "!media-hombre! !media-mujer!" * Everyone laughed.

—Tell me something more. This family name of yours is unusual. What does it mean?

—In the ghettoes and in all of Europe the Jews were known by the work they did, sometimes by the face also. For example, a man with a red face was called Roitman, if he was yellow Gelman, the tailor was Shnaiderman, the shoemaker was called Shuster. I believe that a grandparent of mine, or an earlier ancestor, must have been a very happy man because he was called fréilaj, which means happy. And I would like that my children, Miriam and you, to use this name, when you sign your works in the periodicals.

—Yes, we should, though we don't always write about such happy subjects as you. Gracias, Máximo Freilich, gracias papá, por estos respuestos.

Trans. by Roberta Kalechofsky

---

* literally, half-man, half-woman. He meant a stocking which can be worn by men or women.

The Translators

David Pritchard *received a B.A. in English literature from Yale, in 1969, and an M.F.A. in Creative Writing, from the Iowa Writer's Workshop in 1974. He spent two years in the Caribbean with the Peace Corps, teaching English and learning Spanish in return. He has translated the stories of Felisberto Hernandez, the Uruguayan writer, and work by Vicente Aleixandre, the Nobel Prize winning poet, which will be included in a book of poetry translated by Lewis Hyde (Harper & Row). He is also the husband of the poet, Ellen Wittlinger, whose book of poetry,* Breakers, *was recently published by The Sheep Meadow Press.*

Giovanni Pontiero *was born in Scotland of Italian parents and received his Ph.D. in Glasgow. He is presently a Senior Lecturer in Latin American Literature at the University of Manchester, England. His books include a critical edition of the plays of the Uruguayan dramatist, Florencio Sanches (1972);* An Anthology of Brazilian Modernist Poetry *(1969); and* Family Ties *by Clarice Lispector (1972). His translations have appeared regularly in* New Directions *and* Review *(Center for Inter-American Relations). Soon to be published is a study of Clarice Lispector's work, to mark her death in 1978:* Focus on Clarice Lispector; *a study of the stories of Dalton Trevisan, and a work on Elenora Duse.*

Marilyn Rae *received her B.A. from Boston University in 1975 and has been a freelance translator for The Translation Center, Linguistics Systems, and Transtek Associates, as well as a Spanish teacher in Brookline High School, Brookline, Ma.*

Miriam Varon *is a poet and actress, as well as translator. She has performed in six different languages, and a volume of her poetry,* Thoughtprints, *was recently published. She is also the wife of Benno Weiser Varon, whose article is included in this volume.*

Susan Riva Greenberg *recently graduated from Tufts University and has been a tutor there in Afro-American House. She has also worked with the Hispanic Community in and around Cambridge since 1974 and is presently a Bi-lingual Education Counselor in Roxbury, Ma.*

David Unger, *whose poetry is included in this volume, won the Translation Center Translation Award in 1978. His translations of Latin American and Spanish writers have been published in* Street Magazine, Paris Review, Massachusetts Review, Gumbo, Sun, Unmuzzled Ox *and elsewhere, as well as in* The Prose Poem *(Dell, 1976); and in a book of translation of Enrique Lihn, with J. Cohen and J. Felstiner,* The Dark Room and other Poems, *New Directions, 1978.*

Yishai Tobin *was born in New York in 1946 and has lived in Mexico and in Israel since 1966, where he is now a lecturer at the Ben Gurion University of the Negev. He received a Ph.D. in Linguistics from New York University, was a member of Kibbutz Revivim for five years, and served in the Israeli army for three years. Translations by him have appeared in* Midstream, The Jewish Spectator, Poetry, Modern Poetry in Translation, Dissent, *and elsewhere. He is currently editing a prose anthology of the Israeli writer, Nathan Alterman.*

Shepherd Bliss *was born in California, raised in Panama, and received his doctorate from the University of Chicago Divinity School. His reviews have appeared in the* Guardian; *he has contributed a chapter on religion in Latin America to the book,* From Hope to Liberation *(Fortress Press) and has published articles in Spanish in Latin America. Harper and Row recently published his translation of a poem by the Nobel Laureate, Vicente Aleixandre in the book,* A Longing for the Light, *(edited by Lewis Hyde).*

Antonio Dajer *was born in New York City in 1956, of a Nicaraguan-Lebanese father and a Nicaraguan-Irish mother. He moved to Puerto Rico at the age of seven and lived there until he attended Harvard College, where he majored in English. After graduating, he lived in Ireland and in Israel for a year. He has translated Vicente Huidobro and various Puerto Rican poets, and is now attending medical school.*

Roberta Kalechofsky *is the author of* George Orwell *(Ungar, 1973), five works of fiction:* Justice, My Brother; Stephen's Passion; La Hoya; Orestes in Progress; *and* Solomon's Wisdom: A Collection of Short Stories. *Her articles and reviews have appeared in* Margins, Stony Hills, The Independent, *and* The American Book Review, *and elsewhere; and her stories have been published in various quarterlies, as well as in several anthologies:* The Best American Short Stories of 1972, *and* The Enduring Legacy, *edited by Douglas Brown. She has labored much with this volume, has been rewarded with many new friends, and brings this work to its close with the pleasure of presenting it to the public.*